The Tyndale Old Testa P9-ECP-556

General Editor: PROFESSOR D. J. WISEMAN, O.B.E., M.A.,
D.LIT., F.B.A., F.S.A.

HAGGAI, ZECHARIAH, MALACHI

HAGGAI, ZECHARIAH, MALACHI

AN INTRODUCTION AND COMMENTARY

by

JOYCE G. BALDWIN, B.A., B.D.
Dean of Women, Trinity College, Bristol

INTER-VARSITY PRESS

© 1972 by The Tyndale Press, London, England. Published in America by
InterVarsity Press, Downers Grove, Illinois, with permission from Universities and
Colleges Christian Fellowship, Leicester, England.

InterVarsity Press is the book-publishing division of Inter-Varsity Christian Fellowship,
a student movement active on campus at hundreds of universities, colleges
and schools of nursing. For information about local and regional activities, write
IVCF, 233 Langdon St., Madison, WI 53703.

Distributed in Canada through InterVarsity Press, 1875 Leslie St., Unit 10,
Don Mills, Ontario M3B 2M5, Canada.

ISBN paper 0-87784-276-0
ISBN cloth 0-87784-908-0
Library of Congress Catalog Card Number: 72-75980

Printed in the United States of America

18   17   16   15   14   13   12   11   10   9   8   7   6   5
93   92   91   90   89   88   87   86   85   84   83

GENERAL PREFACE

THE aim of this series of *Tyndale Old Testament Commentaries*, as it was in the companion volumes on the New Testament, is to provide the student of the Bible with a handy, up-to-date commentary on each book, with the primary emphasis on exegesis. Major critical questions are discussed in the introductions and additional notes, while undue technicalities have been avoided.

In this series individual authors are, of course, free to make their own distinct contributions and express their own point of view on all controversial issues. Within the necessary limits of space they frequently draw attention to interpretations which they themselves do not hold but which represent the stated conclusions of sincere fellow Christians. While she has done all this, the author of this commentary has shown that it is possible to make a book of the Bible – often little read and studied outside a few well-known passages – stand out afresh in its historical and prophetic setting, yet with meaning, relevance and application for the serious reader today.

In the Old Testament in particular no single English translation is adequate to reflect the original text. The authors of these commentaries freely quote various versions, therefore, or give their own translation, in the endeavour to make the more difficult passages or words meaningful today. Where necessary, words from the Hebrew (and Aramaic) Text underlying their studies are transliterated. This will help the reader who may be unfamiliar with the Semitic languages to identify the word under discussion and thus to follow the argument. It is assumed throughout that the reader will have ready access to one, or more, reliable rendering of the Bible in English.

Interest in the meaning and message of the Old Testament continues undiminished and it is hoped that this series will thus further the systematic study of the revelation of God and His will and ways as seen in these records. It is the prayer of the editor and publisher, as of the authors, that these books will help many to understand, and to respond to, the Word of God today.

D. J. WISEMAN

CONTENTS

HAGGAI

ZECHARIAH

MALACHI

AUTHOR'S PREFACE

IT is probably true to say that these last three books of the prophetic canon receive less than their full share of attention, yet there is treasure here as in any other part of Scripture.

So far as Zechariah is concerned, a maze of speculations about the date and authorship of the various oracles in chapters 9–14 tends to lead into by-ways, which so bewilder the reader that he turns gratefully to more familiar territory. It is my hope that others will be helped to understand Zechariah, as I myself have been, by discerning its symmetry of structure. If this is an intrinsic feature of the book its purpose becomes clear and its message coherent. To western minds Haggai and Malachi are easier to follow, and their words are still relevant, especially wherever there is discouragement or lethargy.

My indebtedness to many books and commentaries will be evident from the footnotes. In addition I have greatly benefited from the stimulus and encouragement of meetings of the Tyndale Fellowship Old Testament Study Group, to whose chairman, Professor D. J. Wiseman, I owe the fact that I ever started commentary writing. The Rev. N. Hillyer, Librarian of Tyndale House Library, Cambridge, and his predecessor, Mr A. R. Millard, have always been ready to supply information, and I also wish to thank the Rev. John B. Taylor who has checked the manuscript and made many useful suggestions, though he is not to be held responsible for the imperfections that remain.

May this commentary in some small way serve the cause of Him who is soon to be declared King over all the earth.

Advent 1971   JOYCE BALDWIN

CHIEF ABBREVIATIONS

ANEP   *The Ancient Near East in Pictures* by J. B. Pritchard 1954.

ANET   *Ancient Near Eastern Texts relating to the Old Testament*[2] by J. B. Pritchard, 1955.

ATD   *Das Alte Testament Deutsch. 25, Das Buch der Zwölf Kleinen Propheten*[6] by Karl Elliger, 1967.

AV   English Authorized Version (King James), 1611.

BAT   *Die Botschaft des Alten Testaments. 24, Das Buch der Kirche in der Weltwende*[5] by H. Frey, 1963.

BDB   *Hebrew–English Lexicon of the Old Testament* by F. Brown, S. R. Driver and C. A. Briggs, 1907.

BWAT   *Beiträge zur Wissenschaft vom Alten Testament.*

BZAW   *Beihefte zur Zeitschrift für die alttestamentliche Wissenschaft.*

CB   *Cambridge Bible. Haggai and Zechariah* by T. T. Perowne, 1888; *Haggai, Zechariah and Malachi* by W. E. Barnes, 1917.

CBQ   *Catholic Biblical Quarterly.*

Chary   *Aggée-Zacharie Malachie* by Théophane Chary (Sources Bibliques), 1969.

DOTT   *Documents from Old Testament Times* edited by D. Winton Thomas, 1958.

EB   *Expositor's Bible. The Book of the Twelve Prophets* by G. A. Smith, 1891.

ET   *Expository Times.*

EVV   English Versions.

Fohrer   *Introduction to the Old Testament* by Georg Fohrer, Eng. tr. 1970.

GK	*Hebrew Grammar*[2] by W. Gesenius, E. Kautzsch and A. E. Cowley, 1910.
HAT	*Handbuch zum Alten Testament.* 14, *Die Zwölf Kleinen Propheten, Nahum – Maleachi*[3] by Friedrich Horst, 1964.
IB	*The Interpreter's Bible* VI, 1956.
ICC	*International Critical Commentary. Haggai and Zechariah* by H. G. Mitchell, 1912; *Malachi* by J. M. P. Smith, 1912.
IDB	*The Interpreter's Dictionary of the Bible,* 4 vols., 1962.
Jansma	*Inquiry into the Hebrew Text and the Ancient Versions of Zechariah IX–XIV* by Taeke Jansma, 1949.
JB	*The Jerusalem Bible,* Standard Edition, 1966.
JBL	*Journal of Biblical Literature.*
JJS	*Journal of Jewish Studies.*
JNES	*Journal of Near Eastern Studies.*
JTS	*Journal of Theological Studies.*
KAT	*Kommentar zum Alten Testament. Das Zwölfprophetenbuch übersetzt und erklärt*[3] by E. Sellin, 1930.
Lamarche	*Zacharie IX–XIV, Structure Littéraire et Messianisme* by Paul Lamarche, 1961.
LXX	The Septuagint (pre-Christian Greek version of the Old Testament).
mg.	margin.
Moffatt	*A New Translation of the Bible* by James Moffatt, 1935.
MS	manuscript.
MT	Massoretic Text.
NBC	*The New Bible Commentary Revised* edited by D. Guthrie, J. A. Motyer, A. M. Stibbs and D. J. Wiseman, 1970.

NBD	*The New Bible Dictionary* edited by J. D. Douglas, 1962.
NEB	*The New English Bible Old Testament*, Library Edition, 1970.
Petitjean	*Les Oracles du Proto-Zacharie* by Albert Petitjean (Études Bibliques), 1969.
PCB	*Peake's Commentary on the Bible* edited by A. S. Peake and A. J. Grieve, 1919.
*PCB*²	*Peake's Commentary on the Bible* (Revised Edition) edited by M. Black and H. H. Rowley, 1962.
Pusey	*The Minor Prophets.* VIII, *Zechariah* by E. B. Pusey, 1907.
RB	*Revue Biblique.*
RSV	American Revised Standard Version, 1952.
RV	English Revised Version, 1881.
Soncino	*Soncino Books of the Bible. The Twelve Prophets* edited by A. Cohen, 1948.
TBC	*Torch Bible Commentary. Haggai, Zechariah and Malachi* by D. R. Jones, 1962.
TOTC	*Tyndale Old Testament Commentary.*
VT	*Vetus Testamentum.*
Vulg.	The Vulgate (translation of the Bible into Latin by Jerome).
Wright	*Zechariah and his Prophecies* by C. H. H. Wright, 1879.
ZNW	*Zeitschrift für die Neutestamentliche Wissenschaft.*

GENERAL INTRODUCTION

I. BACKGROUND TO RESTORATION

THE imminence of destruction and exile had filled the horizon of the pre-exilic prophets. Though they were not without their assurances of ultimate triumph for God's cause, the immediate crisis for the nation was such that they had to be watchmen, warning of threatening danger (Je. 4:5; Ezk. 3:17; 33:4; Ho. 5:8; 8:1; Joel 2:1; Am. 3:6). From the time of Amos onwards both nations were presented with a message of doom. Fire was to devour Jerusalem (Am. 2:5) and for Samaria the end had come (Am. 3:15; 8:2). Like the prey in the teeth of a lion the population would be torn and carried away, and there would be no escape (Ho. 5:14; 13:7, 8). The light had gone out (Is. 5:30), the land had been devastated (Is. 6:11), the floods had risen up to the neck (Is. 8:7, 8). Though a reprieve was granted to Judah in Hezekiah's time, the full sentence was imposed in 587 BC, when both Temple and city were plundered and destroyed.

This disaster was the death of the nation. Far from recording an evolutionary spiral of steady progress from Moses to Christ, the Bible presents a high point of revelation at the time of the Exodus, followed by a decline which the occasional reformation was powerless to reverse. The whole tragic story could be summed up in the sequence: chosen, privileged, presumptuous, rebellious. The defeat and captivity of the two kingdoms was a divine judgment, from which the nation would never recover. The carefully tended vine had grown wild (Is. 5:2; Je. 2:21), the tree had been felled (Is. 6:13). Things could never be the same again. The only other event in Jewish history comparable to the exile was the destruction of Jerusalem in AD 70, which foreshadowed final judgment at the end of time (Mt. 24). The exile was the prototype; it was 'the day of the Lord' for Israel and Judah.

The best part of a lifetime separated the deportations of 597 and the first return in 538 BC. The common feeling among the exiles was that they might as well be dead. Their bones were dried up and their hope gone (Ezk. 37:11). From a human standpoint they were right. It would have been hard to find any reasonable ground for hope, but to Ezekiel came a vision of resurrection. God would recreate His people, reunite the two kingdoms under a Davidic head and set His sanctuary among them once and for all (Ezk. 37). The encouragements of Isaiah chapters 40–48 laid new stress on election and covenant. The great Creator still counted Israel His servant and Jacob His chosen (41:8) and therefore they need not fear. He had blotted out their transgressions 'for his own sake' (43:25) and planned their return to Jerusalem to rebuild the Temple (44:28). Cyrus was designated as the anointed of the Lord to fulfil His purpose. Suddenly there was a glorious future ahead because they had an incomparable God who saw fit to forgive the past and plan redemption. The very heavens and earth would witness the declaration, 'The Lord loves him' (48:14).

Such was the prophetic utterance. Jewish history began a new chapter in 539 BC when Cyrus, after twenty years of conquest, established himself as the king of a new world empire by entering Babylon as victor. Ever since the death of Nebuchadrezzar in 562 Babylonian power had been on the wane. A stable government eluded Nebuchadrezzar's successors until 556, when Nabonidus seized the throne, but even he aroused hostility and withdrew to Arabia in *c.* 552 BC, leaving his son Belshazzar to rule. Meanwhile Cyrus, prince of Anshan, had not only assumed power in Persia, but had taken advantage of internal strife in the Median empire to seize the Median throne. This added to his territory not only Media but the countries of Armenia and Cappadocia.[1] From such a wide base he was able to launch military operations to both west and east. After taking the whole of Asia Minor and encountering Greece he moved eastwards through Parthia into Afghanistan. Though the full extent of his conquests in an easterly direction is not known, Cyrus had established the largest empire the world had ever seen.[2] Once Elam and the area formerly known as Assyria had surrendered to him Babylon alone remained, helpless to defend herself. In October 539 BC this last bastion fell and Cyrus's empire was complete.

The next few years as they affected the Jews are recorded in Ezra 1:1 – 4:5. First of all Cyrus is quoted as saying that

---

[1] The extent of the Median empire is shown in Map 7, *NBD*.

[2] See Map 9 in *NBD* or a similar map of the Persian Empire.

the Lord, the God of heaven, had charged him to build Him a house at Jerusalem (Ezr. 1:2). The 'Cyrus Cylinder' sheds light on this statement, for the king records how, after his victorious entry into Babylon, he rebuilt temples and restored gods to their places. His prayer 'May all the gods whom I have placed within their sanctuaries address a daily prayer in my favour . . .',[1] reveals his motive and his syncretistic outlook. By honouring all the gods he hoped to be able to count on the help of all. Thus the Jews were encouraged to return to Jerusalem to rebuild the Temple, and received back the sacred vessels which Nebuchadrezzar had confiscated when the city fell. After a long register of those who returned (Ezr. 2) the setting up of the altar is recorded (Ezr. 3:1–6). Sacrificial ritual was resumed amid the ruins of the Temple. Steps were also taken to obtain the official grant of timber allowed by Cyrus (Ezr. 3:7), and in the second year a ceremony was held to give thanks for the inauguration of the rebuilding of the Temple (3:8–13).

Progress was short-lived, however. The people of mixed descent who had appropriated the land during the Exile wanted to identify themselves with the Jews by co-operating with them in their building projects. They probably hoped to keep a controlling interest in local political issues. Zerubbabel and Joshua appear to have had the support of the repatriates in refusing to compromise with people whose easy-going religion and morals might encourage apostasy. The resulting hostility brought the work to a halt, and the Temple was still a ruin in 520 BC (Ezr. 4:1–5).

Cyrus died in battle in 530 BC, fighting barbarian tribes to the north-east of Persia, but not before he had inaugurated an efficient system of communication throughout the empire, and established effective control through Persian and Median officials, supported by the army. His unusual liberality as a ruler is well known. According to Herodotus, the Persians considered Cyrus to be a father to his people because he was 'in the kindness of his heart always occupied with plans for their well-being'.[2] His son and successor, Cambyses, was by contrast a tyrant, who feared any apparent threat to his

---

[1] *DOTT*, pp. 93, 94; *cf. ANET*, pp. 315, 316. A useful assessment of the Cyrus edict in the light of archaeological evidence is to be found in J. A. Thompson, *The Bible and Archaeology* (Paternoster, 1962), pp. 174–180.

[2] Herodotus III. 89 (Penguin Classics Edition, p. 214).

throne, and secretly assassinated his brother Bardiya, who was popular with the people. Cambyses' outstanding achievement was to add Egypt to the Persian Empire, but in July 522, on his way back from Ethiopia, he heard news that a usurper pretending to be his brother Bardiya had seized the throne in the eastern part of the empire. Though the details are obscure it seems that Cambyses took his own life. In the absence of a direct successor Darius, son of the governor of Susa and an officer in Cambyses' entourage, claimed the throne. Incidentally the march of Cambyses' armies through Palestine, with the consequent looting and damage, may have contributed to the poverty referred to by Haggai (1:6, 9; 2:16f.).

The death of Cambyses sparked off rebellions in many parts of the empire. Darius' first task was to overthrow and execute pseudo-Bardiya. This he did by the end of September 522, but battles remained to be fought against rebel factions in such widely separated areas as Iran to the east, Asia Minor to the west and Egypt to the south. Darius refers to these campaigns in his famous inscriptions on the Behistun cliff in Iran. On the left-hand side stands the figure of Darius with his foot on the prostrate figure of Gautama (pseudo-Bardiya).[1] There are differences of opinion as to how soon these rebellions were quelled (see the commentary on Zc. 1:11), but it is likely that Darius had established himself in the throne by 520 BC, the year in which Haggai and Zechariah began to prophesy.

To what extent were these prophets influenced by world events? Like their predecessors they were given their message at a critical time, but if political revolt against Persia had been in their minds, as K. Elliger suggests,[2] they were too late. Eighteen months earlier would have been the favourable moment. Moreover, there was no evidence of a fighting spirit among those whom Haggai addressed. Though other nations were stirred by nationalistic fervour, that only served to throw into relief the hopelessness and lassitude of the little Jewish community in Judah. The fact that the Persian Empire was in a tumult may have awakened memories of Amos's earthquake prophecies (8:8; 9:5). Judgment on the nations was beginning and prophetic hopes of a Davidic ruler were about to be fulfilled. If he was about to come the Temple must be

---

[1] *ANEP*, plates 249, 250.

[2] *ATD*, p. 83. He thinks that the Jews refused to pay the levy demanded by Persia and used the money for the Temple building.

ready to welcome him. In this way world events helped to give urgency to the prophetic message, but the message itself was not new. Ezekiel had seen that the Temple must be rebuilt, but now the moment for action had come.

The right of the Jews to rebuild was challenged by the pro-Persian governors of Trans-Euphrates, who applied to Darius in writing for confirmation that Cyrus had authorized the project. An official memorandum was discovered at Ecbatana, whereupon Darius not only forbad interference with the work but also ordered material help to be given (Ezr. 5:6 – 6:12). It is remarkable that Darius should have gone to so much trouble, especially if he was hard pressed by threats to his empire. Moreover there is not the slightest hint that he suspected the Jews of sedition or resented the leadership of Zerubbabel in Jerusalem at this time. The lack of information about Zerubbabel's fate, and the fact that he does not seem to have had a successor has led to the conjecture that the Persians objected to the claims made for him (Hg. 2:21–23; Zc. 4:6f.), removed him and stripped the Davidic house of its prerogatives.[1] Whatever may have happened later, the rebuilding of the Temple appears to have proceeded peacefully until its completion in 516 BC, and there is no evidence of official Persian opposition. 'We detect no change of policy, nor of violent action against the Jews such as might have been anticipated if Zerubbabel's claims were looked at askance.'[2]

The biblical records are silent about the Jews of Jerusalem once the Temple was completed. No sequel was written to the books of Kings and Chronicles, and only the two isolated incidents related in Ezra 4:6–23 give any information about the period 515–458 BC. Two aspects of the reign of Darius had a bearing on international relations. In the first place he organized the building of roads to enable royal envoys to cover in a week routes that took caravans ninety days (*cf.* Zechariah's horses that patrolled the earth). In the second place his confrontation with Greece turned the attention of world leaders westwards to the people destined to control the next world empire. It is true that there had been interchange of trade between Greece and the Near East from the second millennium BC, but the clash of Persian and Greek armies

---

[1] J. Bright, *History of Israel* (SCM Press, 1960), p. 355; D. Winton Thomas, *IB*, VI, p. 1039.
[2] P. R. Ackroyd, *Exile and Restoration* (SCM Press, 1968), p. 165.

brought large numbers of Asians on to Greek soil. There was nothing surprising therefore about references to Greece in biblical literature from this time on (*cf.* Zc. 9:13).

As a subject people the Jews' political history was to be bound up with that of the great world empires. During the fifth century they were answerable to officials in Samaria who were out of sympathy with them, taxed them beyond their income (Ne. 5:4), and made exorbitant personal demands upon them (Ne. 5:15). Under continual threat of being accused to the central government, as happened during the reigns of Ahasuerus (Ezr. 4:6) and Artaxerxes (Ezr. 4:7–23),[1] and having no means of self-defence, the Jews must have felt keenly their helplessness. Once hopes for the future faded, morale became low, and the religious and moral laxity presupposed by the prophecy of Malachi prevailed.

It was not that the prophets had been mistaken in presenting their glowing pictures of what God was going to do. It was rather that they had been given a very long view, ranging from the coming of Christ as man to His coming again in judgment and including the final ushering in of His kingdom. The baffling element was the time and manner of the fulfilment of their prophecies (1 Pet. 1:10–12).

II. THEOLOGICAL SIGNIFICANCE OF THE TEMPLE

The fact that Haggai and Zechariah had the primary task of ensuring the rebuilding of the Temple raises the question of its place in the theological thinking of the period. No prophet initiated the building of Solomon's Temple; Nathan gave permission rather than instruction to David's successor to build it (2 Sa. 7:12). In Nathan's eyes a tent was a more appropriate symbol of the Lord's presence than a temple because it was mobile, and therefore allowed freedom for the living, dynamic relationship which characterizes God's dealings with men (2 Sa. 7:6). So far as the ritual was concerned it could be performed equally well in the Tabernacle as in a more permanent structure.

---

[1] Artaxerxes I, 464–423 BC. Later in his reign the building of the city walls, about which the complaint was lodged, was completed (Ne. 6:15; *cf.* 2:1).

Moreover the efficacy of sacrifice had often been questioned. It was axiomatic for the eighth-century prophets that there could be no forgiveness of sin without confession and repentance, evidenced by a reformed daily life (*e.g.* Is. 1:11–20). At best sacrifices dealt only with overt sins, not with the whole range of sins of the mind and heart. 'It is not surprising, therefore, that there were individuals in Israel who saw beyond the ritual of the sacrificial system and its concern with outward acts to the possibility of reconciliation with God.'[1] Individuals found assurance of forgiveness apart from sacrifice (2 Sa. 12:13; Ps. 32:5) and certain Psalms go so far as to assert that sacrifices were not required by God (Ps. 40:6; 51:16,17). Add to this the prophetic assurances that the Lord was to be found in exile (Je. 29:12–14), and would be to them a sanctuary (Ezk. 11:16) even though no sacrifices could be offered, and it becomes obvious that there must have been a more fundamental reason for the rebuilding of the Temple than resumption of the ritual.[2]

A whole complex of ideas had grown up around the name Zion, which first occurs in the narrative recording David's conquest of Jerusalem (2 Sa. 5:7). (*a*) Mount Zion became symbolic of the throne of the Davidic king, whose dynasty was for ever (2 Sa. 7:16). This theme is developed under the heading 'Messianic Hopes'. (*b*) The Lord had chosen Zion as His own resting place for ever (Ps. 132:13,14), and therefore the sanctuary was 'sanctified for ever' (2 Ch. 30:8). The Lord chose 'Mount Zion, which he loves. He built his sanctuary like the heavens' (Ps. 78:68, 69). Though the heaven of heavens could not contain Him, the Lord had deigned to call His own one particular hill on the face of the earth, and let it be known by His name (Je. 7:11). No wonder Jeremiah's contemporaries could not believe that the Temple would ever be destroyed (Je. 7:3). (*c*) The nations were aware of the Lord's choice of Mount Zion, and yet they were allowed to profane it (Ezk. 7:21). By implication the name of the Lord was blasphemed among the heathen, for they were not to know that His glory had been withdrawn before it was destroyed (Ezk. 11:23).

It follows that the honour of the Lord was bound up with the rebuilding of the Temple. The nations had to know beyond

---

[1] I. H. Marshall, *Kept by the Power of God* (Epworth, 1969), p. 17.

[2] The last two verses of Psalm 51, which reflect a different viewpoint from that of verses 16, 17, appear to be a prayer added during the exile.

any doubt that the God of Israel had not gone out of existence when the Israelites were removed from their land. 'Then the nations will know that I the Lord sanctify Israel, when my sanctuary is in the midst of them for evermore' (Ezk. 37:28). Israel had to know that God did not go back on His election, hence Zechariah's assurance, 'Cry out, Thus says the Lord of hosts: I am exceedingly jealous for Jerusalem and for Zion' (Zc. 1:14); 'The Lord . . . will again choose Jerusalem' (Zc. 2:12).

In the thinking of Ezekiel there was a close link between the Temple and the covenant. 'I will make a covenant of peace with them; it shall be an everlasting covenant with them; and I will bless them and multiply them, and will set my sanctuary in the midst of them for evermore' (Ezk. 37:26). While the Temple lay in ruins there was no outward sign of the Lord's presence with the restored community. To judge by Haggai's assurance, given as soon as the rebuilding started, 'I am with you, says the Lord' (Hg. 1:13; 2:4), there had been considerable doubt whether God was among them at all. Ezekiel had seen that the glory of the Lord would return to Jerusalem, but he also envisaged the Temple there to receive Him (Ezk. 43:1–5). In the event building was made possible by the work of God's Spirit, not by human initiative (Zc. 4:6). The Lord had overruled international events (Zc. 1:18–21) and stirred up enthusiasm through Haggai and Zechariah. The completion of the Temple was to be proof that Zechariah had been His instrument (Zc. 4:9) and therefore a sign that the covenant had been renewed. The Lord was once more with them in the way that He had been with Moses and Joshua (Jos. 1:5) and therefore hope in the ancient promises revived.

Finally there was an eschatological reason why the Temple was indispensable. When Micah first pronounced the destruction of Jerusalem (Mi. 3:12), he went on immediately to describe a new Temple, higher than the hills, into which all the nations would flock to hear the transforming word which would bring peace to the world (Mi. 4:1–4; *cf.* Is. 2:2–4). The sequence of events appeared to be destruction, desolation for a time, and then, with the Lord's house re-established, the 'latter days' would dawn with their Messianic hopes. Similarly in Isaiah 40–55, once Jerusalem's punishment was complete (40:2), city and Temple would be rebuilt (44:28) amid great joy. Nothing appeared to stand between the restoration of the city and ecstatic experiences of God's reign (Is. 52:1,2,7). The rebuilding of the Temple was the condition on which the dawning of the Messianic age depended. Haggai implied as much (Hg. 2:6–9) and Malachi proclaimed that the Lord would suddenly come to His Temple (Mal. 3:1).

The rebuilding of the Temple was at once an act of dedication and of faith. It was a symbol of the continuity of the present with the past, and expressed the longing of the community that, despite the exile, the old covenant promises still stood. What the Temple was to symbolize in God's purpose the prophets themselves could hardly be expected to appreciate, for Jesus spoke of His own body as the Temple (Mk. 14:58; Jn. 2:19), which in its turn would be destroyed. Raised from the dead it was to be the corner stone of a holy temple made up of living stones, believers who become 'a dwelling place of God in the Spirit' (Eph. 2:19–22; 1 Pet. 2:4,5), a church to be presented before Him in splendour. For all this the rebuilding of the Temple in the time of Haggai and Zechariah was a necessary preparation.

III. MESSIANIC HOPES

There is evidence that expectation of salvation was characteristic of Israel from the earliest days. Before the monarchy Israel had already experienced salvation from Egypt and had entered into a promised land. In the fierce battles for conquest and occupation 'saviours' led them and fought through to deliverance and victory. Spectacular saving events became the subject of early psalms, such as Exodus 15:1–18 and Judges 5:2–31, which, by regular choral repetition, would keep alive through every generation the memory of God's great acts. Two particular strands of tradition were established: (i) belief in a coming age of peace and plenty, (ii) belief in a coming superhuman ruler, miraculously provided and endowed.

The latter hope, encouraged by the *charisma* bestowed on the judges and even on Saul the king (1 Sa. 10:10), became identified at the foundation of the Davidic dynasty with the royal house of Judah. The promise of Nathan, 'And your house and your kingdom shall be made sure for ever before me; your throne shall be established for ever', was later confirmed and given covenant status (2 Sa. 23:5). At times this was no doubt interpreted in purely nationalistic terms, but the Psalmists rejoiced that the coming king would claim dominion over the nations by divine right (Ps. 2:7,8) and establish God's law throughout the earth (Ps. 45:4–7; 72:1–4). When he had routed his enemies righteousness and peace would flourish, for the conditions on which God's kingdom could come would have been fulfilled. Then nature would provide abundantly the food man needed and an age of bliss would be ushered in (Ps. 72:3,7,9–11,16).

Pre-exilic prophets had been unable to encourage an optimistic outlook in a nation that showed not a vestige of allegiance to the Lord it professed to serve, and yet expected to enjoy all the covenant privileges. The immediate prospect was exile, and only after that experience had humbled Israel into repentance and submission would there be hope of seeing God's day of deliverance. Moreover, the coming king of whom these prophets spoke became more clearly superhuman (Is. 9:6), and his impartial rule would be sought by all nations (Is. 11:10) for the underprivileged would have their rights and even animals would no longer prey upon one another (Is. 11:6f.). Jeremiah, who was prevented by the false optimism of his contemporaries from giving grounds for hope, referred nevertheless to the coming Davidic king as the righteous Branch, whose name was to be 'The Lord is our righteousness' (Je. 23:5, 6; 33:15,16). This hint of the king's mediatorial role was to be developed after the exile.

Cyrus's appointment of 'the prince of Judah' to take charge of the caravans returning to Jerusalem (Ezr. 1:8f.), and of Zerubbabel, one of Jehoiachin's grandsons (1 Ch. 3:16–19), to leadership in the restored community, revived hopes in the Davidic line. Haggai proclaimed him to be the Lord's choice, authoritative as a signet ring (Hg. 2:23). For Zechariah he was not only the one who would complete the Temple building, but also one of the two anointed ones who stand by the Lord of the whole earth (Zc. 4:14). The other was Joshua the high priest, linked in 3:8 and 6:12 with the mediatorial Branch of Jeremiah. The partnership of prince and high-priest brought together two strands in the traditional leadership of Israel and made a creative contribution to the Messianic concept.

The only explicit reference to the coming king in these post-exilic prophets is in Zechariah 9:9,10. This triumphant poem makes use of imagery drawn from the ancient Blessings of Jacob (Gn. 49:11) and from Psalm 72. Unlike most human rulers who experience deliverance and ride in triumph he is 'humble', identified with the poor of the land. The Lord vindicates him, disarms the nations and gives him dominion over the earth. When next the king is mentioned it is the Lord who is king over all the earth (Zc. 14:9).

But this glorious hope is not the only theme of Zechariah 9–14. In contrast there are battle scenes described in the vivid language of early war poetry. Promised deliverance implies catastrophic disasters like Egyptian bondage and Babylonian exile (Zc. 10:8–12). Furthermore, the leader figure was rejected (Zc. 11:8), murdered (Zc. 12:10), with the result that the bewildered nation was no match for its foes (Zc. 13:7–9). Yet, through suffering voluntarily accepted he opened a way of forgiveness and cleansing for those who said 'The Lord is my God' (Zc. 13:1,9). Victory has to be won in the lives of men, and for this military weapons are useless and human resources inadequate. Moreover, its achievement will mark the end of history. Haggai describes a cataclysmic shaking, suggested by an earthquake, but involving outer space (Hg. 2:21,22), before Zerubbabel is to see the outworking of his election. Zechariah envisages changes in the landscape round Jerusalem, but implies cosmic changes also, because alternation of day and night ceases. Nothing less than divine intervention will bring about the longed-for age of peace and prosperity (Zc. 14:3–9).

Malachi is the prophet of the waiting period. He believed the end was near, and though there would be one last warning messenger to prepare the way the Lord's coming would be as drastic as bleach and as inescapable as fire (3:1–3). It would not be enough then to belong by descent to the covenant nation. All who had defied God would perish (4:1) and all moral disorders in Judah and Jerusalem would receive just sentence (3:5). Deliverance would be granted only to those who allied themselves to the Lord (4:2). Thus Malachi corrected any purely nationalistic ideas, and at the same time indicated that enjoyment of peace and prosperity would not come till after the Lord's personal intervention in history. The execution of justice in Israel and among the nations, and the provision of bliss for the righteous was reserved for God alone.

The Old Testament ends on this solemn but expectant note, its intent longing set on the fulfilment of hopes built up over a thousand years of history and revelation. Not that these hopes were clearly defined or integrated. Though the implications of some of the imagery were clear enough, unified interpretation remained uncertain, and therefore the tendency during the inter-testamental period was to concentrate on aspects that seemed attractive and unambiguous. Only in retrospect could it be seen that Jesus of Nazareth brought together in His person the divergent strands of prophetic teaching concerning the Messianic hope.

HAGGAI

INTRODUCTION

THE year 520 BC was one of crisis for Jerusalem. It was not the kind of crisis obvious to all, as when a threat of invasion shocks a whole population into action, but the dangerous state of moral paralysis which accepts as normal conditions that demand drastic changes. Unless a man of vision and determination can intervene in time there is no hope of recovery.

The Jews who returned from Babylon had been given to expect the very desert to burst into flower (Is. 35:1). Instead they found the desert encroaching on their fields and orchards as one year of drought succeeded another. The consequent food shortage and poverty had taken the heart out of those who might otherwise have been eager to rebuild. Three centuries earlier Amos had commented on freak weather conditions and blighted harvests (Am. 4:6f.), teaching that these had been God's warning signs, which Israel had been too self-confident to recognize. Though the circumstances were different Haggai saw in the recurrent droughts a divine rebuke. Unlike Amos he found himself confronted with a people conscious of their need and prepared to admit their failure. They accepted Haggai's diagnosis of their situation as from God, reorganized their lives accordingly, and set to work.

I. THE PROPHET

Haggai apparently needed neither introduction nor identification (1:1), for both here and in Ezra 5:1; 6:14 he is simply 'the prophet', and to judge by the repetition in the Aramaic of Ezra 5:1 'the prophets, Haggai the prophet...' he was usually referred to in this way (*cf.* 'Habakkuk the prophet', Hab. 1:1). The absence of a patronym may indicate that his father was already forgotten, that prophets were few and therefore 'the prophet' was sufficiently specific, and that he was well known in the small Judean community. His name is one of several in the Old Testament derived from *hag*, 'festival': Haggi (Gn. 46:16; Nu. 26:15), Haggith (2 Sa. 3:4), Haggiah

(1 Ch. 6:30). He was probably born on a feast day and therefore named 'my feast' (Lat. Festus, Gk. Hilary). It is even
possible that Haggai was a nickname.

It is hardly surprising that so short a book reveals little about
the prophet's life. Was he a young man, who had returned
with his parents in 538 BC? If he was a child at that time the
omission of his name from the list in Ezra 2 would be understandable. Had he been in Babylon at all? According to
Jewish tradition he had lived the greater part of his life in
Babylon.[1] Partly on this tradition and partly on inference from
Haggai 2:3 is based the opinion that when he prophesied he
was a very old man who had seen the Temple before its
destruction, and was given the most important task of his life
just before his death. The authority he commanded and his
single-minded preoccupation with the Temple rather tend to
bear this out.

According to an early Christian tradition Haggai was a
priest, and was buried with honour near the sepulchres of the
priests.[2] The fact that in the Versions certain Psalms are
attributed to Haggai may add support to his priestly lineage.
The LXX, for example, prefaces Psalms 138 and 146–149
with the names Haggai and Zechariah, indicating perhaps
that they were responsible for the recension from which the
Greek translation was being made. Hebrew tradition on the
other hand did not reckon Haggai among the priests, and the
modern Rabbi Eli Cashdan writes: 'Evidently he was not of
the priestly tribe, seeing that he called on the priests of his day
for a ruling on levitical uncleanness (ii.11).'[3] The point is
hardly proved on this evidence, however. The one thing of
which we may be certain is that, like all the great prophets
before him, he had a consuming passion for God's cause. Just
as Elijah faced his contemporaries with one fundamental
decision on Mount Carmel, so Haggai saw that for his generation everything depended on the rebuilding of the Temple. It
'was in fact a kind of incarnation of all that God stood for and
all that He required and all that He could do for His people
in the age that was about to dawn'.[4]

---

[1] Rabbi Eli Cashdan, *The Twelve Prophets* (Soncino Press, 1948), p. 254.
[2] H. G. Mitchell, *ICC*, p. 26, quotes Dorotheus and Hesychius to this
effect.
[3] *Op. cit.*, p. 252.
[4] J. B. Taylor, *Ezekiel* (*TOTC*, 1969), p. 253.

From the precise dates given in the text we discover that Haggai preached the sermons recorded in his book within the space of fifteen weeks during the second year of Darius I (521–486 BC). It has proved possible with the help of evidence from well over a hundred Babylonian texts, and from new-moon tables calculated from astronomical data, to synchronize the old lunar calendar with the Julian calendar. The results are accurate to within one day.[1] The dates given in Haggai and Zechariah and their equivalents are shown in the following table. In column four is given the date in the Julian calendar on which the new moon fell in the particular year named.

Reference	Year of Darius	Month	Date of new moon	Day	Equivalent date, BC
Hg. 1:1	second	sixth	29 Aug.	1st	29 Aug. 520
Hg. 1:15	„	„	„	24th	21 Sept. 520
Hg. 2:1	„	seventh	27 Sept.	21st	17 Oct. 520
Zc. 1:1	„	eighth	27 Oct.	–	–
Hg. 2:10,20	„	ninth	25 Nov.	24th	18 Dec. 520
Zc. 1:7	„	eleventh	23 Jan.	24th	15 Feb. 519
Zc. 7:1	fourth	ninth	4 Dec.	4th	7 Dec. 518

There is no means of knowing what happened to Haggai after 18 December 520. Once Temple building began in earnest he had fulfilled his mission, and, having in Zechariah a successor to continue the work, he withdrew from the scene.

II. HIS BOOK

In this short book only the basic essentials of the prophet's four messages have been recorded. By enclosing the actual words of the prophet in inverted commas RSV distinguishes plainly between the sermons and the editorial framework in which they are set. The dated introductions (1:1; 2:1,10,20), the narrative (1:12), and the abbreviated introductions (2:13,14) all refer to Haggai in the third person, suggesting that someone

[1] For relevant material, together with tables giving the dates on which the months began, see R. A. Parker and W. H. Dubberstein, *Babylonian Chronology* 626 BC – AD 75 (Brown University Press, 1956).

other than the prophet was responsible for putting the book together. There is every likelihood that the book was compiled soon after 520 BC. That Haggai was too well remembered to need any introduction has been pointed out already.

O. Eissfeldt is impressed with the 'very exact and clearly very reliable details of the report', which he thinks must go back to personal notes of the prophet, who may also be the editor. 'It is only that this prophet, in order to enhance the impression of the complete objectivity of his report, has chosen not the first person but the third person form.'[1] A very different view is taken by P. R. Ackroyd himself. He regards the compiler as responsible for the dating and arrangement of the oracles, possibly one century or even two centuries after the time of Haggai. 'In the case of Haggai, we may assume that the oracles were transmitted for a period, probably orally, though possibly committed to writing, before they came into their present form. The length of that period cannot be determined, but in view of the similarities already indicated between the dates in Haggai and those of the Chronicler, we can estimate that it was not much less than a century, and possibly as much as two centuries.'[2]

Recently W. A. M. Beuken has argued that Haggai and Zechariah 1–8 were edited 'in a Chronistic milieu'.[3] His argument is that the same major interest in the Temple, its ritual, and the continuity of the Davidic line dominate both these prophets and the books of Chronicles. This is true, but if Beuken is implying that the editors selected according to their individual preference the themes they would record, this is to undermine confidence in the books as they have come down to us. We believe it to be both more likely and more logical that Haggai was edited early, possibly before 500 BC, and that he and Zechariah together moulded the thinking of those who edited the books of Chronicles.

Like his predecessors Haggai may have put his prophetic oracles into poetic form to make them as vivid and memorable as possible. The uncertainty arises because Hebrew poetry did

---

[1] O. Eissfeldt, *The Old Testament An Introduction.* Trans. P. R. Ackroyd (Blackwell, 1965), p. 428.

[2] P. R. Ackroyd, 'Studies in the Book of Haggai', *JJS*, II, 4, 1951, pp. 163–176.

[3] W. A. M. Beuken, *Haggai-Sacharja 1–8* (Assen, 1967), reviewed by R. J. Coggins in *JTS*, 20, 1969, pp. 264–266.

not rhyme, and, just as much modern English poetry would pass as prose if it were not written in verse lines, so it is not always possible to identify Hebrew poetry with certainty. Parallelism (the same or contrasting ideas set alongside in parallel clauses) is clearly seen in verse 6, and a distinct rhythm is felt even in the translation of 1:9–11.[1] Whether he used poetry or prose, Haggai was forthright and uncompromising. He had the qualities of an Elijah as he challenged his contemporaries. No-one could fail to grasp his meaning, for he constantly repeated his favourite imperatives: 'consider' (1:5,7; 2:15,18), 'take courage', 'work' (2:4). He made frequent reference to the words of earlier prophets (*e.g.* 1:6, *cf.* Ho. 4:10; Mi. 6:15; and 1:11, *cf.* Ho. 2:9, *etc.*) and could introduce an apt metaphor (1:6e).

One characteristic of Haggai's style is his very free use of the 'messenger formula'. He is not content to introduce his sermons with 'Thus says the Lord of hosts', but often concludes with it (2:7,9,23) and even inserts it elsewhere (2:4,14,23). He is conscious of being a mouthpiece, a voice for his God, and guards against obtruding his own personality. As 'the messenger of the Lord' (1:13) he has to make the message plain and see that it is understood, and no prophet met with a more prompt response. The pattern of the book reflects the fact. First there is accusation (1:1–11), then response (1:12–14), followed by assurance of ultimate success (2:1–9). The pattern repeats: accusation (2:10–17), response (2:18,19), assurance of God's triumph (2:20–23). The proportion of the book devoted to 'the judgment speech' is equal to that devoted to 'the announcement of salvation'.[2]

Though the book is so short, queries have been raised concerning the order of the text. NEB, in a footnote to 1:13, states that the original order of verses may have been 1:14,15,13; 2:15–19, 10–14,1–9,20–23. The suggestion that 2:15–19 should follow chapter 1 originated with J. W. Rothstein,[3] and found acceptance, especially on the Continent, but also in

---

[1] Two writers who think Haggai's oracles were in poetry are A. Bentzen, *Introduction to the Old Testament* (OUP, 1958), p. 156; H. G. Mitchell, *ICC*, pp. 38, 39.

[2] For these terms see Claus Westermann, *Basic Forms of Prophetic Speech* (Lutterworth, 1967), and Klaus Koch, *The Growth of the Biblical Tradition* (A. & C. Black, 1969).

[3] 'Juden und Samaritaner' (*BWAT*, 3, 1908).

England.[1] The date in verse 18 is either omitted as a gloss or brought into line by altering the word 'ninth' into 'sixth' (month). The effect is to leave verses 10–14 isolated and make possible the identification of 'this people' (verse 14) with the Samaritans. The removal of 2:1–9 to precede 2:20 puts at the end the two prophecies that contain an eschatological element. Such dislocation radically alters the book and is quite unsupported by any known text or version.

The publication of the Scroll of the Twelve from the caves of Murabba'at has provided the earliest known Hebrew manuscript of Haggai.[2] It contains about two-thirds of the book (1:12 – 2:10 and 2:12–23), and strongly supports the MT, from which it differs in only two minor points. Since the order of verses is the same as in our Bibles all the evidence previously available is confirmed.

III. HIS MESSAGE

Haggai was a man of one message. He represented the God whom he loved to call the Lord of hosts, the source of all power, the controller of armies, on earth and in heaven (see Additional Note on 'the Lord of hosts', p. 44). It followed that His word had authority; the weather obeyed His commands (1:11); the whole universe was in His grasp and would one day be shaken by His hand (2:6,21).

This same God was consistent in His dealings with men. Though they disregarded Him, He never gave them up. When they failed to fulfil His will He made life hard for them so that they would seek Him (1:5). When they committed themselves to His service He took pleasure in the fact and was glorified (1:8). He changed men's attitudes (1:14) and by His Spirit abode among them (2:5). He would transform the work they did for Him, and cause the nations to supply gifts of gold and silver, all of which belonged to Him by right (2:8).

Haggai listed no catalogue of gross sins. The Jews who returned to Jerusalem appear to have been law-abiding at this

[1] *E.g.* among Continental scholars F. Horst, *HAT*; K. Elliger, *ATD*; O. Eissfeldt, *Introduction*, p. 427. In England L. E. Brown, *Early Judaism* (CUP, 1920), pp. 61f.; D. Winton Thomas, *IB*.
[2] P. Benoît, J. T. Milik, R. de Vaux, *Les Grottes de Murabba'at* (Oxford, 1961), pp. 203–205.

time, restrained still by continuing memories of the exile. What was lacking was dissatisfaction with things as they were, and the consequent drive to initiate action. Resignation killed faith. The ruined skeleton of the Temple was like a dead body decaying in Jerusalem and making everything contaminated (2:10–14). How could the offence be removed? By a concerted effort to rebuild, which would be proof and pledge of a change of attitude from resignation to faith. Once priorities had been put right the presence of the Lord among them would be evident from the prosperity that would accompany both their building and their agriculture (2:9,19).

This assurance of the Lord's present salvation and future purpose pervades Haggai's message and marks him out as a genuine prophet. The bare walls of the present Temple he can see clothed with the silver and gold presented by the nations (2:7–9). Zerubbabel the Temple builder is the coming Davidic ruler, or at least his representative in the contemporary scene (2:21–23). God's universal kingdom, in which the warring nations find their peace in capitulating to Him (2:22; *cf.* 7–9), is the ultimate goal of history, but Haggai sees it beginning in his own time as personal and community affairs are submitted to God's rule. It is not just that everything will turn out right in the end, but that the unchanging God is working out His purposes now: 'My Spirit abides among you; fear not' (2:5). Thus present obedience sets God's people in line with fulfilment of His ultimate purpose, and His Spirit fills them with the conviction that they are experiencing in a small measure 'realized eschatology'.

ANALYSIS

I. AUGUST 520: NOW OR NEVER (1:1-15)
    a. Challenge (1:1-11)
    b. Response (1:12-15)

II. OCTOBER 520: TAKE HEART AND WORK (2:1-9)

III. DECEMBER 520: PROMISE AND PREDICTION (2:10-23)
    a. From now on, blessing (2:10-19)
    b. Zerubbabel, chosen and precious (2:20-23)

COMMENTARY

1. AUGUST 520: NOW OR NEVER (1:1-15)

a. Challenge (1:1-11)

Haggai challenges his compatriots to review their experience since they came back to Jerusalem, and to account for their poverty-stricken conditions of living. Disillusionment had set in after the first exhilarating sense of adventure had passed.

1. This introductory verse takes the place of the customary heading (*cf.* Na. 1:1; Hab. 1:1, *etc.*). The date with which the book begins must have stood out as one of momentous importance, because on that day, for the first time in the post-exilic era, the authentic voice of prophecy was heard. *The first day of the month* was the day of the new moon in the lunar calendar, and there is evidence that it was customary to observe new moon as a holiday, or more literally, as a holy day (Ps. 81:3; Is. 1:13,14; 66:23; Ho. 2:11; Am. 8:5). It was therefore an occasion when it would be possible to gain the ear of this farming community, for there would be festivities in Jerusalem. *The sixth month* at this period would have been the equivalent of our August/September,[1] the time of year when grapes, figs and pomegranates were being harvested.

The use of numbers rather than names to denote the months

---

[1] See the tabulated data in the Introduction (p. 29). The Babylonian system of dating was adopted by the Jews during the exile, and from then on the new year began in the spring. In pre-exilic times there is evidence that the year ended in the autumn after the ingathering of the harvest (Ex. 23:16; 34:22); the so-called Gezer Calendar (*DOTT*, pp. 201–203) also indicates an autumn new year, though it begins with the ingathering and not after it. The idiom 'former rains' (in October/November) and 'latter rains' (March/April) bears out that it was usual to think of new year in the autumn. On the other hand Ex. 12:2, concerning the institution of the Passover, says the new year was to be in the spring. It may be that texts which indicate that the year began in the spring were edited during the exile. 2 Ki. 22–23 presupposes that the year began in the autumn because discovery of the law book, reforms and Passover all happened in Josiah's eighteenth year (R. de Vaux, *Ancient Israel*, Darton, Longman and Todd, 1961, pp. 190–192). Another possibility is that before the exile the civil and agricultural year began in the autumn, and the ritual year in the spring (*cf. NBD*, article 'Calendar').

is usual in the books of Ezekiel and Haggai, but in Zechariah, Esther and Nehemiah Babylonian names are used. During the exile the pre-exilic names for the months fell out of use, and there was reluctance at first to adopt the Babylonian names, associated as they were with heathen worship. Evidently by the fifth century BC heathen connections had been forgotten. Either Zechariah was younger than Haggai and less conservative, or his book was edited later. The omission of the names tends to support the early editing of Haggai's book (see Introduction, p. 30).

The word of the Lord came *by Haggai* (lit. 'by the hand of'). This is a common Hebrew idiom, which means no more than 'by the instrumentality of'. All the same it is unusual in the prophetic books, where the only other occurrence is Malachi 1:1. The normal expression is 'the word of the Lord came to . . . ' (*'el*), and in the scroll from Murabba'at *'el* is the reading in 2:1. The expression 'by the hand of' is frequently used of Moses in the Pentateuch, and of Moses and others in the historical books (Lv. 8:36; 10:11; Nu. 4:37,45; Jos. 14:2; 1 Ki. 16:7, *etc.*, AV, RV). It is therefore unlikely that any doubt is cast on the degree of inspiration of the prophet Haggai. In this sentence the less usual preposition may have been used to avoid repetition of the word 'to'.

The first word was addressed to the two leaders, Zerubbabel and Joshua, but from verse 4 onwards it becomes clear that everyone is involved. *Zerubbabel*, grandson of King Jehoiachin, who had been taken captive to Babylon in 597 BC (2 Ki. 24:15), was the heir apparent to the throne of David. According to the genealogy in 1 Chronicles 3:19 Zerubbabel was son of Jehoiachin's third son, Pedaiah, whereas *Shealtiel*, the eldest, appears to have been childless. Shealtiel most probably adopted his eldest nephew, who from then on would be called by his name; another possibility is that he was born to Shealtiel's widow by levirate marriage.[1] Zerubbabel, a Babylonian name, means 'Seed of Babylon' or, according to S. Mowinckel, 'Shoot from Babylon'.[2]

Governor (peḥâ) of Judah. The extent of Zerubbabel's governorship has been questioned in the light of the fact that there was a governor in Samaria, the provincial centre. As late as the

[1] So W. Rudolph, *Chronikbücher* (*HAT*, 1955).
[2] S. Mowinckel, *He That Cometh.* Trans. G. W. Anderson (Blackwell, 1956), p. 119.

time of Nehemiah the relationship between these two centres of government was still not clearly defined, and we do not know whether there was a succession of governors in Jerusalem between Zerubbabel and Nehemiah. If Zerubbabel's territory was not defined it is easy to see this as a potential source of dispute between Jerusalem and Samaria. *Peḥâ, governor*, is a loan word from Akkadian, and is a reminder that Zerubbabel's appointment had been made by the Persian king.

Joshua (in Ezr.–Ne., Jeshua; LXX *Iēsous, i.e.* Jesus) was son of Jehozadak (Ezr.–Ne., Jozadak), who was taken captive in 587 (1 Ch. 6:15). His famous name meant 'Yahu (a short form of Yahweh) is salvation', and as a descendant of Zadok he came as *high priest*, to be responsible for ecclesiastical affairs in the Jerusalem community. Apart from references to him in the visions of Zechariah, the only other information we have about him is that some of his descendants were among those who married foreign wives in the time of Ezra (Ezr. 10:18).

There is no reason to doubt the impression given in Ezra 3:1–13 that Zerubbabel and Joshua came to Jerusalem with the first caravan to return in the reign of Cyrus. The lists in Ezra 2 and Nehemiah 7 may be the aggregate of several groups of names, representing several repatriations, but even so the fact that the same two names head the list would suggest that Zerubbabel and Joshua were the first two to lead such a return. It is true that, in the legendary story of 1 Esdras, Zerubbabel is in Babylon during the reign of Darius (1 Esdras 3–4), but according to 5:65–73 he was there also in Cyrus's reign. The Ezra account is consistent, whereas that of 1 Esdras is not.

2. Haggai spoke in the name of *the Lord of hosts* (Heb. *ṣebā'ôṯ*), a title which emphasized the invincible might behind the Lord's commands. (See Additional Note, p. 44.) For the returned remnant to be addressed as *this people* rather than 'my people' was a rebuke in itself. Did God disown them? Then He taunted them with their own words *the time has not yet come . . .*, which were realistic. There was much to be done and there were few to do it. The same able-bodied men were in demand for everything, and how could they make a living on their farms as well as build the Temple? It is conceivable that some had questioned whether the rebuilding of the Temple justified all the expenditure involved, and whether God expected it, for it was Cyrus, the Persian king, who had ordered it to be done (Ezr. 1:2,3; but *cf.* Is. 44:28; 45:13). It has even been suggested that a miraculous provision of a new Temple was expected because Ezekiel was 'shown' the Temple he described (Ezk. 40–43), and made no mention of its reconstruction. 'Rebuilding was a betrayal of the eschatological hope.'[1]

Difficulties in the Hebrew of this verse are reflected in the AV and RV. RSV emends the text to obtain a smooth translation, altering the infinitive of the verb *to come* (*bo'*) into the finite *has . . . come* (*ba'*), and deleting the first occurrence of the word 'time' (*'et*). The latter has the support of the LXX, but the repetition in the Hebrew may represent remarks being interjected by the crowd.

3. When the reader is expecting to hear a comment on the attitude of the people the repetition of the messenger formula in this verse is an anticlimax. If, however, the spokesmen of the people had been heckling the prophet, the emphatic introduction is understandable. What follows is the master-stroke that carried the day. The dialogue between the Lord and His people has reached its climax.

4. He challenges their priorities. The pronoun *you* is repeated in the Hebrew, so adding emphasis: 'Is it a time for you, you I say, to dwell in your roofed-in houses?' The reply might have been that it was unreasonable to expect anyone to live in a roofless house, but the question made its point. What worth did they set on their God when they left His Temple in ruins?

The word translated 'roofed-in' (Heb. *sāp̄an*) means both 'to cover in' and 'to panel' (*cf.* RSV). Its root provides the noun for 'ceiling' (*cf.* AV, RV). Haggai probably implies that the people had completed their homes rather than that they had gone to the lengths of adorning them with wood panelling, but it could be that the governor's residence was being reconstructed with some of the elegance of Solomon's palace. If so there was particular point in addressing Zerubbabel and Joshua. The conflict between expenditure on luxury homes and worthy support of God's work is still with us.

5–7. *Consider* is one of Haggai's characteristic expressions (2:15,18 twice, as well as twice in these verses). The north-country expression 'think on' captures the note of rebuke and warning in the original here. Reflection on events in the light

[1] R. G. Hamerton-Kelly, 'The temple and the origins of Jewish apocalyptic', *VT*, XX, 1, 1970, p. 12.

of God's word is indispensable if God's people are to know the meaning of His providential ordering of their everyday affairs. Thus Moses reflected on the Exodus events in Deuteronomy 1–11, drawing out salutary guide-lines from past failures and disappointments. It was no surprise to Haggai that for all their hard work the people found no satisfaction, and that their money disappeared like flour through a sieve. God was speaking to them through such circumstances as rising prices and inflation.

Though minted coins were in use to a limited extent in this period (Ezr. 2:69), it is unlikely that a workman's wages would be paid in coinage as early as this. The money bags referred to would contain wedges or discs of copper or silver, approximately defined in value, but since forgery was not unknown, and metal was often pared away, it was necessary to weigh out the sum for each transaction (*cf.* Zc. 11:12, where the shekels of silver still had to be weighed out).

8. After this assessment comes the central part of the message, with its command to collect timber from the hills and build. There is no specific mention of repentance, but by obeying they will be turning their backs on apathy and indifference, so demonstrating their repentance in action. In the long run it is the deed that matters (Mt. 21:28–32). No mention is made of bringing stone, probably because this was available locally, whereas wood was not. The hills of Judah were well wooded in Old Testament times, and from Nehemiah 8:15 we know that olive, myrtle and palm were available. It was customary to set layers of wood in stone walls to minimize earthquake damage (*cf.* Ezr. 5:8); this wood, and heavy timber, long enough to stretch from wall to wall of the Temple to support the roof, would probably have to be imported (Ezr. 3:7). Solomon had introduced conscription in order to force the population to hew stone and carry loads (1 Ki. 5:13–18). Haggai was expecting voluntary service.

That I may take pleasure in it. When work is gladly done in order to please God it also brings Him glory. The RSV translation of the last clause, *that I may appear in my glory*, changes the strict sense of the Hebrew which means literally 'I will get glory to myself' (*cf.* AV, RV), and the link which is sometimes made with Ezekiel 10:18 and 43:4 on the grounds of that translation is not justified.

9. Reverting now to the economic plight of the people, Haggai maintains that there is a direct connection between their poverty and their neglect of the Temple (*cf.* Ho. 2:8, where gold and silver as well as crops are the direct gift of God).

10. They could not plead ignorance for failing to recognize God's hand in the failure of their harvests. They were expected to know and apply Amos 4:6–10 (*cf.* also Hg. 2:17), Hosea 4:10 and Micah 6:15. The heavens and the earth obeyed their Creator's word but His people did not (*cf.* Is. 1:2,3; Je. 18:14–17). *Dew* was important, especially in August and September, to prevent ripening grain from wilting in the heat.

11. By the simple expedient of withholding rain or dew God can reduce human pride and self-sufficiency. A play on words links *drought* (*ḥōreḇ*) with the Temple 'ruin' (*ḥārēḇ*, 1:4,9).

b. Response (1:12–15)

Though the impact of Haggai's sermon was such that a unanimous decision was taken to resume work on the Temple, he took none of the credit. It was the Lord's doing.

12. With Zerubbabel and Joshua in the lead *all the remnant of the people* obeyed. The 'remnant' theme had been especially characteristic of Isaiah's prophecy. In the Temple vision he was warned of destruction, which only a small proportion would survive (Is. 6:11–13), and his son's name, Shear-jashub (meaning 'a remnant shall return'), became a *motif* in his preaching (Is. 7:3; 10:21; 11:11). Both Haggai and Zechariah recognized in the small group of repatriated Jews fulfilment of Isaiah's prophecy, but more was required of them than mere physical presence in the land if they were to fulfil Isaiah's hopes. The verb 'return' (*šûḇ*) also meant 'repent' (*cf.* Zc. 1:3), and it is significant that in Haggai the word 'remnant' is applied to them when they respond in obedience to *the voice of the Lord their God*. There is no quibbling as to Haggai's authority (*cf.* 1 Ki. 22:24; Mi. 2:6). *The people feared before the Lord.* This fear is in contrast to the careless indifference which had faced the pre-exilic prophets. When God has spoken, apathy is evidence of practical atheism. They 'feared' in the sense that they had been startled wide awake by the voice of God.

13. Once the people had registered their intention of carrying out Haggai's instructions they received the encouraging word *I am with you, says the Lord.* So God endorses and strengthens our good resolves. Haggai may have been referring to Isaiah 42:18 – 43:7, a passage in which the prophet reviewed Israel's past and then in glowing terms spoke of the return from exile saying 'Fear not, for I am with you' (verse 5). If so, the reference to Haggai as *the messenger of the Lord* may have been suggested by the use of the same phrase in Isaiah 42:19. Though Haggai is not referred to elsewhere in this way, there is no need to consider this verse as a later interpolation. The phraseology is explained by association of ideas. Israel, for so long deaf and dumb, was at last responding. The translation of H. L. Ellison,[1] 'Then spake Haggai, The Angel of the Lord is *here* with a message for the people, saying I am with you, saith the Lord', is possible, and would be a natural way of understanding the text if the book were Zechariah. Haggai nowhere suggests a supernatural messenger.

14. Behind the willing response of both leaders and people was the silent working of the Lord, creating a willing attitude by His Spirit (*cf.* Zc. 4:6). The turning-point had come and work began again *in the house of the Lord* (AV, RV). The preposition 'in' (*be*) implies that the shell of the building remained.

15. According to the date given here there was a delay of twenty-three days between the original prophecy and the resumption of work. For this reason it has been suggested that the day of the month was inserted by mistake from 2:10. According to J. W. Rothstein, 2:15-19 should now follow, to bring forward to the sixth month the ceremony marking the new rebuilding project.[2] It is possible to make good sense of the text, however, without rearranging it. The *sixth month* was a month of harvesting, when urgent tasks in the orchards and fields would have to be completed. Twenty-three days would allow that work to be finished, after which every able-bodied man could be expected to report at the Temple site.

[1] H. L. Ellison, *Men Spake from God* (Paternoster Press, 1952), pp. 120, 121.
[2] See Introduction p. 31 and the commentary on 2:14.

Additional Note on 'the Lord of hosts'

This title for God occurs nearly 300 times in the Old Testament, predominantly in the prophetic books (247 times), and is particularly frequent in Haggai (14 times), Zechariah (53 times) and Malachi (24 times). It is relevant, therefore, in a study of the post-exilic prophets to examine the significance of this popular traditional name for God.

The Hebrew *ṣᵉbā'ôṭ* ('hosts') has the primary meaning 'army' (hence the Latin *Dominus exercituum*, 'Lord of armies'), and in a few contexts the Lord is spoken of as God of Israel's armies (1 Sa. 17:45; Ps. 24:7–10). Yet there are many passages on the subject of the Lord's help in war where this title does not occur (notably Dt. 1:30; 7:18,19, *etc.*), and a merely nationalistic interpretation fails to do justice to the theology of even early historical passages. Israel's armies were not always victorious, and the ark of the covenant of the Lord of hosts itself was captured (1 Sa. 4:4–11), after which it is referred to as 'the ark of God' (verse 13, *etc.*). The prophets were certainly not disposed to teach that Israel's armies could expect divine favour in battle, and they are not likely to have used the title with that in mind.

The name 'Lord of hosts' does not occur at all in the books Genesis to Judges, but first occurs in 1 Samuel 1:3, which tells how Elkanah went 'to worship and to sacrifice to the Lord of hosts at Shiloh'. It occurs again in Hannah's prayer (1:11) and in the description of the ark (4:4). Why it should have been coined in the eleventh century at Shiloh is so far unexplained, but the original connection was evidently with worship rather than with battles, in which case the 'hosts' were angelic beings. It is in this way that the LXX translator of Psalms and the translator of the Qumran Greek scroll of Zechariah understood the name, translating *kurios tōn dunameōn*, that is, 'Lord of the powers of heaven', though LXX of Haggai and Zechariah has the more general *kurios pantokratōr*, 'Almighty Lord'. These angelic hosts were symbolized by the golden cherubim which covered the ark, and on which the Lord of hosts was enthroned (1 Sa. 4:4). When David transferred the ark to Jerusalem he blessed the people in the name of the Lord of hosts (2 Sa. 6:18; *cf.* verse 2), and his prayer concerning the building of the Temple asked that it might be said, 'The Lord of hosts is over Israel' (2 Sa. 7:26; *cf.* verse 27). From David's time on there was this particular link between this title and the city of

Jerusalem, 'the city of the Lord of hosts' (Ps. 48:8). Isaiah, who in the Temple saw 'the King, the Lord of hosts' (Is. 6:1–6), frequently used this name in his ministry in Jerusalem.

There is, therefore, some evidence for the view that the title is the peculiar Temple and cultic title for the deity, and its occurrence in the antiphonal Psalm 24, proclaiming that the King of glory is entering His holy place, would support this. On the other hand the title is used by prophets who were not connected with Jerusalem. Elijah on Mount Carmel had been 'very jealous for the Lord, the God of hosts' (1 Ki. 19:10,14); Elisha spoke to the Northern Kingdom in the name of the Lord of hosts (2 Ki. 3:14), and Amos confronted Israel with the word of 'the Lord God, the God of hosts' (Am. 9:5), and was about to judge and condemn them to exile (Am. 3:13; 4:12,13; 5:27; 6:14).

One further possibility is that the created 'hosts', the stars, were primarily in mind when this title was used. Isaiah 40:26 (*cf.* Gn. 2:1) would support this, while in 45:12,13 it is clearly the Creator who is identified with the Lord of hosts. During and after the exile, when the ark was no more and the Temple lay in ruins a cosmic reference may well have predominated. It is the thesis of B. N. Wambacq[1] that it is possible to trace the development of the idea from an original military association to the cosmic understanding of it in the prophets.

Reaction against an evolutionary approach is well represented by G. von Rad, who argues that we must abandon the attempt at rational explanation of a name for God as old as this,[2] and implies that the name will have had different connotations for each period and each author. A very different conclusion follows from the argument of O. Eissfeldt[3] that the plural 'hosts' is an intensive abstract plural, of which there are other examples in Hebrew. The translation would then be 'Lord of might' or 'mighty Lord'. This view, which is tending to become accepted, cuts across the various possible meanings of the word 'hosts' and arrives at a generalization which, in translation, loses the vivid references of the original. The One in whose name the prophets spoke was Lord of all powers, seen and unseen, in the universe and in heaven.

[1] *L'Épithète Divine Jahvé Seba'ôt* (Bruges, 1947).
[2] G. von Rad, *Old Testament Theology.* Trans. D. M. G. Stalker (Oliver and Boyd, 1962), pp. 18f.
[3] O. Eissfeldt, 'Jahwe Zebaoth', *Miscellanea Academica Berolinensia*, II, 2 (1950).

II. OCTOBER 520: TAKE HEART AND WORK (2:1–9)

It was nearly a month after work started when Haggai was
given a new word from the Lord. We can guess that during
the intervening weeks efforts were concentrated on clearing
the site of rubble, re-dressing stone that was fit for use, testing
for safety the walls that still remained (for we know that even
after bombing a surprising amount of a stone building may
remain standing), and organizing teams of workmen for their
particular tasks. Such preparations on a sixty-year-old ruin,
without any mechanical aids, would tax the endurance of even
the most enthusiastic; hence the need of encouragement. But
there was another factor.

Progress would have been delayed during the seventh month
by the major festivals on which no work would be allowed. In
addition to sabbath rest days, the first day of the month was
the Feast of Trumpets, and the tenth the Day of Atonement
(Lv. 23:23–32). Then on the fifteenth day the Feast of Booths
began, when the whole population moved out of their homes
to live in leafy shelters for a week in memory of the Exodus
wanderings. It was also an occasion of rejoicing in the harvest,
through which, year by year, they proved God's faithfulness
to His promises (Lv. 23:33–36,39–44; Dt. 16:13–15). It would
be understandable if the enthusiastic, longing to see some
evidence of progress, were impatient with holy days.

1, 2. As though to reassure such people Haggai delivered
his second major sermon on the last ordinary day of the Feast
of Booths. The twenty-second day of the month was a solemn
rest-day (Lv. 23:39). Once again he was instructed to address
Zerubbabel and Joshua, who are again given their full official
titles, but this time *the remnant of the people* are included (*cf.* the
commentary on 1:12).

3. The revered elders who remembered the Temple before
its destruction must often have spoken nostalgically of its
splendour. Some of them no doubt took part in the abortive
attempt to rebuild in 538 BC (Ezr. 3:8–13). Past disappointment was making them gloomy about the present and future.
The new Temple would never be like the old; they had no
resources to pay skilled craftsmen from abroad, as Solomon had
done, and they could not begin to think of covering the interior
with gold (1 Ki. 6:21,22). In spite of the work they had already

put in there was nothing to show for it. Unfavourable comparison between the present and the past undermined all incentive to persevere.

4, 5. *Be strong* (AV, RV; *take courage*, RSV) was the command repeated many times to the earlier Joshua (Dt. 31:7; Jos. 1:6, 7,9,18) and to Israel (Dt. 31:6; Jos. 10:25), as they went into the land for the first time. One of these passages might even have been the theme of the day's meditations at the end of this week during which the events of the Exodus had been commemorated (verse 5). There is an echo of Haggai's oratory in the threefold command in verse 4. *All you people of the land* means here and in Zechariah 7:5 all the ordinary people as opposed to the leaders. Contrast this with the meaning of the phrase in Ezra 4:4, where it refers to the adversaries of Judah and Benjamin (verse 1).

There is a striking parallel between Haggai's exhortation and the words of Jesus in Mark 6:50, 'Take heart, it is I; have no fear.' The personal presence of the Lord gives courage, determination, and the conviction that He will not permit His cause to fail. If the exile had seemed to annul the covenant, here was the sure word that, just as God had been present with His people during all the events of the Exodus (Ex. 29:45), so He was with them still by His Spirit. *My Spirit abides among you* (*abode among you*, RV). Both translations are justified. The Hebrew participle, which denotes continuous action, includes both past and present within its meaning. God had been present even in apparent disaster, and He made His presence known the moment they repented.

Some commentators have considered verse 5a to be a gloss; indeed it is omitted from the text in NEB and JB, which follow LXX here. The Hebrew means 'the matter which I covenanted with you when you went out of Egypt', but it is not the usual idiom, and, moreover, the clause interrupts the sense, separating the parallel statements 'I am with you' and 'My Spirit abides among you'. A scribe's marginal reference to Exodus 29:45,46 may have become incorporated into the text.

6, 7. The Lord proceeds to make His purpose more explicit. *Once again, in a little while* does not quite convey the meaning. The prophet is saying 'Wait, just one little while'. The interval will not be long before the Lord begins to *shake* all creation. The verb is the Hiphil participle, which conveys that the Lord

47

will cause a series of shakings. Earthquake had early become
a symbol for God's supernatural intervention, especially after
the severe one in the eighth century, by which the prophecy of
Amos is dated (Am. 1:1), and from which he found imagery
for his message (8:8; 9:15). Isaiah took it up (Is. 2:13–21;
13:13; 29:6), as did Joel (3:16) and Ezekiel (38:20). Earthquakes come without warning and there is no escaping their
terrors. Haggai foresees the whole universe in such a series of
convulsions that every nation will gladly part with its treasures.
These will be brought to add beauty upon beauty to the
Temple until it is filled with splendour. Unspectacular service
in a time of financial stringency played its part in God's final
purpose (*cf.* Is. 60:5–22). He was never short of funds.

And the desire of all nations shall come (AV). This familiar translation with its Messianic expectations has rightly been abandoned in the more recent translations. The reason is that,
whereas the Vulgate (and hence AV) has a singular subject,
the Hebrew verb is plural and requires a plural subject: *the
treasures (desirable things*, RV) *of all nations shall come in.* Thus the
Gentiles are seen to have a part to play in the achievement of
God's purposes by bringing their wealth in homage to Him.

8. In the days of Solomon gold had been so plentiful that
silver counted for little (1 Ki. 10:21). By the sixth century it
was the Persians who had inherited the world's wealth, but
they too would pass it on eventually, and the ultimate owner
was the One who made it, the Lord of hosts. Since He owned
it He was well able to transfer it as and when He willed. A
demonstration of this occurred about this time. Opponents
who hoped to bring the building to a halt were ordered to pay
in full the cost of the Temple from the royal revenue in their
own taxation district (Ezr. 6:8–12). This financial provision
probably arrived just after Haggai's daring claim that their
God owned all wealth and would meet their need. Later
Herod the Great and his successors were to lavish wealth on
the Temple. Parts of this structure still remain, identifiable by
the huge, smooth stones used.[1] Its pinnacles glistened with gold
to greet One who was 'greater than the Temple'.

9. *The latter splendour of this house shall be greater than the former*
was literally true under the Herods (Mk. 13:1), but chiefly

[1] André Parrot, *The Temple of Jerusalem.* Trans. B. Hooke (SCM Press,
1957), pp. 76–96.

because the Lord of the Temple came (Mt. 12:6) and super-
seded it (Jn. 2:13–22). *And in this place* (*māqôm*) *will I give
peace* (*šālôm*) (AV, RV). Since the name Jerusalem probably
means 'city of peace', the prophet is making a play on the
word, and at the same time connecting it by assonance to
māqôm, place, a word which in certain contexts has a cultic
meaning (*e.g.* Dt. 12:5,14; 14:23, *etc.*; Ne. 1:9; Je. 17:12;
Ezk. 43:7). *Šālôm* (still used as a greeting 'may you have
peace') sums up all the blessings of the Messianic age, when
reconciliation with God and His righteous rule will ensure a
just and lasting peace. The Temple was the source from which
all blessing would flow (Ezk. 47:1) to make Jerusalem the
centre of the world's well-being, the 'city of peace'. Since
salvation in the end-days was so involved with the Temple,
its rebuilding could not possibly be neglected.

III. DECEMBER 520: PROMISE AND PREDICTION (2:10–23)

a. From now on, blessing (2:10–19)

Before Haggai develops more fully his vision for the future he
recapitulates his earlier sermon (1:2–11). He looks back
(2:10–18) in order to lay stress on the complete change that
will be observable from the very day on which he is speaking.
In order to be precise he supplies the date. Every one of the
prophet's hearers will have such a successful season on his farm
that it will be obvious that God is blessing.

Some commentators divide this passage into two sections
and transfer verses 15–19 to follow 1:15 (*cf.* Introduction,
p. 31). The intended advantage is that the promise of blessing
follows the start of work on the Temple, whereas in the text
as we have it the promise is given when the new crop is planted.
The disadvantage is that verses 10–14 are then left without
explanation or application. To say that they apply to the
Samaritans is an unwarranted assumption. (See below on
verse 14.) Furthermore, such a rearrangement of the text is
entirely arbitrary.

10. The new date (18 December by our calendar) marks a
two month interval since Haggai's previous sermon (2:1). The
early rains began in mid-October round Jerusalem, and once

the ground had become sufficiently soft seed was sown and ploughing begun.[1] By the middle of December this work would have been completed, with all the accompanying hopes of a good year, free from drought and pests. This was exactly what God was planning to give because they had put Him first (verse 19).

Zechariah had begun his ministry in Jerusalem a few weeks previously (Zc. 1:1).

11. Haggai, preaching evidently in the Temple, calls on the priests for an official ruling (*tôrâ*) on a matter of ritual (*cf.* Zc. 7:3; Mal. 2:7). This use of *tôrâ* for a short instruction of the priest was probably the original meaning of the word, which continued alongside the wider application to the Law of God, the Torah, the body of precepts through which God's way of life for man was made known. Eventually the Torah was what we know as the Pentateuch. This development accounts for the older translations (*e.g. Ask now the priests concerning the law* (RV)).[2]

12. Haggai's question is not asking for information, but is a methodological device familiar to every teacher. The exchange of question and answer arouses and sustains interest. *Holy flesh* became 'holy' by being set apart to fulfil a sacrificial purpose. The animal used for a sin offering was 'most holy' (Lv. 6:25). At the end of a Nazirite vow part of the ram of the peace offering, together with tokens from the meal offering, was waved as a gesture of presentation to the Lord, 'a holy portion for the priest' (Nu. 6:20). Such holy portions must frequently have been carried in the robes of the priests. According to Leviticus 6:27 the garment itself would be holy, but holiness would not be passed on from the garment to anything it might touch.

13. By contrast ritual defilement was passed on by contact, like a contagious disease (Lv. 11:28; 22:4-7).

14. *So it is with this people.* The application is twofold. (i) Israel had originally been set apart for the Lord and was therefore holy (Ex. 19:6), but (ii) the nation had been defiled,

---

[1] Evidence that sowing preceded ploughing is given by J. Jeremias, *The Parables of Jesus.* Trans. S. H. Hooke (SCM Press, Revised Edn. 1963), p. 11.
[2] On the meaning of *tôrâ* see R. de Vaux, *Ancient Israel.* Trans. J. McHugh (Darton, Longman and Todd, 1961), pp. 353-357.

and everything it touched, including its offerings, became unclean. The ruined Temple, a witness to sins of negligence, stood like a corpse in the midst. How could the defilement be purged away if every offering was itself defiled? The Levitical law provided rituals for certain emergencies, but these dealt only with outward uncleanness, for which the passing of time, together with ceremonial washing, was sufficient to provide cleansing. For Israel there was no known remedy. The only hope lay in free acceptance by God, and the promised blessing (verse 19) implies that such acceptance was granted. By heeding the prophet's rebuke and by turning good intentions into actions Israel exercised faith and experienced saving grace.

The rearrangement of the text which allows 'this people' to refer to the Samaritans is given in the Introduction, pp. 31f., where it is pointed out that no known text deviates from the traditional order. The suggestion arose because the Samaritans were responsible for causing the original attempt at rebuilding to cease (Ezr. 4:1–5), and therefore Haggai might have been expected to refer to their opposition. If, however, this was his intention, why was he not more explicit? Why did he not mention the Samaritans by name and drive home his point with one of his favourite imperatives? Morever, the expression 'this people' was used by Jeremiah to reproach the inhabitants of Judah (Je. 6:19,21; 14:10,11), and by Haggai himself (1:2) to rebuke his compatriots. There is no evidence that he uses the expression with a different reference in this verse. 'If the Samaritan schism lies behind Haggai's oracle in ii 10–14, it is more implicit than explicit. The burden of proof lies on those who presume it.'[1]

15. *From this day onward.* The Hebrew idiom was capable of reference backwards as well as forwards in time.[2] Like a signpost it stood at the parting of the ways, pointing back over the road already travelled and on to the way ahead. First Haggai observed that things had gone from bad to worse ever since work on the Temple had been deferred (Ezr. 4:24). *How did you fare?* is taken from LXX, and replaces the opening words of verse 16 in AV, RV. JB also borrows from LXX and translates *What state were you in?*

[1] Herbert H. May, ' "This People" and "This Nation" in Haggai', *VT*, XVIII (April 1968), p. 192.
[2] BDB, p. 751, but see also Addenda et Corrigenda, p. 1125.

16. *Since those days were* (AV), *through all that time* (RV) are attempts to translate a problematic expression, which even the earliest translators found difficult (*cf.* LXX, verse 15, which is a guess). For years the grain had given only a fifty per cent yield and the vines even less. The word translated *winevat* is strictly 'winepress' (*cf.* Is. 63:3, the only other place where it is used), but the vat underneath, which collected the juice, was included by metonymy.

17. *I smote you.* The Lord of the harvest had power to withhold it and so give warning of His displeasure (Dt. 28:22; Am. 4:9). Haggai is referring to Amos here, and therefore the defective Hebrew at the end of the verse (lit. 'not you to me') is justifiably emended from Amos 4:9.

18. Having looked back, Haggai now looks ahead *from this day onward.* He makes a solemn declaration, dated with the precision of a legal document, that the newly-sown seed will yield abundantly. *Since the day that the foundation . . . was laid.* Once again Haggai sees the rebuilding of the Temple as the event of crucial importance. For the significance of the phraseology see Additional Note on 'the day that the foundation of the Lord's temple was laid', below.

19. The seed was in the soil and not *in the barn,* but in the middle of winter no-one would have dared forecast the quality of the next year's harvest. Haggai's boldness proves how certain he was that his revelation was authentic.

Additional Note on 'the day that the foundation of the Lord's temple was laid' (2:18)

It is frequently pointed out that, whereas a foundation-laying ceremony is recorded in Ezra 3:10–13, in Haggai no knowledge of such an event is evident. Indeed verse 18 is said to refer to another foundation-laying ceremony in the year 520 BC. Since the book Haggai is reckoned a good historical source, while the work of the Chronicler is late and shows evidence of special interests (Ezra–Nehemiah is generally considered to be part of the Chronicler's work), it has sometimes been assumed that Haggai's silence proves that there was no foundation-laying ceremony in 538.

The Hebrew word used both in Haggai 2:18 and in Ezra 3:6 for 'the foundation . . . was laid' is the verb *yāsaḏ*, which means in most contexts 'to found'. Note that the Hebrew employs no noun corresponding to the English 'foundations'. Two sentences in which the Chronicler uses this verb are particularly instructive: 'Now concerning . . . the rebuilding of the house of God . . . ' (2 Ch. 24:27, RV), and, speaking of the collection of tithes, 'In the third month they began to lay the foundation of the heaps' (2 Ch. 31:7, RV) or 'they began to pile up the heaps' (RSV). These examples show that the word 'foundation' is not essential; in fact it has been a very misleading translation. In both the sentences quoted *yāsaḏ* could have been adequately translated by the simple verb 'build'.

Similarly in Ezra 3:10,11 it would be equally correct and less misleading to translate, 'And when the builders began the restoration' (verse 10), and 'because the restoration of the house of the Lord had begun' (verse 11). Understood in this way the text presents no contradiction between the account of Ezra and the prophecy of Haggai. Work did begin on the Temple site in 538, only to cease shortly afterwards until, as a result of Haggai's rebuke, it was resumed in 520 BC.

This interpretation explains the fact that the rebuilding was accomplished in four and a half years,[1] whereas it had taken Solomon, with all his resources of manpower and materials, seven and a half years (1 Ki. 6:37,38) to complete the original Temple. Far from being razed to the ground much of the stonework remained intact after the fire (2 Ki. 25:9). The main need was for wood (Hg. 1:8) to replace what had been burnt. There was no question of relaying foundations.

b. Zerubbabel, chosen and precious (2:20–23)

Haggai's last recorded word is addressed to an individual, Zerubbabel, the Davidic prince. In traditional eschatological language he presents a new phase of world history, when thrones will fall before neighbouring armies, and Zerubbabel will become God's chosen man of the hour.

It is natural to assume that Haggai (and Zechariah) expected this new age to dawn in their own time as a result of

---

[1] It began in the sixth month of the second year of Darius (Hg. 1:1, 24) and was finished in the twelfth month (Adar) of the sixth year of Darius (Ezr. 6:15).

the upheavals at the beginning of the reign of Darius. As time passed, and Zerubbabel was not honoured as had been expected, the Messianic hopes were transferred to his descendants. As the writer to the Hebrews realized there was an important principle, amply illustrated in Old Testament story, in the deferment of the promise (Heb. 11:13). Zerubbabel might have been added to the list of those who by faith looked longingly for its fulfilment.

20. This last word is said to come *to Haggai* and not 'by' him, a fact which bears out the argument that there is no particular significance in the less usual 'by'. (*Cf.* the comment on 1:1.) There is no reason to doubt that the prophet could receive two separate messages on one day (*cf.* 2:10).

21. The shaking of *the heavens and the earth* would not only be a signal for the nations to bring their wealth (2:7-9), but also an indication that the last days had come.

22. The prophet uses traditional vocabulary for God's miraculous intervention. As at the Exodus horses, chariots and riders will *go down* (Ex. 15:1,5); kingdoms will be *overthrown* as were Sodom and Gomorrah (Dt. 29:23; Is. 13:19; Je. 20:16; Am. 4:11); men will fall *every one by the sword of his fellow* (Jdg. 7:22; Ezk. 38:21, Zc. 14:13). The fact that Judah is small and defenceless makes no difference when God says *I will overthrow*. He will act, and Judah will not need to fight.

23. The vocabulary continues to have special significance. *I will take you* (*lāqaḥ*); the verb is here used in the sense of special selection (Ex. 6:7; Jos. 24:3; 2 Sa. 7:8). Zerubbabel is not only governor (verse 21) but also *my servant*, a title used of David (Ezk. 34:23; 37:24) and prominent in Isaiah 40-55. Moreover, 'servant' and *chosen* are in juxtaposition in Isaiah 41:8; 42:1; 44:1. The tribe of Judah, Mount Zion and David were similarly 'chosen' (Ps. 78:68-70) to fulfil God's purposes. Zerubbabel's grandfather, Jehoiachin (Coniah), had apparently been rejected, 'Though Coniah ... were the signet ring on my right hand, yet I would tear you off' (Je. 22:24). Now the sentence is reversed. The signet ring, engraved with the king's seal, was used to endorse all official documents (*cf.* Est. 8:10). It was so precious that, to guard it against theft, it was usually worn on the king's person. This vivid figure attested the renewed election of the Davidic line, represented

54

in Haggai's day by Zerubbabel. He too would be kept safe to fulfil his God-appointed destiny.

Later generations thought very highly of Zerubbabel. His name is included with that of Joshua among the famous men of the fathers of Israel (Ecclesiasticus 49:11), and even today it occurs in the Hanukkah hymn recounting God's deliverances: 'Well nigh had I perished, when Babylon's end drew near; through Zerubbabel I was saved after seventy years.'[1]

Haggai continues to call God's people to zealous service. Half-hearted allegiance is no allegiance. To think that any time will do to become serious about His cause is to fail Him completely. He is waiting to bless, but He cannot do so while His people are apathetic and self-centred. Moreover, in this mood they experience only shortfall, whereas He wants to shower them with good things. Haggai's remedy for today, as for his own day, is a church mobilized for action, to which he would say, 'Take courage, work, fear not.' God's future purpose will be achieved and will prove to be more glorious in fulfilment than in prospect by the degree to which Jesus Christ was more glorious than the Temple.

[1] *Daily Authorised Prayer Book of the United Hebrew Congregations of the British Empire.* A New Translation by Rev. S. Singer (London, 1891), p. 275.

ZECHARIAH

INTRODUCTION

THERE is a marked contrast between Haggai and his contemporary Zechariah. If Haggai was the builder, responsible for the solid structure of the new Temple, Zechariah was more like the artist, adding colourful windows with their symbolism, gaiety and light. To make sure that their symbolism is rightly understood an interpreting angel acts as guide, adding in some cases a message that goes far beyond what could be deduced from the visions. The short introduction (1:1–6), and the two chapters dealing with the relevance of current fast days (7; 8), form the framework enclosing the 'book of visions'.

The last six chapters are very different. Gone are the bold outlines, and instead there are enigmatic references to enemies of former days, grim battles, betrayal, bitter weeping, interspersed with assurances of peace, prosperity and ultimate victory. It is probably with these chapters in mind that Jerome wrote, ' . . . that most obscure book of the prophet Zechariah, and of the Twelve the longest . . . '.[1] Obscure though it is in places, chapters 9–14 are the most quoted section of the prophets in the passion narratives of the Gospels[2] and, next to Ezekiel, Zechariah has influenced the author of Revelation more than any other Old Testament writer.[3] For this reason alone the book deserves careful study.

Though Zechariah supplements Haggai and Malachi, he makes a contribution all his own to post-exilic prophecy. While they are firmly based on present realities, Zechariah, though as aware as they of the spiritual needs of his contemporaries, goes on to introduce glimpses of things as they are from a heavenly standpoint. The transcendent God is working out His eternal purpose for Judah and Jerusalem, equipping His covenant people to fulfil the spiritual role for which He chose them (Zc. 1:7 – 6:15). The prophet goes on

[1] Quoted by P. Lamarche, *Zacharie IX–XIV. Structure Littéraire et Messianisme* (Gabalda, Paris, 1961), p. 7, ' . . . obscurissimus liber Zachariae prophetae, et inter duodecim longissimus . . . '.
[2] P. Lamarche tabulates a comparison between the number of quotations from Isaiah 40–55 and Zechariah 9–14 (p. 9).
[3] P. Carrington, *The Meaning of Revelation* (SPCK, 1931), pp. 268–271.

to spell out in everyday terms the quality of life which they are to display (7:1 – 8:23). But he knew it would be misleading to give the impression that the goal would be reached through a gentle evolutionary process. The last six chapters are dominated by struggle and tension. At first the battle is local and God's people triumph, but later the rejection of the good shepherd (11:4–17), mourning (12:10 – 13:1) and the slaughter of the shepherd (13:7–9) intensify the sinister impression that evil forces are gaining control. Finally they capture Jerusalem, and that is the signal for the Lord's intervention to establish His kingdom over all the earth.

The book prepares God's people for the worst calamity they can ever face, the triumph of evil over good. Even God's representative dies at the hand of evil men. There is no room in Zechariah's thinking for glib optimism, but when evil has done its worst the Lord remains King, and will be seen to be King by all the nations.

I. AUTHORSHIP

a. Zechariah the Prophet

The book is called after Zechariah (Gk. *Zacharias*), whose genealogy, given in the opening verse and repeated in 1:7, is 'son of Berechiah, son of Iddo', but when he is referred to in Ezra 5:1 and 6:14 he is called 'son of Iddo'. The simplest explanation of this discrepancy is that the writer of Ezra omitted a generation and used the idiom 'son of' to stand for grandson, as it frequently does in the Old Testament. The matter is dealt with more fully in the commentary on 1:1. While nothing is known about Berechiah, an Iddo who could be the prophet's grandfather is named in the list of priests and Levites who accompanied Joshua and Zerubbabel in the original return from exile (Ne. 12:4). Later in the same chapter (verse 16) the name Zechariah appears as head of the house of Iddo in the time of the high priest Joiakim, who held office between Joshua and Eliashib. There is no means of knowing the dates of these high priests; we only know that Eliashib was high priest in 445/4 (Ne. 3:1), and if Joshua held office till about the turn of the century, Joiakim might have been high priest from about 500 to 460 BC. Clearly Zechariah would have been a young man in 520, and would have become head of the family some thirty or forty years later.

While it is quite possible, and even likely, that the prophet is to be identified with the Zechariah of the priestly family of Iddo, the fact that Zechariah was a common name, borne by over thirty Old Testament characters,[1] points to the need for caution before jumping to conclusions. All the same, though the prophet reveals little information about himself in his book, there is a certain amount of internal evidence for thinking that he was a priest. Not only was he deeply concerned that the Temple should be rebuilt, but he also appreciated the responsibilities of the high priest, as the fourth vision shows. Access to God's presence was assured to Joshua (3:7); guilt had been removed (3:4,9), and after the long interval without Temple or officiating priest Zechariah still believed that the priest was indispensable if men were to be brought into living relationship with the Lord of hosts. When he envisaged the glorious future he thought in terms of two 'sons of oil' (4:14), priest and prince forming a dyarchy or rule of two.[2] Then again, like Ezekiel the priest-prophet, he was concerned for the cleansing of the land, the removal of its defilement (3:9; 5:3,6–11).

It is clear from the messages which accompany the visions that Zechariah was steeped in the language of the pre-exilic prophets. He does not simply quote. It is rather that their language has become his own and bursts from him under the stress of the message welling up within him. Something of the range of his emotions is reflected in the imperatives he uses: 'cry out' (1:14), 'flee' (2:6), 'escape' (2:7), 'sing and rejoice' (2:10), 'be silent . . . before the Lord' (2:13). Zechariah is no passive observer in these visions, but is fully involved in all that is going on, interjecting remarks, questions, suggestions. His call for silence is reminiscent of Habakkuk 2:20; another near quotation is the reference to a brand plucked from the fire (3:2; cf. Am. 4:11); the picture of men at peace under their vine and fig tree (3:10) recalls Micah 4:4 (cf. 1 Ki. 4:25). Over twenty other allusions to pre-exilic prophets are listed by H. G. Mitchell,[3] including several from both parts of Isaiah, from Hosea, Amos and Micah in the eighth century,

---

[1] Thirty-one people bearing the name Zechariah are identified by T. M. Mauch, *IDB*, IV, pp. 941–943.
[2] G. von Rad, *Old Testament Theology*, II. Trans. D. M. G. Stalker (Oliver and Boyd, 1965), p. 287.
[3] *ICC*, pp. 101, 102.

from Jeremiah and Ezekiel, his immediate predecessors. If Zechariah was typical of the priests in general, the cessation of cultic duties at the fall of the Temple had enabled them to concentrate on their study of the holy books committed to them, and equipped them to carry out their role as teachers and interpreters of the law (Zc. 7:3; *cf.* Dt. 31:9-13).

The dates given in the text link Zechariah's ministry with that of Haggai, showing that they overlapped by one month. (See the table on p. 29.) The last date mentioned (7:1) is the equivalent of 7 December, 518 BC. The historical setting, therefore, is the same as that of Haggai, and Zechariah's first task was to support Haggai in encouraging the completion of the Temple.

b. Zechariah and chapters 9-14

In the attempt to glean such information as the book discloses about its author, no reference was made to chapters 9-14. The reason is that critical scholars have been almost unanimous in thinking that these chapters are of different authorship. Whereas Zechariah's name appears three times in the first eight chapters (1:1; 1:7; 7:1) it is nowhere mentioned in the last six. There are neither dates nor plain references to known events, such as the completion of the Temple, to make clear the historical setting. The fact that these chapters are included under the name of Zechariah in our Bibles could mean no more than that they were anonymous writings, known to be authentic prophetic words but, because of their fragmentary nature, in danger of being lost and needing to be included on the scroll allocated to another prophet to save them from extinction. The Jewish Rabbis have written of cases in the prophets where they believed this principle to have operated.[1]

Arguments against unity of authorship centre round three main issues: contents, style, vocabulary. *a.* The specific purpose of chapters 1-8, namely to rebuild the Temple and city, plays no part in the last six. It is claimed, moreover, that hope of restoring the royal dynasty vanishes from the last chapters. The royal figure of 9:9-10 is not connected with a contemporary prince, and hopes are placed on other Messianic figures, the good shepherd (11:4-14) and the pierced one (12:10 –

---

[1] *Baba Bathra* 14b; *Vayyiqra Rabba* xv. 2; T. B. *Maccoth* 24b. Cited by W. H. Lowe, *The Hebrew Student's Commentary on Zechariah* (Macmillan, 1882), p. 16.

13:1). Whereas power had been divided between prince and priest, now only the priest remains, though this interpretation of the shepherd (11:8,15–17) is suggested by the subsequent history of Judah rather than by the use of shepherd imagery in the prophets. *b*. In the latter part of the book there are no visions. It follows that there is no interpreting angel, nor does the angel of the Lord appear. Instead there are apparently disconnected eschatological glimpses. The first eight chapters are said to be almost entirely prose (but 2:6–13 and 8:1–8 are poetic), and chapters 9–11 poetry, except for 11:4–16, while the last three chapters are prose apart from 13:7–9. In the book as we have it there is in fact both poetry and prose in each section. *c*. The characteristic turns of phrase used in chapters 1–8, such as 'Thus says the Lord', 'The word of the Lord came to me' do not occur later, whereas the opening words of chapters 9 and 12, 'The burden of the word of the Lord' (AV, RV), are not used in the earlier part of the book. 'The Lord of the whole earth' is twice used as a title for God in chapters 1–8, but not at all in 9–14, though it would have been appropriate. Other differences of vocabulary are listed by H. G. Mitchell.[1]

c. A summary of critical views

1. *Date*. It is interesting that the question of Zechariah's authorship of chapters 9–14 was first raised in defence of the accuracy of the New Testament. Joseph Mede (1586–1638), a Cambridge scholar and writer on prophecy, noted the statement in Matthew 27:9 that Jeremiah was the source of the quotation that follows. The words are a free translation of Zechariah 11:13, which led him to conclude that chapters 9–11 were the work of Jeremiah, and therefore pre-exilic.[2] Early in the eighteenth century other British scholars supported this viewpoint, though Bishop Richard Kidder, writing in 1700, attributed all the last six chapters to Jeremiah, and William Whiston, in 1722, agreed with him. Later in the century Archbishop William Newcome, noting the presupposition of chapters 9–11 that Ephraim existed as a separate people and that the named enemies included Assyria and Egypt, assigned

---

[1] *ICC*, p. 236.
[2] The connection of Jeremiah with potters (Je. 18:1–3; 19:1), and his purchase of a field (32:6–15), shows how Jeremiah became associated with the text.

these three chapters to the eighth century, just before the fall of Samaria. The last three chapters, speaking only of Judah, were assigned to the period 609–587 on the ground that 12:11 looked back to the death of Josiah. Newcome's work, published in 1785, exerted a wide influence in Germany during the nineteenth century. L. Berthold argued for an eighth-century date for chapters 9-14, suggesting that the author could have been the Zechariah, son of Jeberechiah (LXX Berechiah), of Isaiah 8:2.

The pre-exilic date had been challenged as early as 1792 by H. Corrodi, another German scholar, who was the first to express the opinion that chapters 9–14 were written long after Zechariah's time, though J. G. Eichhorn, in the second edition of his *Introduction to the Old Testament* (1787), had already hinted at a connection between 9:1–8 and the conquest of Alexander. In a later edition (1824) he attributed chapters 9 and 10 to the Greek period, and chapter 14 to a time just before the Maccabean uprising. Two German scholars who advocated a Maccabean date and became largely responsible for the popularity of this view in the twentieth century were K. Marti (1904) and B. Duhm (1911). Prior to 1935 it went almost unchallenged.

Three main arguments were put forward in favour of the Maccabean dating: linguistic, theological, historical, and their cumulative force was considered incontestable. The language was late, for it contained more Aramaisms than chapters 1–8;[1] the apocalyptic *genre* was thought to have arisen only in the second century; most convincing of all, Maccabean leaders and their fate had inspired the shepherd imagery of 11:4–17 and 13:7–9, as well as the murder in 12:10. W. O. E. Oesterley, for instance, dated the seven sections into which he divided these chapters between about 218 and some time after 134 BC.[2] Two recent writers who continue to argue for a Maccabean date are S. Lasalle and M. Trèves.[3]

Though the case for a Maccabean date might have seemed

[1] G. A. Smith, *The Book of the Twelve Prophets*, EB (Hodder and Stoughton, 1901), p. 459.

[2] W. O. E. Oesterley (and T. H. Robinson), *An Introduction to the Books of the Old Testament* (SPCK, 1934), pp. 419–425; *History of Israel*, II (Oxford, 1932), pp. 212f., 242f., *etc.*

[3] S. Lasalle, 'Le Deutéro-Zacharie date du temps des Macchabées', *Bulletin Renan*, 87, 1962, pp. 1–4; M. Trèves, 'Conjectures Concerning the Date and Authorship of Zechariah IX–XIV', *VT*, 13, 1963, pp. 196–207.

in 1935 to have been established, scholarly opinion soon began to swing in another direction. O. Eissfeldt, who in the first German edition of his *Einleitung in Das Alte Testament* (1934) accepted it, later defended a fourth-century date. 'The view which has come to prevail is rather that ix–xiv should be assigned to the end of the Persian period, or the beginning of the Greek.'[1] Similarly, A. Weiser has modified his views since 1930, and is non-committal about a Maccabean date.[2] Scholars now admit that too little information is available for linguistic evidence to provide any sure basis for the date of a book,[3] and whereas it used to be assumed that theological ideas must have developed in a discernible evolutionary pattern, it is now acknowledged that this is not so.[4] Nor are the apocalyptic traits necessarily as late as the second century. There are apocalyptic elements in the visions of chapters 1–6, and yet these are generally agreed to be sixth-century writings. Even on the identification of the shepherds with Maccabean leaders there was no unanimity (see commentary on 11:4–17; 12:10–14).

At the present time the consensus of opinion favours the Greek period. The opening poem (9:1–8) is thought to reflect the swift advance of Alexander the Great in 332.[5] In subsequent passages there are references to Egypt (9:11; 10:10–11; 14:18, 19), and, according to this view, these reflect conditions during the third century, when Palestine was ruled by the Ptolemies. The reference to Greece (Javan) in 9:13 is taken as an indication that the unified Greek empire, seen now as the enemy of the eschatological future, had already passed into history. Between the death of Alexander in 323 and the establishment of Ptolemy Lagi as master of Palestine in 301 BC, there were two decades of unrest and war such as could have formed the military background of these chapters and given rise to Messianic longings. Among those who favour the Greek period

[1] O. Eissfeldt, *The Old Testament An Introduction*. Trans. P. R. Ackroyd (Basil Blackwell, 1965), p. 436.
[2] A. Weiser, *Introduction to the Old Testament*. Trans. D. M. Barton (Darton, Longman and Todd, 1961), pp. 273–275.
[3] P. R. Ackroyd, 'Criteria for the Maccabean Dating of the Old Testament Literature', *VT*, III, 1953, p. 121. *Cf.* D. Winton Thomas in *Record and Revelation*. Ed. H. W. Robinson (Oxford, 1938), p. 386.
[4] P. R. Ackroyd, *op. cit.*, p. 121; G. W. Anderson in *The Old Testament and Modern Study*. Ed. H. H. Rowley (Oxford, 1951), p. 309.
[5] M. Delcor, 'Les Allusions à Alexandre le Grand dans Zacharie 9:1–8', *VT*, I, 1951, pp. 110–124.

for most or all of chapters 9–14 are G. H. Box, K. Elliger, R. H. Pfeiffer, D. W. Thomas, Th. Chary and the editors of the Jerusalem Bible.[1]

Finally mention must be made of recent scholars who, while not attributing authorship of these chapters to Zechariah, would date all or part of chapters 9–14 early in the fifth century, within the possible lifetime of the prophet. M. Bič[2] thinks they belong roughly to the time of Zechariah. D. R. Jones dates chapters 9–11 between 500 and 450 and P. Lamarche suggests that Zerubbabel may have been the one around whom the Messianic hopes of these chapters are woven, so supporting a date before 500 for the whole section.[3]

2. *Unity.* Once Joseph Mede had attributed chapters 9–11 to Jeremiah the unity of chapters 9–14 was called in question, and it is clear from all that has been said concerning the dates suggested for different sections that many further subdivisions have been made since then.

The simplest was into the two sections, 9–11 and 12–14, each introduced by the words 'The burden of the word of the Lord', a heading which they shared with Malachi. The view was widely held that the formula pointed to three little books of anonymous prophecy, two of which came to be appended to the book of Zechariah, while Malachi became the twelfth of the 'Book of the Twelve'.[4] But whereas the two sections in Zechariah have much in common, Malachi is quite different, and there can never have been any question of its being put together with them.

The occurrence of the shepherd theme in both sections was one of the most obvious links between them. H. G. A. Ewald, writing in 1840, moved 13:7–9 to follow 11:17, so bringing together themes which he thought to have been accidentally separated. Some scholars continue to follow Ewald in this,

---

[1] G. H. Box, *Judaism in the Greek Period*, Clarendon Bible (Oxford, 1932), p. 88; K. Elliger, *ATD*, p. 143; R. H. Pfeiffer, *Introduction to the Old Testament* (A. & C. Black, 1952), p. 1092; D. W. Thomas, *IB*, VI, p. 611; Chary, p. 137; JB, p. 1139.

[2] M. Bič, *Das Buch Sacharja* (Berlin, 1964).

[3] D. R. Jones, 'A Fresh Interpretation of Zechariah IX–XI', *VT*, 12, 1962, pp. 241f.; Lamarche, p. 121.

[4] See, for instance, S. R. Driver, *An Introduction to the Literature of the Old Testament* (T. & T. Clark, 1898), p. 355; G. Fohrer, *Introduction to the Old Testament*. Trans. D. Green (SPCK, 1970), p. 465.

including the translators of NEB, who have rearranged the text. There is, however, strong opinion against this suggestion. K. Elliger keeps the passages distinct because the role of the shepherd in 13:7 is to be identified neither with the good shepherd nor with the foolish shepherds of 11:4–17.[1] Eissfeldt points out that Ewald's suggestion cannot be proved to be correct,[2] a viewpoint shared by Fohrer.[3] All these three writers adopt the distinction between the two booklets, referring to them as Deutero- and Trito-Zechariah, though this does not necessarily imply that there are only two authors. Fohrer, for example, says the last three chapters are 'more likely supplements by one or several authors than a single composition'.[4] Chapter 14 has particular characteristics which, according to several writers, require it to be attributed to a different origin from the rest.

A different way of looking at these chapters is to see them as a mosaic to which many people have contributed. This is the view of Oesterley[5] and of several more recent writers. 'It is a disorderly collection of possibly ancient passages' says the introduction to Zechariah in JB.[6] B. Otzen regards chapters 9–14 as deriving from Judean circles, chapters 9 and 10 in the time of Josiah, chapter 11 immediately prior to 587, chapters 12 and 13 from the early exilic period, and chapter 14 from the last years of the exile.[7] J. Bright thinks of these chapters as an anthology of prophetic oracles.[8] Those who adopt the anthology theory would attribute any orderly arrangement in these chapters to editorial skill; in practice the theory has resulted in detailed studies of small sections taken in isolation, and presumed to be unrelated to the rest.

During the last decade at least two commentators have swung away from the anthology hypothesis. D. R. Jones argues for the unity of authorship, at least for chapters 9–11.[9] He thinks they are the autobiographical framework of a prophet

[1] *ATD*, p. 175.
[2] O. Eissfeldt, *op. cit.*, p. 438.
[3] G. Fohrer, *op. cit.*, p. 468.
[4] *Ibid.*, p. 467.
[5] W. O. E. Oesterley (and T. H. Robinson), *Introduction*, p. 419.
[6] JB, p. 1139.
[7] *Studien über Deuterosacharja* (1964), summarized by O. Eissfeldt, *op. cit.*, p. 762, and by G. Fohrer, *op. cit.*, p. 466.
[8] J. Bright, *A History of Israel* (SCM Press, 1960), p. 417.
[9] 'A Fresh Interpretation of Zechariah IX–XI', *VT*, XII, 1962, pp. 241–259; *TBC*, pp. 117, 118.

living in or near Damascus, and taking pastoral responsibility for Israelites of the northern dispersion in this region. P. Lamarche argues for the unity of chapters 9–14 on the ground that they exhibit a deliberate and well-thought-out structure.

Such a bewildering variety of views on both date and unity leaves the reader at a loss to know what to believe. The very fact that there is such diversity undermines confidence in the methodology used. As P. R. Ackroyd observes, 'It may be wondered whether the attempt to date is the most useful approach to the material.'[1] Historical allusions are vague and defy attempts to refer them to specific people or events. Moreover, the author makes free use of his sources, so that, whatever may have been their origin, they become a vehicle through which to convey persisting truths. If it were necessary to know the historical setting in order to understand their message, these chapters would have to be put aside as an unsolved enigma, but it is hoped to show that the meaning can be known, and that the historical allusions can be interpreted even if the precise event that prompted them cannot be known.

Finally, the question must at least be asked whether after all Zechariah may have been responsible for chapters 9–14. W. E. Barnes, while thinking it unlikely that the two halves of the book proceed from the same author, argues that the second followed the first after only a short interval of time.[2] He points to the centrality of Jerusalem, the sympathetic attitude to Ephraim together with the prominent place given to David as connections between the two parts, and speaks of the 'close bond of union in the common standpoint and the common aim of their authors', whom he designates 'Zechariah the prophet' and 'Zechariah the disciple'. H. G. Mitchell was prepared to state that the metre of the verse in 13:7–9, which he thought should follow 11:17, resembled that of 3:7, the use of which here 'is favourable rather than unfavourable to the authorship of Zechariah'.[3]

Much has already been said about the differences between the two halves of the book, but there are further similarities. In both parts earlier prophets are frequently referred to and quoted. Characteristic phrases in chapters 1–8 recur in 9–14. Compare, for instance, 2:10 with 9:9, and 9:8 with 7:14. This

[1] *PCB²*, p. 651.
[2] *CB*, pp. xviiif.
[3] *ICC*, p. 235.

68

last is a telling example because, though RSV translates 'none shall march to and fro' and 'no one went to and fro', the wording is identical in the Hebrew, and the exact phrase occurs nowhere else in the Old Testament, the nearest equivalent being in Ezekiel 35:7. Stylistic devices common to both parts must be accounted for. There is the idiosyncrasy of dwelling on an idea, as in 6:10,11,13 (take ... take, crown, throne, throne); 8:4,5 (streets ... streets); and in 11:17 (his arm, his right eye, each repeated); 14:5 (ye shall flee ... ye shall flee as ye fled ..., RV); 14:9 (the Lord will be one and his name one). Though some of these repetitions have been excised as glosses enough examples remain to prove the point. Another stylistic device is to achieve emphasis by mentioning the whole and then the part, as in 5:4 (the house ... his house ... both timber and stones) or 12:11-13 (every family, specified in 12, 13). Metaphors are followed by their meaning, as in 10:4. The unusual fivefold development of an idea is found both in 6:13 and in 9:5,7. In both parts there is a fondness for the vocative. There are also similarities of thought, including the need for cleansing (1:4; 3:4,9; 5:1-11; 13:1,9); the promise that the nations will return (2:6,7; 8:7; 10:6-12); the overthrow and conversion of Israel's enemies (1:21; 2:8,9; 8:20-23; 9:1-8; 12:4; 14:16); the hope of a Messianic deliverer and ruler (6:12,13; 9:9,10).

The force of these similarities is admitted by those who postulate that the second part was the work of a disciple of Zechariah, as well as by those scholars, such as C. H. H. Wright, E. B. Pusey, W. H. Lowe, A. van Hoonacker, who have attributed the whole book to Zechariah.[1] In recent years the cogency of the arguments in favour of the unity of the book has been acknowledged by W. F. Albright, E. J. Young, J. Ridderbos and R. K. Harrison.[2] In the nature of the case it is not possible to prove conclusively who wrote chapters 9-14, but when every argument has been considered the fact remains that all fourteen chapters have been handed down to us as one book in every manuscript so far discovered. Even the tiny fragment of the Greek manuscript found at Qumran,

[1] C. H. H. Wright, *op. cit.*, pp. xxxv-xlii; E. B. Pusey, pp. 4-37; W. H. Lowe, *op. cit.*, p. xix; A. van Hoonacker, *RB*, XI (1902), pp. 61ff.

[2] W. F. Albright, *JBL*, 61, 1942, p. 121; E. J. Young, *An Introduction to the Old Testament* (Tyndale Press, 1949) pp. 271-273; J. Ridderbos, *De kleine profeten*, III, 1935; R. K. Harrison, *Introduction to the Old Testament* Tyndale Press, 1970), p. 956.

which includes the end of chapter 8 and the beginning of chapter 9, shows no gap or spacing whatsoever to suggest a break between the two parts.[1] Again, as P. R. Ackroyd comments, 'The very fact that this linking of 9–14 with 1–8 took place argues for some recognition of common ideas or interests'.[2]

If the book is taken to pieces and studied in watertight sections this common interest is likely to be overlooked. In this commentary an attempt will be made to see the book as an artistic whole, with an over-all plan and unity of message. Whether the unity results from the master mind of one prophet or from a redactor or redactors is in the last analysis immaterial. What is urgent is that the whole book, after being fragmented for so long, should once again make its full impact on the church.

II. LITERARY GENRE

At first sight it might seem impossible to describe this book in terms of one literary genre. After a short introduction urging repentance (1:1–6) a series of eight visions, together with explanatory oracles, forms a self-contained unit (1:7 – 6:15). This is followed by two chapters of sermon material which comes to a climax in 8:20–23 with the clamouring of the nations to know God. Chapters 9–14 divide into two halves and bear many signs of apocalyptic, but so do the visions. If it can be demonstrated that the whole book is in some sense apocalyptic, one unifying factor will have been established.

Derived from the Greek name for the last book of the Bible, the 'Apocalypse', apocalyptic is best defined in terms of the contents of that book, though a whole library of books in a similar style preceded it in time, including the book of Daniel in the Old Testament. Both these biblical books taken together provide the characteristics of apocalyptic that apply in the Scriptures.

In each of these books there is a clear arrangement of material, so that it is not difficult to divide them into sections. Each begins at a given point in history. The periods referred to can be identified and described, and yet the content of the

[1] See section on Text, pp. 81ff.
[2] *PCB*[2], p. 651.

70

chapters has a universal application. In Daniel the experiences of Babylonian kings confront them with the God of history who has their lives, their kingdoms and all kingdoms in His control. In Revelation the seven local churches of Asia Minor represent the universal church of every age. Moreover, there is progression in the course of the book from the local scene in Babylon or Asia Minor to the world scene, from a point in time to the end of time. There is much to be said for the description 'progressive parallelism' applied to Revelation by W. Hendriksen.[1] In the briefest terms this understanding of Revelation sees the main division at the end of chapter 11. The two parts are parallel in that they both cover the whole of time between Christ's first and second coming, but in the second part there is progress in intensity of spiritual conflict and in eschatological emphasis.

Though in Revelation this literary form is fully developed to express the advanced stage of apocalyptic there revealed, in Zechariah we have the rudimentary stage of the same literary form. Chapters 1–8 are set in the prophet's own time, but there is eschatology in the pictures of the submission of the nations (1:21; 2:9; 8:20–23), the exaltation of Jerusalem (1:17; 2:4,5, 10–12; 7:3), and the work of the Branch (3:8; 6:12). In chapters 9–14 the starting-point is episodes in Israel's history, but the submission of the nations and the exaltation of God's people are conveyed with deep emotion in highly poetic language, full of allusions. The note of conflict is suggested throughout by the battle imagery, but it becomes centred in the good shepherd of 11:4–14. In chapters 12–14 a pierced one reduces the land to mourning (12:10–14), and the sword strikes the Lord's shepherd (13:7–9). Intense hatred has concentrated itself on one individual, but the final lines of the little poem show men in communion with God(13:9).Chapter 14 leaps to the day when the Lord will reign over all the earth, and so to the end of time (14:7).

Visions are a characteristic feature of apocalyptic. Daniel saw beasts that represented the nations, angels that communicated to him the course of history, and on one occasion he saw the throne-room of God. John in Revelation also saw these things, together with many other symbolic features, drawn from Old Testament literature, but particularly from Isaiah, Ezekiel and Zechariah. Amos and Jeremiah had also

---

[1] *More Than Conquerors* (Tyndale Press, 1962), pp. 34–36.

seen visions of a relatively simple 'impressionist' type, pictures which conveyed their own message. The contrast between these and the involved imagery of Ezekiel marks one distinct step in the direction of apocalyptic. Zechariah's visions are less involved and avoid the grotesque, but to meet his need of an interpreter, angelic beings play a prominent part in chapters 1–6. Where Zechariah's visions go a stage further than those of his predecessors is in declaring as accomplished the pattern for the future which they depict. 'He became aware that Jahweh was jealous for Jerusalem and that he had already made all the preparations for his own advent – he had appointed his representatives and provided for and overcome all complications and opposition. . . . Indeed, even the events which must necessarily precede the advent of the kingdom of God – as, for example, the removal of evil – are already accomplished in the sight of the world above, so that they have anticipated the course of events on earth.'[1] This conviction that God had already worked out His purposes in heaven so that all that remained was for the same pattern to be repeated on earth was to dominate apocalyptic, and is seen in both Daniel and Revelation.

Other significant features of chapters 1–6 include animal symbolism (horses, horns) and symbolic numbers: the numbers two, four and seven are prominent, and are used in Revelation, especially seven, which occurs fifty-four times.[2] The four horses of the first and eighth visions reappear in Revelation 6:1, even the question 'how long?' (1:12) being repeated (Rev. 6:10). The measuring of the city (2:1) features in two passages (Rev. 11:1f.; 21:15f.). The lampstand (4:2f.) becomes a symbol of the church (Rev. 1:20), while two olive trees and two lampstands stand before the Lord of the whole earth in Revelation 11:4 (*cf.* Zc. 4:14). The woman representing wickedness and symbolic horns are the subject matter of Revelation 17, and the seven eyes (Zc. 3:9) represent the seven Spirits of God in Revelation 5:6. As the 'third dimension' of prophetic vision became clearer, these powerful symbols expressed the spiritual significance of everyday, human experience.

Even in the sermon material of these chapters there are apocalyptic trends. The introduction (1:1–6) and chapters 7,

---

[1] G. von Rad, *Old Testament Theology*, II, p. 288.
[2] W. Hendriksen, *op. cit.*, p. 55.

8, with their historical retrospect, aim to show that there is a pattern in Israel's history which makes sense of her past experience of exile. But there is also a future for Israel, thanks to God's jealousy for Zion, and the end He purposes for her (Zc. 8:2f.). She has not completely perished. Numerically she will again become strong (8:4–8), God's presence will bring unprecedented prosperity (8:8–15), and the nations will seek Him for themselves (8:20–23). A blend of history and eschatology provided the thought-forms for the prophet here.

Prophetic eschatology had developed a technical vocabulary before the time of Zechariah. As early as the eighth century BC Amos was proclaiming a day of inescapable judgment in terms of an earthquake (8:8; 9:5), eclipse (8:9), bitter mourning (8:10). Isaiah had foretold the destruction of Jerusalem (3:8), and yet in the eleventh hour she would be delivered (10:28–34; 29:1–8). In chapter 34 Isaiah draws a picture of the Lord's sacrificial feast at which the victims are all the nations, His sword slays the sacrifices, and the land becomes drunken with their blood. Closely related to this is the great battle imagery. Sometimes the nations are summoned by name to the last great battle (Zp. 2), but Ezekiel (38; 39) addresses Gog, prince of legendary lands on the edge of civilization, and conjures up a frightening picture of ill-defined hordes of invaders, coming to fight against the Lord's land. The Lord intervenes to bring them to judgment, deliver His people and glorify His name. All this imagery became the stuff of which apocalyptic is made. Zechariah 9–14 takes up the earthquake theme (14:4–6); the miraculous intervention of the Lord (9:14; 12:3, 4); the eschatological battle (12:1–9; 14:1–15), and the divine deliverance of Jerusalem (9:8; 12:7; 14:1–8); bitter mourning (12:10–14) but ultimate joy (9:9; 14:16). The book of the Revelation uses these among other themes to depict the end of history.

Whereas in chapters 1–8 Zechariah was using the medium of visions to convey his message, in 9–14 the medium is prophetic-apocalyptic, a term coined by G. E. Ladd.[1] Its style had already been developed, and its imagery and vocabulary could be recognized. It is this fact that causes an analytical examination of the language of chapters 9–14 to give such different results from similar tests on chapters 1–8. It is also this apocalyptic strain that strikes the modern reader as strange

[1] 'Why not Prophetic-Apocalyptic?', *JBL*, LXXVII, 1957, pp. 192ff.

and unfamiliar, and makes the book difficult to appreciate. 'There is a language not only of the tongue but also of thought and we must learn to read not only the one but also the other, so that we become familiar with an author's thought forms and ideals and, what is more important, his unconscious assumptions; for until we have achieved this we are not in a position to judge his work.' These words of S. B. Frost[1] sum up the task of understanding and interpreting this book.

III. STRUCTURE

One of the important contributions of modern scholarship to our understanding of the Bible is the realization that its truth is expressed in literary forms and structures as well as in words. The 'shape' of a poem, the artistic arrangement of a book are instruments used by the Holy Spirit to convey His message. It is a great gain that many modern versions of the Bible keep artificial reference numbers as unobtrusive as possible, take a fresh look at the divisions in the text, and endeavour to bring out the poetic structure of the original.[2]

The main divisions in Zechariah are clear enough. After the introduction (1:1–6) come three blocks of material: the visions (1:7 – 6:15); oracles connected with fasting (7:1 – 8:23); eschatological writings, subdivided into two parts (9–11; 12–14). It is obvious that someone has arranged the material systematically, on the general plan of progression from the known to the unknown. The introductory verses appeal for repentance in the year 520 BC, while the closing verses look ahead to the time when all men will worship the true God (cf. the books of Daniel and Revelation in which there is a similar progression). The vast majority of scholars have assumed that the component parts of the book are not homogeneous, and have concentrated on finding the life-setting of each part. Comparatively few have attempted to treat the book as a unity, to see whether there is any over-all plan in its arrangement, whatever the origin of different sections. There is little difficulty in chapters 1–8, for most scholars are prepared to see these as a genuine collection of the prophecies of Zechariah. The problematic chapters are 9–14, which, as has

---

[1] *Old Testament Apocalyptic* (Epworth, 1952), p. 15.
[2] JB excels in this respect, but NEB is a close second.

been evident from a review of suggested dates and authors, are assigned to many different eras.

A fresh approach to the second part of the book has been made by P. Lamarche.[1] His point of departure was the quest for an explanation of the apparently chaotic order of events, and the abrupt changes of subject-matter, and he found his explanation in a literary unity built on a chiastic pattern. It is understandable that scholars should be wary of accepting too readily a conclusion so different from that which has been held for 200 years, but preliminary reviews, while not accepting it without question, have admitted its contribution to an understanding of the text.[2]

The reader unfamiliar with classical terms may be puzzled by the word 'chiastic' and its noun 'chiasmus', but the underlying idea is simple. The Greek letter *chi* is in the form of a cross and, just as the hand in writing that letter moves from left to right and right to left, so the rhyme or thought-pattern indicated by chiasmus is *a b b a*. A simple example from the AV, though not paralleled in the Greek, is 'I cannot dig; to beg I am ashamed' (Lk. 16:3). Charles Wesley demonstrates his mastery of the form in the third verse of his hymn 'Jesu, Lover of my soul':

> Just and holy is Thy name,
> I am all unrighteousness;
> Vile and full of sin I am,
> Thou art full of truth and grace.

[1] P. Lamarche, *Zacharie IX–XIV, Structure Littéraire et Messianisme* (Gabalda, Paris, 1961).

[2] F. Buck, *CBQ*, XXIV, 1962, pp. 319, 320: 'Not every reader may agree with every answer of the author.' . . . 'The study, nevertheless, throws better light on these obscure chapters and introduces the reader to the best of modern literature on Zachariah.' W. Harrelson, *JBL*, 1963, p. 117, writes: 'It seems to me a more probable thesis that a single author is responsible for the remarkable messianic picture found in these chapters, as this picture is explained by Lamarche, but that the six chapters derive from a prophetic circle associated with the older prophet Zechariah. The author of the messianic passages was in all probability a disciple of Zechariah. The followers of this disciple may then have brought together the miscellaneous materials that surround the messianic passages. The pattern found by Lamarche may be the product of such a circle of prophets.' Though he questions the authorship, Harrelson does not deny the pattern. H. H. Rowley, *ET*, 74, 1962, p. 94, commented: 'It will be agreed that the evidence he sets forth has a real impressiveness. What adds to its impressiveness is that he does not have to rearrange the text to make it fit into his scheme, but treats it as it stands.' See also R. Tournay in *RB*, 1962, pp. 588f.

Here the quatrain is a chiasmus (Thy name . . . I . . . I . . .
Thou), and each couplet is also a chiasmus (just and holy . . .
Thy name . . . I . . . unrighteousness; Vile . . . I am . . . Thou
art . . . full of truth and grace).[1] The substitutionary meaning
underlying the words here is conveyed most effectively: form
and content are beautifully matched. In fact the example
illustrates the importance of appreciating the structure of a
piece of writing as a vehicle of the writer's meaning. Such an
appreciation is, of course, quite as important in the case of
biblical literature.

The question will immediately be asked whether Old
Testament writers would be likely to employ such a form.
There is an example as early as Genesis 9:6, 'Whoso sheddeth
man's blood, by man shall his blood be shed' (RV). The
Hebrew is a six-word sentence, 3+3 exactly balancing in the
pattern *a b c c b a*. Again the form is appropriate to the sense,
and lays stress on the exact justice of retribution. An example
from the prophets (Ho. 5:3,4) illustrates how effective chiasmus
can be in drawing a contrast.

> *I know Ephraim*, and Israel is not hid from me;   *a*
>   for now, O Ephraim, you have played the harlot,
>   Israel is defiled.   *b*
>   Their deeds do not permit them to return to their God. *b*
> For the spirit of harlotry is within them,
>   and *they know not the Lord*.   *a*

In a more developed poetic form Psalm 2 demonstrates how,
in the process of thrust and counter-thrust, a dialectic may
express new revelation. The first of the four stanzas reveals the
revolutionary intent of the kings of the nations. In the second
this is countered by the assertion that the Lord will have the
laugh over them and bring forth His king. The decree of the
third stanza establishes His world-wide victory, which, in the
fourth, entails the submission of every rebel king. Psalm 1,
with its contrast between the godly and the wicked man, ends
in a chiastic summary (verse 6). Enough has been said to show
that, far from being foreign to Old Testament writers, chiasmus

[1] I am indebted to Mr H. C. Oakley, formerly a tutor at the London
Bible College, for these examples. *Cf.* Bernard Lord Manning, *The Hymns of
Wesley and Watts* (Epworth, 1942), pp. 21–23.

was a form which they knew how to adapt with great versatility to their particular needs.[1]

Would a book, or a section of a book, be likely to be so designed? Isaiah 2–4 seems to provide an example of chiastic structure. The framework provided by 2:2–4 and 4:2–6 tells of an ideal Jerusalem. Isaiah begins with a Utopian picture of mount Zion exalted to be the focal point of the whole earth, and the Temple as the centre of God's just rule over an effective league of nations. The rest of the chapter is a devastating exposure of actual Jerusalem in its idolatry, pride and materialism, all of which would be reduced to dust when the Lord was exalted in His terror and majesty. Chapters 3:1 – 4:1 declare the downfall of those specially responsible, the leading citizens and their wives. The final section, 4:2–6, ends with an assurance of God's presence in mount Zion, but not before a way of cleansing from all defilement just described is made plain. What remains after that will be called holy. So the Utopian picture with which the prophet began can be seen to have possibility of fulfilment. The general pattern is *a b b a*, but with a progression through accusation, judgment and back to realization of the ideal in spite of all.[2]

P. Lamarche believes that the author of Zechariah 9–14 made use of chiasmus in constructing his prophetic apocalyptic. The pattern is seen most clearly in the plan set out overleaf. The introductory subject, judgment and salvation of neighbouring peoples (9:1–8) *a*, is balanced by the conclusion, in which the theme includes all nations (14:16–21) a^1. In the remaining material, which divides into two sections at the end of chapter 11, three themes may be distinguished: *b* the king, the shepherd and the Lord's representative, all of whom are identified as one and the same person; *c* Israel's war and victory; *d* judgment on idols. These themes form the following pattern in the text: *b* (9:9,10), *c* (9:11 – 10:1), *d* (10:2,3a), c^1 (10:3b – 11:3), b^1 (11:4–17). In the second half the order is inverted: c^2 (12:1–9), b^2 (12:10 – 13:1), d^1 (13:2–6), b^3 (13:7–9), c^3 (14:1–15).[3]

---

[1] H. H. Rowley in his review of Lamarche's book states that A. Condamin some years ago claimed to find chiasmus in the structure of many of the Psalms, as well as in Isaiah and Jeremiah.

[2] Chiasmus has been discerned in the New Testament also by J. Jeremias, 'Chiasmus in den Paulusbriefen', *ZNW*, 1958, pp. 145–156. See also J. C. Fenton, *St. Matthew* (Pelican Gospel Commentaries, 1963), pp. 15f.

[3] The plan is set out by Lamarche, pp. 112, 113. The only alteration is that his headings have been translated, with his permission, into English.

PLAN OF ZE

(according to P. La

a Judgment
and salvation
of neighbouring
peoples (9:1–8)

  b Arrival and
  description of
  the king (9:9–10)

  b^1 The shepherds
  rejected by the
  people (11:4–17)

    c War and victory
    of Israel
    (9:11 – 10:1)

    c^1 War and victory
    of Israel
    (10:3b – 11:3)

      d Presence of idols;
      judgment (10:2,3a)

As in the Isaiah example the glorious picture (the king's arrival) comes first, whereas the inevitable war and the destruction of idolatry are put second. When the prophet refers a second time to the shepherd/king he is rejected. In chapters 12–14 the whole theme is intensified. The war motif is in the first place, and each time it recurs Israel is more helpless. The constant repetition of the ominous 'in that day' is awesome. The Lord's representative is pierced through and the house of David finds repentance and cleansing. In the last shepherd poem, through the smiting of the shepherd and the death of many, a remnant becomes God's people. In each crisis the Lord intervenes to deliver until, on the final occasion, He comes in cataclysmic, transforming power as King. The prophecy ends with all the nations offering true worship in Jerusalem. In the commentary the general chiastic pattern set out by Lamarche has been adopted, though the development

AH 9–14

, pp. 112–113)

a^1 Judgment
and salvation
of all nations
(14:16–21)

c^2 War and victory
of Israel
(12:1–9)

c^3 War and victory
of Israel
(14:1–15)

b^2 Yahweh's representative
pierced; mourning and
purification (12:10 – 13:1)

b^3 Shepherd struck; people
tested, purification and
return to God (13:7–9)

d^1 Suppression of idols
and false prophets (13:2–6)

has been interpreted a little differently with different headings
(*cf.* Analysis, pp. 85 f.).

Some have questioned whether the four passages marked *b*
may legimately be set alongside one another as parallels.
Certainly 9:9,10 and 11:4–17, for example, seem at first sight
to have little in common, but Jeremiah 23:1–8 sets shepherds
and Davidic king side by side, and Ezekiel even more explicitly:
'I will set up over them one shepherd, my servant David, and
he shall feed them: ... and be their shepherd. And I, the
Lord, will be their God, and my servant David shall be prince
among them' (Ezk. 34:23,24). Those who knew the earlier
prophets could not fail to see the connection between king and
shepherd in Zechariah. Similarly 13:7-9, though very different
in form from 11:4–17, clearly declares war on God's king and
people. Chapter 12 centres round the house of David, and to
that extent hints at a Davidic king, though it is true that the

'pierced one' is not clearly identified. The literary arrangement here is not unlike that in Isaiah 40–55, where major themes such as the Servant are first touched on, then expanded, then reverted to, each time with a new insistence and new insights. Interpretation gains much when the Servant passages are seen as part of the total literary scheme, and similarly in Zechariah the progression intensifies the dramatic development of the three themes until they coalesce in the climax at the end of the book.

One great gain in this interpretation is that no rearrangement of the text is called for, nor is it necessary for the reader to know what historical event sparked off the prophet's inspiration. The abundant references to Israel's past suggest that it was here that he discovered his dominant themes. As he meditated on past events he saw 'history in miniature', the conflict between good and evil in which God's people, together with the whole of mankind, were involved. He expressed himself in the highly-coloured language of Old Testament battle-scenes and the contrasting pastoral imagery of the farmer, which had become standard for apocalyptic. Jerusalem, God's dwelling-place on earth, together with its environs, was the centre of his thinking. This metropolis of the spiritual universe would both suffer most and exult most in the final consummation of history, when evil had done its worst.[1]

It is significant that a chiastic structure is not limited to the second part of the book. The eight visions follow the pattern *a b b c c b b a*, with the theological climax in the fourth and fifth. At the same time there is a progression as God's purposes are accomplished for His people and the patrols go out to compass the earth. As is only to be expected in the first section the eschatological emphasis is less marked than in chapters 9–14. The historical situation in 520 BC localizes the references and confines them mainly to that period. Divine intervention accomplishes the rebuilding of Temple and city, scatters the nations, and provides cleansing from sin. A promised leader will combine the roles of priest and prince. His divine resources are made plain, but no mention is made of his suffering. As

[1] See H. Thielicke, *Theological Ethics*, I (A. & C. Black, 1968), p. 439: 'By nature, that is, in its innermost structure, history is implicated in the fall. This is why it cannot sever itself from its own roots and approximate more and more to the kingdom of God. On the contrary, its demonic potentiality is never more fully disclosed than at the very end.'

in 9–14 the visions begin and end with the nations. In the first and eighth visions they are under God's domination, but His saving purpose for them is not referred to (though see 2:11).

The introductory call to hear the words of the former prophets (1:1–6) is repeated in the sermons 7:4–14; 8:9–17, which are themselves part of a chiastic pattern, as the Analysis shows. The climax of chapters 1–8 concerns the nations (8:20–23), who flock to worship the Lord of hosts in Jerusalem alongside the Jew. This is the theme of 14:16–29, though the eschatology of those chapters envisages the nations barely surviving after judgment. A chiastic pattern is discernible in pericopes of both parts of the book. These are noted in the commentary on the text, but examples are 1:14–17 (Jerusalem ... Zion, 14; Zion ... Jerusalem, 17); 8:9–13, beginning and ending with 'let your hands be strong'; 10:10,11, Egypt ... Assyria; Assyria ... Egypt; 14:1–15, where the series of misfortunes related in 1–6 are balanced by the joys of 7–14.

The chiastic pattern, though most prominent in the second part of the book, is present in the whole. This presupposes deliberate intention on the part of the editor, but in view of the fact that the chiastic language and style characterized the prophet Zechariah in his oracles there is reason to believe either that the prophet was also the editor or that the editor was intimately aware of the prophet's style and built faithfully upon it – unless we are to suppose that the chiastic pattern has been imposed by the editor on original material which lacked it (which is a most unlikely assumption). Chiasmus is a stylistic device particularly well suited to the prophet's theme when he deals with the justice of retribution and the miracle of God's grace. It is capable of expressing exact equivalents or startling contrasts. Used as a pattern for the framework of the book it also welds together the prophet's own day and the end of time. The connecting links are the need of repentance, the certainty of judgment, the continuing mercy of God, and the Messianic figure who accomplishes His purposes.

IV. TEXT

So far as chapters 1–8 are concerned the Massoretic Text of the Hebrew is well preserved, but, as the footnotes in the RV and RSV indicate, this does not mean that there are no matters of dispute. Not that the vocabulary is unusual, but occasionally the sense is obscure (see, *e.g.*, 2:8; 5:6), or there seems to be a word missing (as at the beginning of 6:6), or there is a word too many (*e.g.* 1:7, where the word 'saying' is inappropriate). Unfortunately the Hebrew MSS discovered at Qumran include only a fragment of Zechariah (1:1–4), and therefore the only available independent source of information on the original text remains the early Versions.

In chapters 9–14 there are many more problem verses, chiefly on account of the highly allusive, poetic language. This does not necessarily mean that the text is suspect. Pungent, vigorous poetry in our own language is often difficult to interpret. Variations on the meaning of the Hebrew made by the early translations suggest that certain verses have always presented difficulties. One classic example is 11:13, where the Hebrew has 'potter', Syriac 'treasury', LXX 'furnace', and Jerome translated it 'sculptor'. Another verse which became modified in the Versions is 12:10. The tendency was to weaken the sense in order to make the meaning more acceptable. For this reason one rule of textual criticism is that the more difficult reading is likely to be original,[1] a point worth bearing in mind in these chapters. A translation which is easy to understand is not necessarily the one which is closest to the Hebrew.

How much weight can be given to the early translations? The answer to that question is far from simple. It all depends on the accuracy of the manuscript from which the translation was made and on the ability of the translator both to understand the Hebrew and to be faithful to it. In general the more literal the translation the easier it is to guess the Hebrew that lies behind it, but each document has to be assessed by comparison with other Versions, and with variants on the MT. In the case of Zechariah 9–14 a very useful tool has been prepared by T. Jansma, who has collected for each verse a comparison of variations on the Hebrew text, together with those of the early Versions.[2] He sets out the evidence without taking exegesis into account, working solely according to the principles of textual criticism. This erudite work highlights the immense amount of knowledge and painstaking work required if the

[1] 'Difficilior lectio potior'. formulated by J. A. Bengel (1687–1753).
[2] T. Jansma, *Inquiry into the Hebrew Text and the Ancient Versions of Zechariah IX–XIV* (Brill, Leiden, 1949).

linguistic evidence alone is adequately to be taken into account. The four Versions to which reference is made in the RSV margin are Greek, Syriac, Vulgate and Targums.

By *Greek* is meant the 'Septuagint' (LXX), a translation begun in the third century BC, and therefore likely to bear witness to a pre-Massoretic Hebrew text. Though on occasion it keeps close to the Hebrew as we know it, in general it is a free translation. The number, tense and mood of a verb are sometimes altered, metaphors are adapted, several Greek words represent one in Hebrew, and the vocalization of the Hebrew may be changed. For these reasons it is not always possible when the texts diverge to know whether the underlying manuscript was different from our MT or whether the translator had misread or adapted the text. An important check on the LXX has recently been provided by fragments of a Greek translation of Zechariah, found among the Dead Sea Scrolls.[1] This is much closer to the MT than is the LXX, and Barthélemy is of the opinion that this is a recension of the LXX, intended to bring it more closely into line with the Hebrew. Where the Qumran manuscript differs from the LXX, therefore, the former is likely to be nearer to the pre-Massoretic Hebrew, and is to be preferred.

The *Syriac* 'Peshitta' originated with the help of Jewish Christians for the use of the Syrian church in the first or second century AD. It was based on the Hebrew but made reference to the LXX. T. Jansma's general assessment is that 'there exist no essential differences between M (MT) and the Hebrew text underlying S (Syriac)',[2] that is, in Zechariah 9–14. Jerome's *Latin* version (fourth century), known as the 'Vulgate', was also based on a Hebrew original, and was little influenced by the Old Latin or by the LXX. The Aramaic *Targums*, which originated as oral translations, though they paraphrase and sometimes digress slightly, are nevertheless a useful independent witness to the meaning of the Hebrew from which they were translated. However it is true that, whereas errors in the Versions are fairly numerous, it is difficult to prove the MT to be at fault.

The whole discipline of comparative philology in Semitic

---

[1] Published by D. Barthélemy, *Les Devanciers d'Aquila* (Brill, Leiden, 1963), pp. 170–178. It includes the following verses: 1:1,3,4,13,14; 2:2,7, 16,17; 3:1,4–7; 8:19–21, 23; 9:1–4.
[2] T. Jansma, *op. cit.*, p. 23.

languages has developed over the last thirty to forty years as a result of the discovery of a multitude of texts and inscriptions. With new understanding has come the solution of problems, and an admission that our knowledge of Hebrew is still incomplete. Moreover, though the Versions are important, and not to be neglected, scholars hesitate to use them as a ground for emending the Hebrew text unless the evidence is very strongly in their favour. Emendation must be a last resort. 'This revolt against emendation of the Hebrew text has restored the reputation of the Massoretic Text – a reputation which has been strengthened further by the study of the ancient Versions, especially of the Septuagint.'[1] In the commentary it will be necessary to make frequent reference to suggested emendations, but for the most part the MT reading will be found to be upheld.

Lest the non-specialist should be bewildered by the whole subject, it must be made plain that there is a vast area of agreement between all the manuscripts. The variants concern details which in most cases do not alter the general sense. It can also be said categorically that there is no MS evidence for transposing sections of a chapter, nor for rearranging the order of verses. Our task is to interpret the text as it has come down to us without attempting to avoid difficulties by reconstructing it.

[1] D. Winton Thomas, 'The Language of the Old Testament' in *Record and Revelation*, ed. H. W. Robinson (Oxford, 1938), p. 401.

ANALYSIS

PART I

I. INTRODUCTION: THE COVENANT STILL STANDS (1:1–6)

II. EIGHT VISIONS AND ACCOMPANYING ORACLES
(1:7 – 6:15)
a. Vision 1. A patrol of the whole earth reports (1:7–17)
  b. Vision 2. The nations meet retribution (1:18–21)
    (Hebrew 2:1–4)
  b¹. Vision 3. Jerusalem has a divine protector (2:1–13)
    (Hebrew 2:5–17)
    c. Vision 4. The high priest reinstated (3:1–10)
    c¹. Vision 5. Divine resources for high priest and
      prince (4:1–14)
  b². Vision 6. Evil meets retribution (5:1–4)
  b³. Vision 7. Jerusalem is purified (5:5–11)
a¹. Vision 8. God's patrols compass the earth (6:1–15)

III. MESSAGES PROMPTED BY THE QUESTION ON FASTING
(7:1 – 8:19)
a. The question (7:1–3)
  b. The first sermon (7:4–14)
    c. Relevant sayings (8:1–8)
  b¹. The second sermon (8:9–17)
a¹. The answer (8:18,19)

IV. CONCLUSION: UNIVERSAL LONGING FOR GOD
(8:20–23)

PART II

I. TRIUMPHANT INTERVENTION OF THE LORD: HIS
SHEPHERD REJECTED (9:1 – 11:17)
a. The Lord triumphs from the north (9:1–8)
  b. Arrival of the king (9:9,10)
    c. Jubilation and prosperity (9:11 – 10:1)
      d. Rebuke for sham leaders (10:2,3a)
    c¹. Jubilation and restoration (10:3b – 11:3)
  b¹. The fate of the good shepherd (11:4–17)

II. FINAL INTERVENTION OF THE LORD AND
   SUFFERING INVOLVED (12:1 – 14:21)
    c^2. Jubilation in Jerusalem (12:1–9)
     b^2. Mourning for the pierced one (12:10 – 13:1)
      d^1. Rejection of sham leaders (13:2–6)
     b^3. The shepherd slaughtered, the people scattered
       (13:7–9)
    c^3. Cataclysm in Jerusalem (14:1–15)
   a^1. The Lord worshipped as King over all (14:16–21)

COMMENTARY

PART I

I. INTRODUCTION: THE COVENANT STILL STANDS
(1:1-6)

This general introduction to chapters 1–8 calls for repentance
and confession. If the hortatory tone, the reminder of judgment
and reference to the anger of the Lord appear to be an
inappropriate way to encourage a downcast people and spur
them to action, the purpose is to provide solid ground for the
promises to come. Without God's absolution they could be no
more than pious sentiment. The key words are 'Return to me,
says the Lord of hosts, and I will return to you'. This was the
reassurance needed after discipline. The new generation was
free to make a new start (Ezk. 18:14ff.); the Lord would
return to them, despite the covenant-breaking of past generations, if they would return to Him.

1. *The eighth month* in the year 520 BC began on 27 October
(*cf.* the table on p. 29), but of the seven dates given in Haggai
and Zechariah, only in this one is the day of the month
omitted. This fact has led to the conjecture that originally the
day of the month was included, and indeed the Syriac version
has 'in the eighth month, on the first day of the month . . . ',
but a comparison between this and the other dates shows that
the Syriac is out of step in putting month, day, year. The other
dates are in the order day, month, year, or year, month, day.
In view of the tendency of the Syriac version to clarify,
amplify and harmonize verses, it seems most likely that in this
case the original did not include the day of the month. The
omission argues for its genuineness, for anyone fabricating a
date would have brought it into line with the others.

The word of the Lord came to . . . This introductory phrase is
used in the first verse of Hosea, Joel, Jonah (and in 3:1),
Micah, Zephaniah, but only in the heading, and not by the
prophets themselves to preface their oracles. The idiom does
not occur in Amos, Nahum or Habakkuk, and Isaiah most
often plunges straight into his message; when he uses a heading

it is 'thus says the Lord'. By contrast the phrase comes thirty times in Jeremiah and fifty times in Ezekiel.[1] A. Petitjean finds that Zechariah uses the heading exactly as does Ezekiel, that is, followed by two other idioms 'and say' and 'thus saith the Lord'.[2] Compare, for example, 1:1,3 with Ezekiel 6:1,3; 11:14,16,17. Thus, originally, this oracle would have begun 'The word of the Lord came to me, saying', as in 4:8; 6:9; 7:4; 8:18; but when these words became part of the heading to the book, 'to me' was replaced by 'to Zechariah'.

Zechariah . . . the prophet. No prophet is recorded as giving himself this title. It occurs in the headings of Habakkuk and Haggai, and elsewhere (*e.g.* Is. 37–39; Je. 20:2; 25:2, *etc.*) always in the third person. *The son of Berechiah, son of Iddo.* These same members of Zechariah's family tree are named in verse 7, but in Ezra 5:1 and 6:14 Zechariah is said to be simply 'son of Iddo'. This difference has been accounted for in three ways. (*a*) Some patristic commentators said he was son of Berechiah according to the flesh, but son of Iddo according to the spirit, that is, he was brought up in the entourage of Iddo in such a way as to adopt his way of life. In other words, a double lineage is given, a physical and a spiritual one.[3] The Hebrew, however, indicates that three generations are meant. (*b*) Another explanation is that 'son of Berechiah' is a gloss, suggested by 'son of Jeberechiah' in Isaiah 8:2. For this reason JB puts the words in parenthesis.[4] A variation on this is the view popular among Continental scholars that two Zechariahs are responsible for the book. Chapters 1–8 were the work of Zechariah son of Iddo, and chapters 9–14 of an anonymous prophet who took the pseudonym Zechariah son of Berechiah. In the heading the two names became conflated.[5] (*c*) The simplest explanation, and one that requires no alteration of the original text, is that in Zechariah 1:1,7, the father and grandfather are named, whereas in Ezra only the better-known grandfather is men-

[1] Petitjean, p. 7, footnote 3.
[2] A. Petitjean, acknowledging a debt to W. Zimmerli's *Ezechiel*, analyses the use of these formulae in forty-seven sections of Ezekiel (pp. 9, 10). The pattern is remarkably uniform.
[3] Jerome's translation followed this interpretation, and it is referred to by S. Bullough, *A Catholic Commentary on Holy Scripture* (Nelson, 1953), p. 689.
[4] So also H. G. Mitchell, *ICC*, p. 82; P. R. Ackroyd, *PCB²*, p. 646; R. E. Higginson, *NBC*, 1970, p. 786, among others.
[5] E. Sellin, *KAT*, pp. 478, 479; F. Horst, *HAT*, p. 217; A. Petitjean, p. 21.

tioned. A parallel is to be found in the case of Jehu, who is called 'son of Nimshi' in 1 Kings 19:16 and 2 Kings 9:20, but 'son of Jehoshaphat, son of Nimshi' in 2 Kings 9:2,14. Ezra then omits a name, whereas Zechariah 1:1 gives the full genealogy, as would be expected in a book that bears his name. English commentators tend to prefer this explanation.[1]

The occurrence of the names Iddo and Zechariah in Nehemiah 12:4,16 has often been noted, but caution is needed in assuming that these names refer to the people in our book. For one thing Iddo is a family name in Nehemiah 12:16,[2] though it could be the same family; for another, Zechariah was a very common name in the post-exilic period, especially among priests and Levites.[3] Though there are reasons for thinking that Zechariah was a priest, there is insufficient evidence to identify him with the Zechariah in this verse.

2. *The Lord was very angry* (Heb. *qāṣap̄*). The writers of Old and New Testaments did not hesitate to attribute anger to God. It was the revulsion of His whole being to the rebellion of those whom He had created and resulted in acts of judgment. In the case of the Flood all mankind was involved (Gn. 6:5–7), but after that, whenever nations thwarted God's purpose for man's salvation, their perversity provoked His anger (Ps. 110:5; Zc. 1:15). Yet it was the privileged nation of Israel that most often became the object of God's displeasure. The whole career of the chosen nation veered away from God's purpose, for social injustice, apostasy and self-seeking became endemic, so that there was no remedy (2 Ch. 36:15,16). Destruction and exile were the outworking of God's anger (Is. 60:10; Je. 21:5), or rather of the Lord's anger, for it is in the covenant name that these statements of divine wrath against Israel are made. There is an association between the wrath of God and the historical election covenant, which still stands in spite of all. God's intention is still salvation, hence Zechariah's call to repentance. 'For God has not destined us for wrath' (1 Thes. 5:9).

Apart from the one occasion when Zechariah sees God's wrath directed against the nations (1:15), it is their *fathers* who

---

[1] *E.g.* D. R. Jones, *TBC*, p. 54; G. A. Smith, *EB*, pp. 264, 265; C. H. H. Wright, p. xiv.

[2] L. H. Brockington, *Ezra, Nehemiah and Esther*, *CB* (Nelson, 1969), p. 200.

[3] H. G. Mitchell, *ICC*, pp. 107, 108: 'Indeed it seems to have been the prime favourite among the names of the Old Testament, being borne by no fewer than twenty-nine different persons.'

have been at fault, as here (*cf.* 7:12; 8:14). He never says God's wrath is directed against his listeners; they still have time to repent. In the Old Testament the wrath of God is directed towards people, not to sin in the abstract, if there could be such a thing. G. A. F. Knight points out that this biblical teaching is 'in contradistinction to much modern preaching, when it is said that God hates the sin, but loves the sinner'.[1] It is instructive also that the prophet laid stress on the failure of the past generation, and saw reason for hope in the present and future.

3. *Therefore say to them* introduces the immediate message to his contemporaries, and marks the fact that a new era has dawned. The message is no longer that judgment is inevitable, as it had been for Jeremiah. Though he had pressed the invitation to 'return' (Je. 3:12,14,22; 4:1, *etc.*), it had been ignored. Now it is issued in a personal form, *Return to me*, not to My law, or My way of life, but to Me, your covenant God. While the approach will involve repentance, which is always appropriate in man's approach to God, the primary emphasis is on establishing a personal relationship, like that of the prodigal with his father (Lk. 15:20), except that here it is God who takes the initiative. He issues the invitation and gives the assurance that He will do His part, *I will return to you*. This is the Old Testament message of conversion. The past can be blotted out (Is. 44:22), and fellowship can be restored. Malachi was to quote this verse in his preaching (Mal. 3:7).

4. Zechariah now takes a text from Jeremiah, probably 35:15, though there is a general resemblance to 18:11 and to 25:5. The same verb *return* (Heb. *šûḇ*) occurs, but with the preposition *from* it is a call first of all to turn from evil ways. This prophetic plea was totally disregarded before the exile, and Jeremiah's frequent complaint was *but they did not hear* (*e.g.* Je. 17:23, 29:19; 36:31) or *heed* (6:10 Heb.; 6:17,19; 18:18; 23:18). Notice that the authenticity of earlier prophets is endorsed both by the fulfilment of what they predicted and by the testimony of the Lord as He speaks through the contemporary prophet. The pre-exilic prophets were already regarded as 'canonical'.[2]

---

[1] G. A. F. Knight, *A Christian Theology of the Old Testament* (SCM Press, 2nd edition 1964), p. 122.

[2] *Cf.* K. Elliger, *ATD*, p. 101.

5. There is no reference to the calamities that followed. The exile was so fresh in everyone's memory that it was unnecessary to mention it. Instead a double question draws attention to the shortness of human life. Even the prophets had passed away.

6. By contrast the *words* of the prophets, because they were God's words, had not passed away. *My words and my statutes.* The prophets continually referred back to the covenant codes, stating in summaries of their own God's requirements from Israel (Is. 1:17; Je. 7:5–7; Ho. 6:6; Am. 5:14,15; Mi. 6:8). Jeremiah made reference to the 'ten words' of the covenant (Ex. 34:28; Dt. 4:13) in 11:7,8; 34:18, but his own prophetic words were no less God's word (3:12; 25:13; 36:4–32). The 'statutes' were specific requirements of the law, and together with the verb *which I commanded* recall the phraseology of Deuteronomy (4:5; 6:1; 7:11, *etc.*). Evidently the prophet is thinking in terms of all pre-exilic Israel when he speaks of *your fathers*; the nation is looked on in its solidarity. 'In' their fathers they had all entered into the covenant (*cf.* Paul's use of the same concept 'in Adam', 'in Christ', 1 Cor. 15:22). Each generation, however, had broken covenant from the Exodus onwards. This was the conviction particularly of Ezekiel (20; 23). God's words, meeting with rebellion, brought curse instead of blessing, in accordance with Deuteronomy 28, until eventually the curse had worked itself out on the immediate predecessors of his hearers. *Did not (my words) overtake your fathers?* The same metaphor is used in Deuteronomy 28:15, 45, where the hunting term 'overtake' (*hiśśîg*) occurs, implying that the curse of God pursues and catches up on the wrongdoer to put him to death. The exile, which involved the removal of leaders and the destruction of national institutions, was the death of the nation (Ezk. 37:11).

So they repented. The verb is the same as 'return' in verse 3, and therefore this statement appears to contradict verse 4, a fact which explains why the JB translators altered the sense to 'This reduced them to such confusion that . . .'. But the context suggests the meaning 'they came to themselves'. Once they were in exile it was impossible to delude themselves any longer into thinking that they were right. Overcome by events, they had to confess that the words of the prophets had been justified, and admit their own failure. The prophet is proving that the word of the Lord has triumphed in the past, and implying that it will do so in the future. Let those who are now hearing it beware, and be sure to listen and heed it. There is, however, another interpretation, arrived at by understanding the 'they' of 'they repented' as the contemporaries of the prophet. In order to have an antecedent to which the new subject could refer, R. Kittel in his *Biblia Hebraica* emended the text from 'overtake your fathers' to 'overtake you', but the alteration is arbitrary.[1] A further suggestion is that the words introduced by *and said* are part of a 'general confession', known and used before the exile by their 'fathers', but still part of the liturgy known and used after the exile. Longer confessions in Ezra 9, Nehemiah 9 and Daniel 9 show awareness of the solidarity felt by later generations with their predecessors and their sins from the Exodus on. The introductory words *So they repented and said* have a liturgical ring, which supports this view. The rest of the statement acknowledges God's right to deal with them as He has. He has been neither arbitrary nor unjust, but utterly righteous.[2]

To sum up this introductory message, Zechariah is making a plea for a whole-hearted response to the Lord's invitation to return to Him. All that happened in 587 BC was entirely in accordance with prophetic foretelling. God did not change, nor did the judgment belie His mercy. On exactly the same terms as had been offered to their fathers, young and old alike are invited to return to God. If they will do so the covenant relationship will be renewed, and spiritual restoration will accompany the material restoration of the Temple.

II. EIGHT VISIONS AND ACCOMPANYING ORACLES
(1:7 – 6:15)

In this 'book of visions' the purpose of God is disclosed for the future of Jerusalem and Judah. The accounts of the eight visions follow a standard pattern. After the introductory words comes a description of the things the prophet sees; then he

---

[1] Among those who adopt this reading are K. Elliger, *ATD*, p. 95, and P. R. Ackroyd, *PCB²*, p. 646.

[2] The view that 6b is characteristic of the cultic confessions of the post-exilic period is expounded in detail by A. Petitjean, pp. 50, 51. He acknowledges his debt to W. Beuken, *Haggai, Sacharja I–VIII* (Assen, 1967), pp. 86–88; 103–110.

asks the angels what these things signify, and the angel gives the prophet the explanation. Accompanying four of the visions is an oracle (1:14-17; 2:6-13; 4:6b-10a; 6:9-15); though this usually follows, in the case of the fifth vision the oracle is inserted within the account of the vision (4:6b-10a). These oracles make specific the message of the visions, and are probably summaries of relevant sermons given by Zechariah on different occasions, as a comparison of 1:14-17 with 8:1-8 indicates.

It has already been pointed out (see Introduction, p. 80) that the arrangement of the visions follows a chiastic pattern. The first and last bear a strong resemblance to one another, the second and third, sixth and seventh are pairs, and the fourth and fifth, with their assurance of God-given authoritative leaders, form the climax. All eight visions are meant to be interpreted as one whole, for each contributes to the total picture of the role of Israel in the new era about to dawn.

a. Vision 1. A patrol of the whole earth reports (1:7-17)

The leading figure on a red horse is standing among myrtle trees in a hollow. Behind him are troops of horses distinguished by their colours as three groups. Presumably they have riders who give the report (verse 11), though these are not specifically mentioned. The fact that there are two angelic beings gives rise to some confusion. The man on the red horse is the same person as the 'angel of the Lord', but the 'angel who talked with me' is an interpreter who accompanies the prophet throughout the night of visions (1:18; 2:3; 4:1,5; 5:5; 6:4), and therefore must be distinguished from the 'angel of the Lord',[1] who does not appear again until the fourth vision (3:1ff.).

Horses feature not only in the visions but also in the symbolism of the second half of the book (9:10; 10:3,5; 12:4; 14:15,20,21). They stand for domination in war (10:3), and for prestige (1 Ki. 10:26). It is fitting therefore that the angel

---

[1] It has been widely held that 'angel of the Lord' is a redactor's attempt to add reverence to the text which read simply 'the man' (verse 10). So Chary, p. 60 and H. G. Mitchell, *ICC*, p. 87. D. Winton Thomas (*IB*, VI, p. 1062) thinks the text should read 'the angel who talked with me'. These changes, however, are conjectural.

of the Lord should have at his disposal horses (and chariots, 6:1–3), to supervise the Lord's world-wide domain.

7. This verse forms a second introduction, identical apart from the date with verse 1, which suggests that originally the book of visions was a separate entity. The date, 15 February 519 BC, is generally taken to apply to all the visions. Three months had elapsed since the date of Zechariah's first oracle, and two since the last recorded messages of Haggai (see Introduction, p. 29). *Shebat*, the Babylonian name for the eleventh month, adopted by the Jews after the exile, is used only here in the Old Testament (*cf.* Chislev in 7:1). In view of the fact that in Haggai and in the two other dates in Zechariah (1:1; 8:18) the months are not named, it may be that the names are later insertions,[1] or, since Ezra–Nehemiah use them more frequently, they may give some slight indication of the dating of Zechariah 1–8 in the transitional period between Ezekiel and Chronicles.

And Zechariah said. RSV has corrected the text, which translated literally reads 'the word of the Lord came to Zechariah . . . saying', so giving the impression that the Lord is recounting what He saw, whereas the author intended the prophet to be speaking. NEB avoids the difficulty by omitting the word 'saying'. This has the effect of making the second half of the verse part of the introductory heading, and makes good sense. The vision which follows, together with its explanation, constitutes the 'word 'of the Lord.

8. *I saw* (Heb. *rā'îtî*) used absolutely like this means 'I received a revelation' (*cf.* Is. 30:10). Though the vision came *in the night* the prophet carefully avoided giving the impression that he had been dreaming. He was intellectually alert, as his questions and interruptions (*e.g.* 3:5) prove. Though there is an element of mystery about the 'how' of this and other methods of revelation, the prophet received the vision and was not subjectively creating it. The view of H. G. Mitchell that these visions are merely 'literary forms in which the prophet clothed his ideas'[2] does less than justice to the plain statement of the prophet.

Zechariah sees *a man*, whose identity is not explained, though

---

[1] So H. G. Mitchell, *ICC*, p. 116.
[2] *ICC*, p. 117.

the reader suspects that he is a superhuman being. This is confirmed as the vision unfolds. He rides a *red horse*, more technically bay, the reddish-brown colour of horses. All is still in the vision; the leading horseman and behind him the different troops of horses, their mission accomplished, seem to be waiting to be dismissed for the night. The question of the possible significance of the colours, and whether there were originally four troops of horses, not three, is discussed in the Additional Note on Zechariah's horses (p. 138).

The scene is set *among the myrtle trees*, fragrant evergreen shrubs that grow well in Palestine, especially beside streams. They were used among other trees to build the rough shelters needed at the feast of booths (Ne. 8:15) but there is no evidence that the myrtle had cultic significance. *The glen* (RSV) or *hollow* (NEB) probably meant the lowest part of the Kidron valley outside Jerusalem, where there was a garden in pre-exilic times (2 Ki. 25:4). If this is correct the Lord had returned to the outskirts of the city but, symbolically speaking, had not yet entered it because the Temple had not yet been completed.[1]

9, 10. The interpreting angel says he will explain the meaning, but it is the man standing among the myrtle trees who speaks. There are those who want to omit as a gloss 'riding upon a red horse' in verse 8 and who note that no horse is mentioned here. The redactor who called the 'man' 'the angel of the Lord' (verse 11; see footnote, p. 93) also provides a steed.[2] There is no textual ground for omitting these words.

The troops of horsemen were emissaries of the Lord sent on a world mission. Like the Persian monarchs who used messengers on swift steeds to keep them informed on all matters concerning their empire, so the Lord knew all about the countries of the earth, including the great Persian state.

11. The prophet now refers to the 'man' as *the angel of the Lord*. Though the word 'angel' (Heb. *mal'āk*) means 'messenger'

---

[1] A rather different view is taken by Th. Chary, p. 57. He sees a mythological background to the 'hollow', which he connects with the 'deep' (Ex. 15:5. *etc.*). This in the myth of Gilgamesh (*ANET*, p. 90) and in a text from Ugarit (W. F. Albright, *Archaeology and the Religion of Israel*[4] (Johns Hopkins Press, 1956), p. 72) is the seat of the gods. According to this interpretation Zechariah is being brought near to the dwelling of the divinity.

[2] H. G. Mitchell, *ICC*, pp. 128, 129.

and may be used of human beings (*cf.* Hg. 1:13; Mal. 1:1, see note), this messenger, with his ability to disclose information normally hidden from men, is superhuman.

All the earth remains at rest. Two questions arise from the report: (*a*) is the news good or bad? (*b*) to what period did the report refer? (*a*) In the light of verse 15 it is evident that the earth's peace was the result of injustice and inhumanity. 'All the earth is seated' (*yošebet*). The same verb is used derogatorily of Egypt (Is. 30:7) in connection with her failure to honour international treaties; 'at rest' (*šoqāṭet*), 'settled', while it is often used in a good sense, refers to selfish inactivity in Moab (Je. 48:11) and in Samaria (Ezk. 16:49, 'prosperous ease'). This state is the very opposite of the Lord's zeal for righteousness (verse 14). It is a peace doomed to be shattered (1:21; *cf.* Hg. 2:7,21). (*b*) Was it a fact that in February 519 BC Darius had succeeded in quelling the riots that broke out on the death of Cambyses (see Introduction, p. 16)? Some think not,[1] and H. G. Mitchell goes on to argue that this vision, together with the second and third, refers to the Babylonian period when the might of Babylonian forces kept the peace.[2] Yet there is no indication that the prophet is transported back in time. Moreover, the report is appropriate for the year 519 BC. Haggai's contemporaries had been unanimous in the opinion that the time was not favourable for building the Temple (Hg. 1:2). They needed government grants such as had been promised (Ezr. 6:4), but Persian wealth was being put to other uses. The world powers were like Egypt of old, 'Rahab who sits still' (Is. 30:7), concerned with their own interests, and unlikely to honour promises to an insignificant group of Jews in Trans-Euphrates. Whether or not every trace of fighting had ended is beside the point. It was sufficiently clear that the riots of 521 had not been the beginning of eschatological battles ushering in the Messianic age. Instead Darius was firmly in control of his empire.

12. The intercession of the angel of the Lord reveals that the return of exiles from Babylon was not in itself regarded as

---

[1] *E.g.* H. G. Mitchell, *ICC*, p. 121: 'It is not probable that the adversaries of Darius were all subdued, and the Persian empire reduced to a state of complete tranquillity, by the month of February, 519 B.C.' See J. Bright, *History of Israel* (SCM Press, 1960), p. 351 footnote, where sources of different viewpoints are listed.
[2] *Ibid.*, p. 122.

fulfilment of the prophecy of Jeremiah 29:10. *Jerusalem and the cities of Judah* needed to be rebuilt. Though there is no specific mention of the Temple, its reconstruction is implied.

The interpretation of Jeremiah's *seventy years* raises questions. It was in the year 605 BC that he first made the statement that Judah would serve the king of Babylon for seventy years (Je. 25:11,12). This was the year of the battle of Carchemish, when Nebuchadrezzar II defeated the Egyptians on the Euphrates, drove them back to Egypt, and claimed as his own the intervening territory, including Judah. Reckoned from that date it was roughly seventy years to 539, when Babylon fell to the Persians. On the other hand Jeremiah gives the impression that he reckons the seventy-year period from the devastation of the land (25:11), in which case the seventy years would be 587–517 BC, and yet Judah was not serving the Babylonians all that time. It is not impossible that there was the double reference (*a*) to the years of Babylonian domination, and (*b*) to the length of time the land was devastated. There is the further consideration that seventy years is roughly a lifetime, and those who heard the prophet would know that they were not likely to live to see the day of rebuilding.

Further light on the question has come from the Near East. The Babylonian king Esarhaddon (681–669 BC) has left an inscription to the effect that the god Marduk should have been angry with his land until seventy years had been accomplished, though in fact he had mercy, and reduced the number to eleven.[1] Tyre was to be laid waste for seventy years (Is. 23:15, 17), and the Chronicler interpreted the seventy years as a sabbath rest for the land (2 Ch. 36:21), a view which may be reflected in Daniel 9:2. Lipinski's conclusion is that seventy years constituted the period of divine anger against a city or a sanctuary. It was a time of penitence intended to appease the divine anger. Once that period had ended there would be no need to continue in acts of penitence; hence the delegation and their question in 7:3.

The evidence suggests that there was symbolism in the number, and that it was meant to be taken as a round figure, but this did not preclude a historical period of desolation for Jerusalem's Temple of seventy years. The number may have

---

[1] E. Lipinski (*VT*, XX, 1970, pp. 38, 39) quotes translations of the actual words and gives details of his sources.

been suggested by commonly-held religious traditions, and yet the fulfilment of the prophecy was remarkably accurate.[1]

13. Though it was the angel of the Lord who had interceded in the previous verse, God's answer comes direct to Zechariah's interpreting angel, through him to the prophet, and finally is proclaimed to the people. This is an interesting example of the role of mediators in the post-exilic period. It is not clear whether the interpreting angel passes on all that he hears or whether he has the more active role of selecting the message. What is noted is that they were *gracious and comforting words* (*cf.* Is. 40:1,2).

14. The vision had lifted the veil which hides the unseen, spiritual world to show that God is in control and active in the earth, but it would not have been of specific comfort without the message in words given by the interpreting angel (verses 14b–17). This oracle is essential to elucidate the implications of the vision.[2]

Having been given the privilege of seeing a vision the prophet is now charged with the duty of proclaiming a message. He is to *cry out*, and not keep the encouragement to himself. It is a startling word: *I am exceedingly jealous for Jerusalem and for Zion.* The divine jealousy is closely related to the divine anger (verse 2). Unrequited love involved God in deep emotion which the Holy Spirit was not afraid to express in terms of human emotions, anger, jealousy, love. Nowhere in the Old Testament is God portrayed as impassive, aloof, uninvolved

---

[1] The claim of C. F. Whitley ('The Term Seventy Years Captivity', *VT*, IV, 1954, pp. 60–72), that the words 'these seventy years' here and in 7:5 are an interpretation by a later editor, is without foundation. It is to be noted that Zechariah does not speak of 'a seventy year captivity'. This is pointed out by A. Orr, *VT*, VI, 1956, pp. 304–306. See also P. R. Ackroyd, 'Two Old Testament Historical Problems of the Early Persian Period', *JNES*, 17, 1958, pp. 23–27.

[2] The view is widely held, especially among Continental scholars, that originally the message consisted of verses 14b, 15 only, and that the rest came from a different setting. See, *e.g.*, K. Elliger, *ATD*, pp. 116f. He concludes the section at verse 15 and takes the introductory words of verses 16 and 17 as indications that they are separate oracles added later. F. Horst (*HAT*, pp. 218–222) takes a similar view. So also P. R. Ackroyd, *PCB²*, pp. 647f. A. Petitjean refutes this by pointing out many parallels between 14b–17 and 8:1–8, from which he concludes that these are two versions of the same prophecy (pp. 73–88), the earlier one being more abbreviated than the later but nonetheless a unity. There does not appear to be any good reason against interpreting the little section as one speech.

with our world.[1] The utter holiness of His love only intensifies
the suffering involved when that love is rejected, and His
desire to save men from the death towards which they are
heading is something we only dimly appreciate (Ezk. 18:23,
31,32). (See Additional Note on The divine jealousy, p.
101.)

The question in the prophet's mind may have been, 'Why
should God intervene now to save Jerusalem?' Why indeed
should God ever be expected to intervene for good in any
human situation? To expect Him to do so would be egocentric
arrogance, were it not for the covenant promises which,
because they are an expression of His unchanging love, He
cannot break (Ho. 2:19,20; Je. 31:31–34; 2 Cor. 5:14,15).
Having chosen Jerusalem to put His name there (1 Ki. 8:29)
the Lord could not merely forget it. His election of the city
endured in spite of human failure which had necessitated its
destruction. Though in 8:3 and 9:9 *Jerusalem* and *Zion* are
synonymous, here the prophet appears to intend some distinction. Zion, the pre-Israelite name of the hill David captured
(2 Sa. 5:7), is often preferred in cultic and religious contexts
(1 Ki. 8:1; 2 Ch. 5:2; Ps. 84:5,7), and it sometimes stands for
the people of Jerusalem in their religious privilege and responsibility (Ps. 97:8; Is. 1:27; 33:5). This last may be the distinction here (*cf.* verse 17).

15. The anger of the Lord is no longer directed towards
Judah, but towards her enemies. This theme is the subject of
the second vision (verses 18-21). The change of direction lends
itself to chiasmus, and there is in the Hebrew chiastic
parallelism (*qinnē'tî . . . qin'â gᵉḏôlâ wᵃqeṣep̄ gāḏôl . . . qōṣēp̄*).

The nations that are at ease is an expression that needs to be
understood in the light of Hebrew usage. The adjective 'at
ease' (*ša'ᵃnān*) is used twice to describe the God-given security
of future Jerusalem (Is. 32:18; 33:20), but in the eight other
places where it occurs it has a derogatory meaning. In Amos
6:1 those who are at ease feel secure but are not. The same
word used as a noun occurs in 2 Kings 19:28 (=Is. 37:29),
'because you have raged against me and your arrogance (ease)

---

[1] This is in no way denied by Article 1 of the Thirty-nine Articles, which
describes God as 'without passions', a Latinism intended to safeguard God's
power and perfection by declaring Him to be 'wholly other than man'. He
is not at the mercy of whims and passions.

has come into my ears'. Assyria has fought successfully against Lybia and Egypt and in arrogant self-confidence presumes that she will take Jerusalem also. The Lord's zeal (2 Ki. 19:31) is aroused against such 'ease'. Similarly in Psalm 123:4 'those who are at ease' is parallel in meaning to 'the proud'. The nations which Zechariah had in mind were those which had harassed Israel and Judah, especially the Assyrians, Babylonians and Edomites. Initially they had been fulfilling a God-given role in punishing the chosen people, and they had unwittingly fulfilled divine prophecy, but they had gone too far and *furthered the disaster*, 'overstepped all limits' JB (*cf.* Is. 47:6). That God's intention was to punish for a moment and then show great compassion (Is. 54:7,8) was beyond their grasp, though His purpose in showing kindness and severity to the nations was likewise to win them (Rom. 11:22,32).

16. Wrongs suffered by God's people in the past are now to be compensated (*cf.* Is. 40:2). There is no need to see in the statements that follow any contradiction of the situation implied in Haggai. Though building had begun a few months before, it would be surprising if no further stimulus were needed to maintain effort and give incentive to persevere, for the task included the city as well as the Temple, and *the measuring line* had not even plotted out the scheme of the city's reconstruction. The rebuilding of the walls would not in fact be completed for another eighty years (Ne. 7:4; 11:1). Meanwhile the words *I have returned to Jerusalem* would recall Ezekiel's vision of the departure of the Lord from the Temple (10:18,19; 11:23) and of His return (43:5). His presence is a pledge that the Temple will be finished. Jeremiah had linked the Lord's *compassion* with the rebuilding of the city (30:18), and that compassion is present among them to bring it about.

17. The word *again*, four times repeated, dominates this verse. It is full of hope, not only for Jerusalem but also for the 'cities' around the capital. With its threefold promise of prosperity, consolation and election it ends the first vision with a fitting climax.

Overflow with prosperity is the sense adopted by all the English versions and by the majority of commentators, in spite of the fact that the verb *pûṣ* almost always means elsewhere 'to scatter in defeat' (*e.g.* Ezk. 34:5; Zc. 13:7).[1] The basic idea expressed by the verb is that of an irresistible force working centrifugally, like a cyclone or anticyclone, for good or ill. Human history being what it is, the effects are more often for ill (Gn. 11:4; Nu. 10:35; 1 Sa. 11:11; Ezk. 34:5; 46:18), but the use of the word in Proverbs 5:16 for a spring gushing out and sending water in all directions links suitably with the thought in this verse. Jerusalem will be like a spring of water, which will overflow to bring to others in the neighbourhood all the *prosperity* (Heb. *tôb*) that results from God's favour.[2]

The Lord will again comfort Zion. In the time of deep distress following the destruction of Jerusalem there was no comforter (La. 1:2,9,16,17,21). Assurances based on past experiences (Pss. 23:4; 71:21; Is. 12:1) no longer satisfied. Against such a background the proclamation of Isaiah 40:1 marked a new beginning, but that comfort would not be complete until the waste places were rebuilt (Is. 51:3; 52:9; 54:11,12). Rebuilding was implied in the words *and again choose Jerusalem*. The election of Jerusalem is prominent in the historical texts that tell of the dedication of the Temple, but A. Petitjean points out that Zechariah is the only prophet to deal with the election of the city (*cf.* 2:12; 3:2).[3] From the words of Solomon, 'the city which thou hast chosen and the house which I have built for thy name' (1 Ki. 8:44,48; 2 Ch. 6:6,34,38), we see that Jerusalem's election was bound up with the presence there of the Temple, and so the future election of Jerusalem involved its rebuilding. Verse 17, therefore, virtually repeats the three-fold message of verse 16, and aptly concludes the account of the first vision by answering the questions asked in verse 12.

Additional Note on The divine jealousy

The Hebrew word *qin'â* is translated in RSV by 'jealousy', 'zeal', 'fury'. Its root is probably connected with an Arabic

---

[1] Some scholars contend that this is the meaning here. The sense would be 'My cities are still despoiled of good things, but . . .'. This is the view, *e.g.*, of H. G. Rignell, *Die Nachtgesichte des Sachar'a* (Lund, 1950), p. 53, and of Th. Chary, p. 63. The Syriac version supported this meaning, and J. Calvin sensed the difficulty, though he translated 'Yet cities shall wear out through abundance of blessings' (Calvin Translation Society, 1849), p. 50.

[2] More detail on the use of the verb *pûṣ* is given by A. Petitjean, pp. 67–69.

[3] Petitjean, pp. 71, 72.

word meaning to become intensely red (or black) with dye, and so by derivation it draws attention to the colour produced in the face by deep emotion.[1] The Greek *zēloō*, 'to be jealous', derived from *zeō*, 'to boil', also expresses deep feeling. From it the English words 'zeal' and 'jealousy' are both derived, so indicating that the emotion can be directed to good or bad ends. When it is self-regarding it results in intense hatred, but when it is concerned for others it becomes a power capable of accomplishing the most noble deeds.

It is significant that God is first spoken of as 'jealous' at the giving of the covenant code (Ex. 20:5; 34:14; Dt. 5:9), when the special relationship was established between the Lord and His people, Israel. Because they are His, they can belong to no-one else, hence the prohibition of idolatry and the sanctions against it in the third commandment; but these are followed by the assurance of 'steadfast love to thousands of those who love me and keep my commandments' (Ex. 20:6). God's jealousy is a measure of the intensity of His love towards those with whom He has entered into covenant. So great is His love that He cannot be indifferent if they spurn Him by disobedience or sheer carelessness.

Reflection on the covenant relationship in Deuteronomy leads to warnings against forgetfulness: 'For the Lord your God is a devouring fire, a jealous God' (Dt. 4:24; *cf.* 6:15; 29:18,19; 32:16,21). The fire of God's jealousy will be experienced in the form of all kinds of calamity, culminating in defeat by enemy armies and total destruction (Dt. 29:20–28). Worse than forgetfulness is presumption (Dt. 29:19), the besetting sin of those who live in a land where the mercy of God is known. This dreaded state of presumption, leading to insensitivity, is the burden of the writer to the Hebrews (Heb. 6:4–6).

Ezekiel, prophesying when the consequences of unfaithfulness were coming on Judah, interpreted the calamities as the expression of God's jealousy (5:13). He had betrothed Jerusalem to Himself (16:8–14) but she had proved unfaithful. The marriage relationship represents the covenant between the Lord and His chosen people, and His jealousy is like that of a husband for an adulterous wife (16:38,42; 23:35). Yet once the nations have carried out the punishment the Lord's jealousy for His people becomes their defence (36:3–7; 38:19–

[1] BDB, p. 888.

23). It will blaze out against the nations who will see His holiness and acknowledge that He is the Lord.

The imagery in Isaiah 40–66, which pictures the Lord as a warrior (42:13), an avenger (59:17), a kinsman-redeemer (*gōʾēl*, 63:15,16), shows His jealousy in the same covenant context. The prophet sets the Lord's zeal and might alongside His compassion and prays that His Father's heart will cause Him to return to His needy people (*cf.* Joel 2:18).

In Zechariah 1:14–17 the jealousy of the Lord is for Jerusalem, the city of His choice (verse 17). His return with compassion, His promise of comfort and His renewed election of the city all suggest a new covenant, to be brought about by the zeal of the Lord of hosts. The longer passage dealing with the same theme (8:1–8) shows even more explicitly the link between the Lord's jealousy and His covenant.[1] God's love is never passive but is always expressing itself in positive encouragement of what is right, or, when it is spurned, in unmistakable judgments, intended to bring the sufferer to his senses, and back to God. His love is so intense that it can do no less.

b. Vision 2. The nations meet retribution (1:18–21) (Hebrew 2:1–4)

The meaning of this vision is straightforward. Hostile powers had overthrown the kingdoms of Israel and Judah, and were still frighteningly strong. Though the returned exiles were vulnerable and had not even a city wall to defend them, any nation threatening Judah would itself be overthrown.

18. The introductory words *And I lifted my eyes and saw* are used in the narration of three other visions (2:1; 5:1; 6:1). They suggest that the prophet was engrossed in thinking over all he had been hearing until another vision caught his attention.

Four horns. Horns, the pride of the young bull, are an obvious choice of symbol to represent invincible strength. J. Mellaart has discovered that in Stone Age settlements in Asia

---

[1] A. Petitjean, to whom I am indebted for the main argument in this note, contends that the divine 'jealousy' considered as a source of His interventions in favour of Israel is attested only from the time of the exile (p. 80). His study of the theme occupies pages 79–81.

Minor the horns of cattle were collected and used to decorate seats, or perhaps to be used as head rests.[1] As trophies of the hunt they represented conquest of strength. Similarly in the 'Blessing of Moses' Joseph is a firstling bull, 'and his horns are the horns of a wild ox' (Dt. 33:17). Horns may be exalted in victory or cut off in defeat (Ps. 75:10). Used figuratively in this way the word has the ordinary form of the plural, and not the dual form for things normally found in pairs. The same is true of the artificial horns of the altar and of the word as it is used in this verse. So the prophet saw four single horns, presumably on the heads of living animals, because they were capable of being terrified (verse 21). Just as in the first vision the riders of the horses were not mentioned, so here the head and body of the animals are left to the imagination.

19. Though the prophet might have arrived at the meaning of the vision without help, he is careful to ask for an interpretation. It is tempting to try to identify *the horns which have scattered Judah, Israel, and Jerusalem* in terms of four particular nations, as patristic commentators did,[1] but 'four[2] here represents the totality of opposition, just as it represents all directions in the eighth vision (see Introduction, p. 72). The order 'Judah, Israel, Jerusalem' is unexpected because historically Israel was the first to be deported. The fact that Israel is omitted in the LXX provides some basis for its omission in NEB, but the Hebrew, which is supported by the Qumran Greek text, should be allowed to stand. Zechariah has in mind the whole people scattered in exile, just as he considers the whole pagan world responsible for the scattering.

20. The *four smiths* clearly correspond to the four horns. The word translated 'smiths' is a general term meaning 'workman'; the context determines the trade intended. Admittedly it is not very clear how they achieve their purpose, but the heavy hammer of the smith is a suitable instrument to supply to the imagery.

21. This time the prophet does not ask who they are, but what their function is. The enemies who had brought about

[1] J. Mellaart, *Çatal Hüyük* (Oxford University Press, 1967), p. 78.
[2] The current view was that the four horns were the Assyrians, Babylonians, Medes and Persians, though Theodore of Mopsuestia considered it fanciful (*Commentarius in XII prophetas minores*, PG 66, col. 513), quoted by Th. Chary, p. 64. Jerome preferred Babylonians, Medes/Persians, Greeks, Romans. See E. B. Pusey, *The Minor Prophets*, VIII, p. 65.

the exile had already been overcome and incorporated into the Persian empire. God's workmen, in the shape of Persian armies, had been casting down horns. It would be better to read the angel's reply, 'Those are the horns' as opposed to 'these' smiths. *Which scattered Judah.* Greek versions add 'Israel', while some MSS add 'Jerusalem and Israel'. NEB arbitrarily translates 'Judah and Jerusalem', so making verse 21 parallel with its own rendering of verse 19. But the vision was moving on from the past to the present. The last world empire, Babylon, itself represented by four horns, had been overthrown by the four workmen, that is, the Persian world empire. In pictorial form the truth is proclaimed that however formidable the enemy may be, there is another enemy who will prove more than a match for it, particularly if God's people are being threatened.

These have come to terrify them, or 'to rout them' (Heb. *ḥārēḏ*). The context shows that the nations are not merely cowed, but defeated.[1] Potential enemies of the immediate or distant future will be no exception. The balance of power among the nations, and the wars that result when that balance is upset, work out God's purpose for the overthrow of those who *lifted up their horns* in arrogant disregard for God, and for the benefit of God's people. Though ferocious attempts to humiliate them continue, they will see the enemies they so much fear reduced to nothing. Thus the second vision adds a further assurance to those of the first.

b¹. Vision 3. Jerusalem has a divine protector (2:1-13) (Hebrew 2:5-17)

1-5. Not only would Jerusalem's enemies become powerless, but also the city would be miraculously guarded by a supernatural wall of fire. Taken together the second and third visions show plainly that timidity is out of place. God is at work in ways appropriate to His people's needs and He guarantees their protection.

1. Though this vision concerns Jerusalem and not the nations, the prophet is still outside the city when he sees *a man with a*

---

[1] Some doubt has been cast on the verb here by LXX *tou oxynai*, 'to sharpen', from a Hebrew verb *ḥāḏaḏ* instead of *ḥaraḏ*. By repointing the text Gunkel arrived at the meaning 'to sharpen axes', but there is little to be said for this reconstruction. NEB *to reunite them* has apparently substituted *yāḥaḏ*, but offers no explanation.

measuring line in his hand. Already in 1:16 the prophet had been given the message that the builder's line would again be stretched out over Jerusalem. The question was, where did one begin? Was it safe to rebuild the Temple while the city remained defenceless? This may have been in the mind of those who advocated first building the walls, in which case the young man would represent the cautious Jew of the day, or he may have been acting out of defiance against Persia.

2. His purpose is to mark out the boundaries of the city. In view of the opposition of the Samaritans (Ezr. 4:1-5) it was necessary to take precautions, and common sense would argue that to fortify the ramparts was in the will of God.

3. The very understandable reasoning of the surveyor is not in keeping with God's purpose, which is declared by *another angel* (Heb. *mal'āk̲*) to Zechariah's interpreting angel.

4. The messenger task of the angel is very clear here, *Run, say to that young man.* He is depicted as young because he has not yet learnt that God's ways cannot be discerned by human reasoning. Legitimate though it must be for men to reason, and take precautions for their own safety, on this occasion their plan was too small. Jerusalem will be *as villages without walls*, open to all who wish to enter (Ezk. 38:11), free from dividing walls and national barriers, knowing no limits on the size of its population. Far from being exclusive, Zechariah opens the city of God to a *multitude of men and cattle.* It cannot become overcrowded (*cf.* Is. 2:2; Zc. 8:20,22).

Eighty years later, in the time of Nehemiah, this hope of an overflowing population was so far from being fulfilled that lots had to be cast and people compelled to move into the city (Ne. 11:1,2; *cf.* 7:4). It is true that Nehemiah's walls enclosed a larger area than that of David's city,[1] perhaps to allow for the expected growth in the population, but increase of size without more people would merely intensify the impression of emptiness. The prophecy was nearer to fulfilment in the time of Jesus, when at festival times the city overflowed with pilgrims from all parts of the known world.[2] More significant

---

[1] Three different theories as to the extent of Nehemiah's Jerusalem are illustrated in *IDB*, II, p. 854, article 'Jerusalem'. What is certain is that the walls of Nehemiah's city were not built over the Jebusite walls. See K. M. Kenyon, 'Excavations in Jerusalem', *BA*, XXVII, 2, 1964, p. 45.

[2] J. Jeremias, *Jerusalem in the Time of Jesus* (SCM Press, 1969), pp. 58-84.

is the expansion of the church to all parts of the world, but even so there is need to 'compel people to come in' (Lk. 14:23), for still there is room.

5. Inviting as the open city was, it took great courage to live without protecting walls, hence the promise, *For I will be to her a wall of fire. I* is emphatic, and so is the verb, which, contrary to usual Hebrew practice with the verb 'to be', is expressed. Th. Chary sees an intentional reference here to Exodus 3:14, and translates 'And I, I shall be to her I AM, oracle of the Lord'.[1] Furthermore the *fire* and the *glory* recalled the Exodus (Ex. 13:22; 14:20; 40:34). Zechariah was being given a message that proved the continuing validity of the covenant made at the Exodus. Whereas Ezekiel had foreseen the return of the glory of the Lord to the Temple (43:2–5), Zechariah sees His glory extending to the whole city, and later (2:12) to the whole land (*cf.* Zc. 14:20,21).

Together the second and third visions guarantee the safety of Jerusalem. God is both dealing with potential enemies and protecting His people, in the same way and on the same covenant basis as He did at the Exodus. Having established this, there follows an oracle which brings out the practical application of the visions for the prophet's contemporaries.

6–13. The fact that the rest of the chapter is poetry is not obvious from the standard English versions. Only Moffatt and JB set it out as poetry. There is a change, not only of *genre*, but also of speaker and destination. Instead of the angel it is now Zechariah who speaks, first to the exiles in Babylon, then to the Jerusalem Jews, and there is nothing now to suggest a vision.

The poem may be divided into two equal stanzas, verses 6–9 and 10–13.[2] In support of such a division there are three main arguments. (*a*) The two halves have a similar structure: an introductory command is followed by a clause beginning 'for . . .' (verses 6,10); after the divine word comes the prophet's comment 'Then you will know . . .' (verses 9,12;

[1] Chary, p. 67.
[2] RSV makes verses 6–12 one paragraph, verse 13 standing alone. Commentators have suggested that this verse was an addition for which liturgical use was responsible. NEB has three sections: 6, 7; 8–12; 13. F. Horst, *HAT*, has two main stanzas: 6–9; 10–12 with 13 as a later addition (pp. 225, 226). A detailed account of theories concerning the structure of these verses is given by A. Petitjean, pp. 89–94.

cf. 4:9; 6:15). (*b*) In each half there is a word of the Lord and that of the prophet. (*c*) From the point of view of ideas the two parts are complementary. The former deals with the over-throw of enemies and so relates to the second vision, while the second half declares the Lord's sovereignty in Zion and relates to the third vision. In short the prophet is reinforcing the implications of the two visions.

6. *Ho! ho!* This exclamation, translated 'Woe' in many contexts, introduces here and in Isaiah 55:1 an exhortation touched with a note of sympathy and pity.[1] It is addressed to the Jews who remained in exile, urging them to *flee from the land of the north*, and to return to strengthen the hands of those rebuilding the community in Jerusalem. They were to escape, not so much from political restrictions as from the danger of becoming too comfortably integrated in the economic life of the countries of their adoption (*cf. Away, away,* NEB). 'The land of the north', Jeremiah's expression to indicate the area from which invasion would come (Je. 6:22; 10:22), and from which the exiles would return (3:18; 16:15; 23:8; 31:8), is used in parallelism with *the four winds* and with 'the daughter of Babylon' (verse 7). Similarly in Isaiah 43:5,6; 49:12 they return from all directions. The 'north' is to be understood figuratively. The call is to exiles wherever they are to return. *For* (*kî*) *I have spread you abroad.* Jewish exiles were *spread abroad* in many countries besides Babylon. Quite apart from the Assyrian policy of deporting Israelites and scattering them over an area from the Gozan river, 200 miles west of Nineveh, to Media 300 miles to the east (2 Ki. 17:6), and Nebucha-drezzar's deportations to Babylon, fugitives had taken refuge in Moab, Ammon and Edom (Je. 40:11,12), while Jeremiah and others went to Egypt (Je. 43:7).

7. If RSV is correct in following the Versions and translating *escape to Zion*, the meaning is that the nations, in spite of their apparent security, are about to experience judgment, and Jews who remain amongst them will inevitably share their fate, hence the urgency of the prophet's command. Th. Chary sees a reference to the Exodus in this urgency (Ex. 12:29; Dt. 16:3) and in the promise that they will spoil their oppressors (verse 9)[2]. The Hebrew, however, reads simply 'Ho! Zion', addressing

[1] BDB, pp. 222, 223.
[2] Chary, p. 69.

the exiles as Zion, as in Isaiah 51:16; 52:2, hence JB *Zion, up!* The idiom *daughter of Babylon* means 'the inhabitants of' the city or the kingdom of Babylon (*cf.* 'daughter of Zion', verse 10; 9:9; but see the footnote to 9:9). Since Babylon in the post-exilic period epitomized all the suffering and indignity inflicted on Judah at the fall of Jerusalem and after, the name could stand for all lands of exile, and was not confined to the geographical area known as Babylon.

8. This is one of the most difficult verses in the book. *After his glory sent me* raises at least two problems. The first concerns the meaning and usage of the word 'after' (*'aḥar*), and the second the significance of the word 'glory' (*kāḇôḏ*). In RSV 'after' is interpreted as a conjunction, and the sense could be expanded to 'after the Lord in his glory sent me'. The prophet would be making reference to a vision of glory at the time of his call to preach to the nations.[1] More frequently the word has been taken as a preposition, *after glory* (RV). H. G. Mitchell, for example, translates 'After the glory (vision) he sent me'.[2] If that is the true reading the prophet was saying, rather obscurely, that this oracle was disclosed to him after seeing the visions. It has been argued that *'aḥar* can also mean 'with'.[3] This meaning would make good sense in Ecclesiastes 12:2, 'before . . . the clouds return *with* the rain' (*cf.* Ex. 11:5, 'the maidservant who is *with* the mill'; Ps. 73:24, 'thou wilt receive me *with* glory'). Th. Chary believes this is the sense here, and by taking *kāḇôḏ* in its other sense 'heaviness' he arrives at the translation 'with insistence he sent me'.[4] Of these interpretations the last makes best sense and is the most convincing.

This mission to the nations gives another glimpse into the call of Zechariah. Though he was sent primarily to Israel, his message had a bearing on other nations concerned. Some think that this oracle was originally preached in exile before 538 BC, which would make this one of the oldest in the book.[5]

[1] A. Petitjean, who adopts this meaning, cites the Hebrew of Leviticus 14:43; Job 42:7; Jeremiah 40:1; 41:16; where *'aḥar* is used as a conjunction.
[2] *ICC*, p. 142. T. C. Vriezen, 'Two Old Cruces' in *Oudtest. Studiën* (Leyden, 1948), pp. 80–91, suggests that *after glory* is a scribal note indicating that what follows should come after 'glory' in verse 5, but he himself admits that such a comment on the disorder of the text has no parallel. See Petitjean, pp. 113, 114.
[3] R. Y. B. Scott, 'Secondary Meanings of *'aḥar*', *JTS*, 50, 1949, pp. 178, 179; M. Dahood, *Biblica*, 44, 1963, pp. 292, 293.
[4] Chary, p. 70. [5] So G. A. Smith, *EB*, pp. 259, 260.

Before quoting the divine message the prophet refers to the simile in Deuteronomy 32:10 ('he kept him as the apple of his eye'), another allusion to the Exodus. Though it had seemed that the Lord did not care when armies plundered Jerusalem, the prophet believed that these events in no way disproved the divine love. By recalling a passage (Dt. 32) which, while centred in the covenant, foresaw the need of chastisement, Zechariah suggested the explanation of their sufferings and the loving purpose for which they had been allowed. The subject led easily into the main affirmation which follows.

9. *Behold* (literally 'for, behold') is used by the prophets to introduce a particularly emphatic statement (*cf.* Is. 3:1; 65:17; Je. 1:15; 25:29; Zc. 2:10; 3:8,9; Mal. 4:1). By a gesture of the hand the Lord is able to overthrow the established order of the nations (*cf.* Is. 11:15; 19:16). The Jews who had been slaves will themselves inherit the prey from their oppressors, but it is important to note that Zechariah sees this emphatically as the Lord's doing, not man's. The proper response for the Jew was to return and prepare for this event. The quotation marks should be closed after 'served them', to indicate that the prophet now speaks. *Then you will know that the Lord of hosts has sent me.* Fulfilment of the prediction will vindicate the authenticity of the messenger. His statement does not necessarily imply that his contemporaries doubted or rejected him, but it does reflect the prophet's unshakable conviction that his word will be fulfilled. On this occasion he does not say 'sent me to you' (*cf.* verse 12; 4:9; 6:15), because he is conscious here of his mission to the nations.

10. *Sing and rejoice.* Imperatives open the second part of the poem as they did the first (verses 6,7). Only here are these two imperatives put together, though in several places songs of praise for deliverance are introduced by 'sing', 'shout', 'cry aloud' (Is. 12:6; 44:23; 54:1; Je. 31:7). The enthronement of the Lord as king in Zion is frequently the setting of exultation (Pss. 84:2; 96; 98; 132; Is. 52:7–10), but most explicitly in Zephaniah 3:14,15. So the joy is associated with many passages which celebrate the enthronement of the Lord in Zion (*cf.* 9:9). *Daughter of Zion* refers to the city of Jerusalem (2:4,5; 8:3), but also to the population round about (Zp. 3:14), and by metonymy to a great company far exceeding the population of Jerusalem, as the next verse shows. *For lo, I come.* As in verses 6, 8 the important disclosure is introduced by 'for' (*kî*). *And I will dwell in the midst of you.* The verb 'dwell' (*šākan*, from which is derived 'shekinah') recalls the making of the tabernacle (*miškān*) 'that I may dwell in their midst' (Ex. 25:8). This same purpose attached in turn to the Temple (1 Ki. 6:13), and when Ezekiel looked forward to the new Temple he saw the coming of the glory of the Lord (43:2,4) and His acceptance of the Temple as the place of His throne (verse 7) for ever (verse 9). Tabernacle and Temple were the visible tokens of the presence of the covenant-keeping Lord God who had delivered them from Egypt (Ex. 29:43–46). With the building of the new Temple in progress this promise involving continuity of the covenant and the enthroning of the Lord in Zion was a major encouragement.

11. The return of the Lord to His throne in Jerusalem is the signal for the nations to come and acknowledge Him, as frequently in the Psalms (*e.g.* 47:9; 96:1; 97:1; 98:4). The prophet's commission to the nations (verse 8) was not limited to the retribution announced in verse 9, but included the long-term purpose of the Lord to incorporate them into His kingdom in a great universal movement centred on the Temple. They *join themselves to the Lord*, deliberately accepting His terms, not urging the claims of their own gods. They *shall be my people* is covenant language, used frequently by Jeremiah when he looks ahead to the day when the law of the covenant will be kept (Je. 31:33; 32:38). God's people must bear a resemblance to Him. It is in this sense that the nations will be His people (*cf.* Is. 56:6–8; 60:3,21). That moral and cultic righteousness is required of these nations is proved by the repetition of the statement that the Lord will dwell in the midst.

12. Just as the major affirmation of verses 6–9 is followed by the prophet's assertion 'you shall know that the Lord of hosts has sent me', so here, though this time he adds *to you. And the Lord will inherit Judah* and so 'come into His own'. It is, of course, the people of Judah and Jerusalem who are His inheritance, not the geographical territory (Ex. 34:9; Dt. 32:9). The bond between them and the Lord is the covenant. *The holy land* is a phrase used only here in the Old Testament. It is an extension of the psalmist's 'holy hill' (Ps. 2:6; 15:1), or

'holy mountain' (the Hebrew is the same) (Pss. 48:2; 99:9; *cf.*
Zc. 8:3). The place of God's sanctuary was by definition 'holy',
but that holiness extended beyond the Temple, and even
beyond the city to the whole land (1:17; *cf.* 14:20,21, where
common things become holy because they are used for God's
service). *And will again choose Jerusalem*, for all the decisive
religious events of the future will take place there: the Temple
will be the place to which God will come (verse 10), and the
centre from which a new covenant embracing the nations
(verse 11) will be proclaimed.

13. *Be silent, all flesh, before the Lord.* In the light of the prophet's two great disclosures, that the Lord is about to reverse
the prosperity of nations and to appear in Jerusalem, it is
appropriate that 'all flesh' (Heb. *bāśār*, emphasizing the weakness of human kind) should react with awe, and keep silence
(*cf.* Hab. 2:20; Zp. 1:7). *He has roused himself*, as a man is
roused from sleep (Zc. 4:1), all his latent powers alert for
action. The prophet may have had in mind passages such as
Psalm 44:23: 'Rouse thyself! Why sleepest thou, O Lord?
Awake! Do not cast us off for ever!' and Isaiah 51:9: 'Awake,
awake, put on strength, O arm of the Lord.' The answer to
such pleas was at hand. *From his holy dwelling* is the heavenly
sanctuary from which the Lord sets out for Jerusalem. Though
in certain contexts the Temple is intended by such a phrase
(Ps. 26:8; 76:2), here the contrast is between the permanent
dwelling of the Lord in heaven and the place to which He is
about to come.[1]

This lyric poem relates first of all to the return from exile
and the completion of the Temple, but it goes beyond these
events in its assurance that the nations will experience God's
power and acknowledge His Lordship, so entering into a new
covenant to be inaugurated in Jerusalem. All men are to look
in expectation for the Lord's coming to dwell amongst them.

c. Vision 4. The high priest reinstated (3:1-10)

The first three visions brought the prophet from a valley
outside the city to a vantage-point from which the dimensions
of the original Jerusalem could be seen. In the fourth and fifth

---

[1] For this reason K. Elliger's claim (*ATD*, p. 119) that this is a liturgical
instruction used in the Temple is rejected.

visions he is in the Temple courts, where the high priest officiated and had access to God's presence. These two visions concern Judah's standing before God and her spiritual resources.

Certain features of the first three visions are no longer present in the fourth. There is nothing mysterious to give rise to the prophet's questions, and no explanation from the interpreting angel is needed. Instead the identity of Joshua is known from the start, and the action is explained as the vision unfolds.[1]

1. *Then he showed me* refers presumably to the interpreting angel who accompanied the prophet. The new way of introducing the vision is probably no more than the writer's attempt to avoid constant repetition of the same formula. The scene is the heavenly court room, where *the angel of the Lord*, called simply 'the Lord' in verse 2, represents God as judge, and *Joshua*, who, in his official capacity as *the high priest*, represents the Jews, stands as prisoner in the dock. His accuser is *Satan*, a transliteration of the Hebrew word meaning 'adversary'. The Hebrew has the definite article, and is not using the word as a name but as a common noun in the sense of 'the accuser' (*cf.* Jb. 1:6–12; 2:1–7; Rev. 12:10), fulfilling a necessary role in the tribunal. The fuller development of the doctrine of a personal and devilish opponent of God is a feature of the New Testament. All the same there is a certain maliciousness about the satan's role even here, and an opposition to God's will, reflected in the Lord's words addressed to him (verse 2).

2. *The Lord rebuke you, O Satan!* When the Lord rebukes there is no gainsaying His word (Ps. 9:5; Is. 17:13). *The Lord who has chosen Jerusalem*. The theme of Jerusalem's election continues to have prominence (1:17; 2:12) and in practical terms makes all the difference to God's relationship with her. The reference to *a brand plucked from the fire* recalls Amos 4:11; evidently this was a proverbial saying to indicate privileged deliverance from God's providential chastisements. To the extent that the slavery in Egypt was referred to as an iron

[1] Many Continental scholars, among them F. Horst (*HAT*, p. 210), K. Elliger (*ATD*, p. 103), Th. Chary (p. 73), consider that originally there were only seven visions, and that this fourth one, which is not quite in line with the rest, is a later addition. Whether that is so or not there is no evidence to suggest that it ever stood in any other context, and indeed it can be shown to belong with the fifth in a comprehensible pattern, as most English commentators agree.

furnace (Dt. 4:20; Je. 11:4) it may contain a specific reference to the Exodus deliverance. By virtue of the fact that Joshua represents all that remains from the furnace of the exile, he is doubly precious, the object of God's electing love.

3. Joshua's *filthy garments* were the robes of the high priest's office. The fact that they are described as 'filthy' has been variously explained. Some have thought that Joshua was in mourning and wearing the customary sackcloth daubed with ash.[1] The simile of verse 2 suggests the possibility that the garments were stained by the furnace experience, that is, polluted by contact with heathen Babylon, but the words spoken to Joshua indicate a connection between 'filthy garments' and 'iniquity' (verse 4), not sufficiently accounted for by ritual impurity nor by the scandal of the uncompleted Temple. Indeed if he was in mourning as a sign of national repentance, that amounted to an admission of personal and corporate guilt. Joshua stands before the judge unable to help himself.

4. Angelic beings not mentioned before are called upon to remove the offending garments and the angel of the Lord explains the significance of the act. The introductory *Behold* is more literally 'look', a different word from the exclamation in 2:3,9,10. It draws attention to the spiritual counterpart of the removal of the filthy garments, *I have taken your iniquity away from you*. 'Iniquity' (Heb. *'āwôn*) is a general term for the whole sinful disposition leading to distress and guilt. Joshua in his high-priestly role stood for the predicament of the whole people, who had incurred the divine wrath, suffered the penalty of the exile, and now knew that they needed a way back to the presence of a holy God. The vision demonstrated that God accepted Joshua, and with him those he represented, having removed from His sight all that offended His holiness. But that was not all. *I will clothe you with rich apparel* promised garments suitable for the heavenly court, which it would have been beyond Joshua's power to provide.

5. *And I said*. So vivid was the scene to Zechariah that he could not refrain from suggesting that the turban be added to complete the special robes of access.[2] The word used for *turban*

---

[1] So JB margin, p. 1533.
[2] The alternative reading in some MSS 'and he said' looks like an accommodation to the expected sense, and so is probably not the original reading.

(*ṣānîp̄*) is not the exact term used in Exodus and Leviticus for the turban of the high priest (*cf.* the comment on 6:11), but a cognate one used in figurative contexts (Jb. 29:14; Is. 62:3). Whether or not the garments were recognizably those prescribed for the high priest, the important thing was that they symbolized acceptance in the heavenly court (*cf.* Mt. 22:11–13; Rev. 19:8).

The vision is related to the rebuke in 1:1–6. The efficacy of animal sacrifices to take away sin was in question. Though no satisfactory explanation was offered, the vision assured those who repented (1:6) that sin had been put away and acceptance with God granted.

6, 7. In recommissioning Joshua the angel of the Lord lays down two conditions. If these are fulfilled the high priest will have two specific privileges which were less clearly applicable to his predecessors before the exile.

If you will walk in my ways implies utter commitment to God's revealed character and intentions, and negatively, rejection of anything that would compromise that commitment. *And keep my charge* (Heb. *mišmeret̄*) involves the faithful performance of the ritual laid down for the priests (*cf.* Nu. 3, where the word is used nine times). In short, he is to fulfil both the moral and ritual requirements. The first privilege will be sole authority in the Temple and its courts. Whereas the king had taken authority in matters concerning worship (1 Ki. 2:27; 2 Ki. 16:10–18; 22:3ff.), from this time on the rights of the high priest will be indisputable. The verb is literally 'judge (*dîn*) my house', and suggests the exercise of judicial functions (Dt. 17:8–13) as well as governing the ritual. The second privilege will be not merely to enter the holy of holies, but to have direct approach to the presence of God Himself *among those who are standing here*, that is, the heavenly beings who wait upon Him (verse 4). Such a high honour was foreseen in the granting of rich apparel, fit for God's presence.

In all this the person and work of Joshua's greater namesake, Jesus, was being anticipated. The faithful high priest of the pre-Christian era entered into God's presence as the Christian does 'by grace through faith'. Whereas the adversary would have accused him (verse 1), the Lord reinstated and recommissioned him, granting a right, now shared by every believer, to direct approach to God (Heb. 4:14–16).

8. *Hear now* leads one to expect a word of special importance (*cf.* Dt. 6:4). It is addressed to *Joshua the high priest, you and your friends who sit before you.* Evidently Joshua presided over conferences of priests as Ezekiel did over those for elders or people (Ezk. 8:1; 14:1; 20:1; 33:31). Zechariah is addressing the whole company of priests, though they are not necessarily all present, hence the third person pronoun, *they are men of good omen*, or strictly, portent (Heb. *môpēṯ*). The word can mean 'a special display of God's power', or 'a token of a future event', which is the meaning in this verse (*cf.* Is. 8:18). The fact that they were priests made them signs of the promised *Branch* (Heb. *ṣemaḥ*), who is also called *my servant* (*cf.* the 'servant' theme of Isaiah 40–55, but especially 52:13 – 53:12). Otherwise there is no clue here to the identity of the Branch, and comment will be reserved for the longer statement about the Branch in 6:12,13.

9. The abrupt change of metaphor from a branch to a stone has seemed to the translators of JB, NEB sufficient ground for rearrangement of the text. In JB verse 9a follows 7, while in NEB it follows 10, but this latter is only part of a drastic rearrangement in NEB of material from chapters 3 and 4. In the absence of textual evidence for such changes, and therefore of objective criteria to act as a control, these changes reflect only the personal judgment of one or more scholars.

The stone (Heb. *'eben*) means a stone of any kind, common or precious. It could have been a building stone for the Temple (*cf.* Isaiah's stone, 28:16), but a stone *with seven facets* would be difficult to use either in the foundations or as a head-stone. *I will engrave its inscription* suggests a commemorative stone of some kind, and the fact that the Assyrian and Babylonian kings set such stones in the foundations of buildings to perpetuate their memory[1] has inclined some commentators to the view that Zechariah had a foundation stone in mind here.[2] The verb 'engrave' is used of work on metal, stone and wood, and so gives no help in defining the type of stone intended, but the only other place where engraving on stone is mentioned

[1] R. S. Ellis, *Foundation Deposits in Ancient Mesopotamia*, Yale N.E. Researches (2) (New Haven–London, 1968), pp. 26–29. Quoted by E. Lipinski, *op. cit.*, p. 31.
[2] So C. H. H. Wright, p. 73; A. Petitjean, p. 185. W. E. Barnes (*CB*, p. 43) thought it was the headstone, but there is no evidence that headstones were ever inscribed.

in a priestly context (Ex. 28:9–12) tells of the names of the tribes of Israel engraved on the onyx stones worn by the high priest, and on the stones of the breastplate (verse 21). While engraving on a building stone could have been intended, there is some evidence in favour of a precious stone with symbolic meaning.[1] Moreover, as P. R. Ackroyd points out, emphasis in this verse is laid on the removal of the land's guilt, and the high priest's turban, in which he thinks this stone was set, was connected with atonement (Ex. 28:36ff.).

The stone is not said to be given to Joshua but *set before* him. It is reasonable, therefore, to suppose that it was larger than a normal gem. *With seven facets*, Heb. 'eyes' (NEB). The word '*ayin* (eye) is extremely versatile in Hebrew usage. Besides denoting the physical eye, it appears in metaphorical contexts, some of which are familiar from translation into English, such as 'the apple of his eye' (Zc. 2:8), 'the eyes of both were opened' (Gn. 3:7), 'his eye shall be evil towards . . .' (Dt. 28:54, AV, RV). In other cases the English has to be more literal or change the metaphor: the eye (face) of the land (Ex. 10:5), the eye (appearance) of manna (Nu. 11:7), the eye (sparkle) of wine (Pr. 23:31), and the eye (gleam) of bronze (Ezk. 1:4). Whether the translation 'facets' can be justified from Hebrew usage is doubtful, though there is some support for it in 'face of the land' (Ex. 10:5; Nu. 22:5).

There is, however, the other word '*ayin* meaning 'spring', and E. Lipinski[2] argues that this is the word used here and in 4:10. A possible translation would then be: 'See the stone which I have set before Joshua. On a single stone (possibly, according to Lipinski, an idiom for "at one and the same time") seven springs! See, I open their openings, says the Lord of hosts, and I will take away the guilt of the land in a single day.' *Open their openings* takes the primary meaning of the verb *pāṭaḥ*, and though the pointing needs revision to give the meaning 'openings' the LXX and other versions support it. The attraction of Lipinski's translation is that it unifies the message of verses 8–10 addressed to Joshua and the priests. The 'living water' of the fountains causes the Branch to shoot up (verse 8),

[1] H. G. Mitchell (*ICC*, p. 157) and P. R. Ackroyd (*PCB*², p. 648) favour this interpretation.
[2] *VT*, XX, 1, 1970, pp. 25–29. On the gender of the word he quotes G. H. Dalman (*Aramäisch-neuhebräisches Handwörterbuch*, 1922, p. 311b) as evidence that, used in the sense 'spring', the word is normally masculine, as in Zechariah.

washes away guilt (9) and ensures prosperity (10). The stone, according to this translation, is no longer an engraved jewel but rather takes its meaning from the rock struck by Moses in the desert (Ex. 17:6; *cf.* Nu. 20:7–11). Moses took his rod to strike the rock. The Lord promises His Branch, and, connected with the stone, living water. Though the vocabulary is different the connection of thought is there. The Branch, like Moses and Joshua, will act in a representative capacity, remove the guilt of the land, and bring true prosperity. It is not impossible that Zechariah was incorporating both meanings, in a play on the word.

10. *In that day.* E. Lipinski[1] cites four authorities to support the translation 'on the same day' for this ancient Hebrew formula, which is usually taken to be a technical term for 'the last day'. 'On the same day' is clearly the meaning in Genesis 15:18. The emphasis in this passage is on the decisive moment in history when these new possibilities will be operative. The proverbial picture of everyone inviting *his neighbour under his vine and under his fig tree* (1 Ki. 4:25; 2 Ki. 18:31; Mi. 4:4) represents the acme of contentment for which the Israelite longed. While every man would have a place to call his own, his joy would be to share it with others, and loneliness would be a thing of the past.

c[1]. Vision 5. Divine resources for high priest and prince (4:1–14)

The lampstand all of gold (Ex. 25:31) stood in the holy place of the Tabernacle. The ten lampstands made by Solomon for the Temple (1 Ki. 7:49) are not heard of again, and were evidently replaced by only one in the post-exilic Temple (1 Macc. 1:21). The prophet might even have had some responsibility in connection with the making of the new lampstand and have had its structure in mind. What it represented is not explained, and the question asked in verse 4 is not dealt with until the end of the chapter. Instead of a direct answer the angel addresses a message to Zerubbabel, which most commentators judge to have been part of a separate oracle that did not originally belong in this chapter. JB and NEB rearrange the text accordingly. In the middle of verse 10 or at the beginning

[1] *Op. cit.*, p. 29.

of verse 11 the narrative broken off in the middle of verse 6 is resumed, and by dint of persistent questioning the prophet finally arrives at the meaning of the two olive trees. They represent two leaders who are shown to be equipped for their tasks by virtue of their relationship to the Lord (verse 14). If the main purpose of the vision may tentatively be stated before the passage is studied in detail, it is to encourage the two leaders, Joshua and Zerubbabel, with a reminder of God's resources, and to vindicate them in the eyes of the community.

1. The particulars of the wakening of the prophet are given only in connection with the fifth vision. It may be that this one was regarded as being of special significance, but too much should not be made of what is probably a stylistic device.

2. The prophet had no difficulty in identifying the object he saw as *a lampstand*, so it must have looked like other lampstands with which he was familiar. Large numbers of lamps have been unearthed in Palestine belonging to the biblical period, and these have a bearing on our understanding of the prophet's description.[1] The first important fact revealed by archaeological studies of lamps is that the seven-branched candlestick pictured on Titus' arch in Rome, and still used by the Jews, the *menôrâ*, is not known earlier than the first century BC. Translations based on the assumption that this was the model confuse the issue. C. H. H. Wright reconstructed the lampstand according to this pattern, but in footnotes admitted the difficulties raised.[2]

Lamp pedestals excavated from Palestine cities were much simpler in design. They were cylindrical in shape, hollow, and looked rather like a tree trunk. They were usually made of pottery, and had a hole in the side, into which a spout could have been fixed.[3] Pedestal lamps have been found not only at Gezer in the south-west of Palestine, but also at Ta'annak on the southern edge of the plain of Esdraelon, and in 1969 at a high place near Dan in the far north. Evidently this was an

[1] R. North includes three pages of lamp diagrams and one of photographs in 'Zechariah's Seven-Spout Lampstand', *Biblica*, 51, 2, 1970.
[2] Wright, pp. 84, 85. See also the diagram, p. 84.
[3] Those illustrated by R. North (*op. cit.*, p. 195, fig. 26, 28) are from Gezer and are dated 1800–1400 or 1400–1000 BC. The remains are up to about 60 cm. high (but the original would have been taller) and about 16 cm. in width.

accepted pattern for a lamp.[1] Zechariah's lampstand (*mᵉnôrâ*) was probably just a cylindrical column, tapering slightly towards the top, on which was *a bowl*. Innumerable pottery versions of bowl lamps show how the rim was pinched together to form a holder for the wick, the better the light needed the more the places for wicks, seven being the most popular number. The bowl of the lamp found near Dan, dated *c.* 900 BC, had seven flutes, as did the one from Ta'annak. Whether or not Zechariah's large bowl had seven flutes, it had *seven lamps on it, with seven lips on each of the lamps*. The picture is of seven small bowls, each with a place for seven wicks, arranged round the rim of the main bowl.[2] A vessel like this, but probably an incense burner rather than a lamp, was excavated north of Akko by Moshe Dothan in 1954/58. He dated it *c.* 1750 BC. Though N. Glueck dates seven-spouted pedestal lamps tenth century and not before,[3] this would appear to have been the pattern on which the Temple lampstand was constructed. What would be unusual would be such a lampstand in gold.[4] With its seven times seven lights it would be both impressive and effective.

3. *Two olive trees by it*, or more exactly, above ('*al*), that is, overshadowing it, stand on either side of the bowl. The pedestals would probably be about the same height as the trunk of the olive trees, say two metres, and the branches would be above the lights.

4. It is the olive trees that puzzle the prophet and prompt his question (*cf.* verses 11, 12).

5. The interpreting angel twice delays his reply (*cf.* verse 13), and the effect is to concentrate interest on the final verse of the chapter.

6. Meanwhile Zechariah is given *the word of the Lord to Zerubbabel*. There is no reference to the vision in the next few

[1] R. North, *op. cit.*, plate opposite p. 192. The right-hand figure shows the lamp found at Dan.

[2] A drawing of Kurt Galling's suggested reconstruction has been reproduced in *IDB*, III, p. 66. R. North, however, thinks that each of the seven lamps had only one light.

[3] *Israel Albright Festschrift*, 1969, referred to by R. North, p. 198.

[4] A photograph of a seven-lipped saucer lamp in metal, but dated second century AD, appears in D. J. Wiseman, *Illustrations from Biblical Archaeology* (Tyndale Press, 1958), p. 102.

verses, but the connection of thought is that the two olive trees stand for the two leaders. Joshua had been given a special word in the previous vision, hence the concentration on Zerubbabel. The two visions belong together.

Temple building, already in hand, will be completed, but *not by might* (Heb. *ḥayil*), that is military strength, human prowess, such as the 'army' of workers Solomon had had to enable him to build (1 Ki. 5:13–18), *nor by power* (Heb. *koaḥ*), a word used for the 'strength' of the load-carriers in Nehemiah 4:10. Looked at from a human point of view the manpower available was inadequate for the task. *But by my spirit* (Heb. *rûaḥ*), *says the Lord of hosts*. It was the breath (*rûaḥ*) of the Lord that worked in creation (Gn. 1:2), and that opened the Red Sea and closed it again (Ex. 15:8,10; 2 Sa. 22:16). In Ezekiel's vision (37:1–14) the wind (*rûaḥ*) brought a dead people to life. Was such intervention needed in order to complete the building of the Temple? Yes, because the work, and the way it was done, and the provision of material resources as well as the finished building, were all a witness to God, the Lord of hosts. Only if His Spirit governs every detail can service be glorifying to Him.

7. *What are you, O great mountain?* (Heb. 'who (*mî*) are you?'). Either Zerubbabel had personified the obstacles or the principal difficulties revolved round human obstructionists who wanted their own way (Ezr. 4:2,4). The 'great mountain' is evidently not to be limited to mounds of rubble that impeded building, any more than Isaiah's mountains are meant to be taken literally (Is. 40:4; 41:15). The mountains of opposition to God's work, both practical and personal, *shall become a plain*, which cannot hinder progress (*cf.* Mk. 11:23).

He shall bring forward the top stone (Heb. 'head stone', an expression used only here and signifying 'stone of primary importance'). It has been argued that the foundation stone is meant, largely because in ancient Near-Eastern texts no mention is made of a top stone, whereas the foundation stone is known to have been laid during a public ceremony.[1] The strongest argument in favour of a completion stone is the demand of the sense of the passage. The foundation has been laid

---

[1] A. Petitjean (pp. 243–251) summarizes discussion on the meaning of the expression and decides in favour of the foundation stone. See also *ANET*, pp. 340, 341.

(verse 9) and the promise is that the building will be finished. Whether or not it was customary,[1] in this case there will be a ceremony of rejoicing when the last stone has been laid, for this is no ordinary building. Its completion is symbolic of victory by God's Spirit (verse 6), hence the exclamations *Grace, grace to it!* Hebrew *ḥēn*, 'grace', 'beauty', draws attention both to the attractiveness of the building and to the grace God has shown and will show in future.

8, 9. The second word to Zerubbabel puts the same message in plain terms. Zerubbabel will certainly finish the work, and the fulfilment of this prophecy will provide further vindication of the prophet's authority (*cf.* 2:9,11; 6:15). For a comment on *laid the foundation* see Additional Note on 'the day that the foundation of the Lord's temple was laid', p. 52.

10. Zechariah, like Haggai, implies that the 'realists' were pessimistic about the building project (Hg. 2:3), and so *despised the day of small things*. They wanted to see it succeed and were glad when it did, but their faith was too small. They would be surprised into rejoicing. The end of the verse is an anticlimax in RSV: to *see the plummet in the hand of Zerubbabel* would indicate no more than that he was supervising the work. This translation is based on early Greek, Latin and Aramaic versions rather than on the Hebrew, which does not use the technical term for a plumbline, but a strange juxtaposition of two nouns, 'the stone the tin' (*bᵉdîl*). In spite of Numbers 31:22, where *bᵉdîl* is translated 'lead', 'tin' is correct, and since tin is unsuitable for use as a weight 'plumbline' is unlikely to be right. NEB has 'the stone called Separation', parallel with 'the stone called Possession' (verse 7). This is based on the opinion of G. R. Driver,[2] suggested by the Syriac version. The verb *bādal*, from which the noun *bᵉdîl* is derived, means 'to separate', and evidently the Syriac translators understood the term as an adjectival form of this verb. The stone would then symbolize the separated, 'holy' nature of the Jewish community. It is but a short step from this to JB 'the chosen stone'. The same stone

---

[1] Th. Chary (p. 96) cites two passages in the Babylonian Chronicles where the king proclaims loudly that he has raised the 'head' (*reshu*) of the Temple to its height (Chronique de Nabopolassar, No. 1, col. III, 24, 25; St. Langdon, *Neubabylonische Königsinschriften*, p. 65; Chronique de Nabonide, No. 3, col. III, 8, 9; St. Langdon, *ibid.*, p. 241). See also Ps. 118:22, 'the headstone of the corner'.

[2] 'Babylonian and Hebrew Notes', in *Die Welt des Orients*, II, 1954, p. 22.

is meant as in verse 9, a specially prepared stone, set apart for a special place in the coping stones of the Temple. Zerubbabel's stone is not to be confused with that of Joshua in 3:9. The cause of rejoicing, therefore, is the placing of this last ceremonial stone, the crown of all their work, on the height of the Temple walls, by Zerubbabel.

Having delivered the word to Zerubbabel, the angel returns to the question put by Zechariah as to the meaning of the vision. *These seven are the eyes of the Lord,* but which 'seven'? The majority of commentators take it that the reference is to the seven lamps (verse 3), which seems obvious. Indeed the symbolism of the number seven, standing as it does for completeness and perfection, would make the lamps a fitting symbol for the Lord's presence in the Temple. It would teach that His eyes watch over the interests of restored Israel, but at the same time *range through the whole earth.* The difficulty with this interpretation is that the oil apparently flows from the trees into the lamps (verse 12), that is, God's servants would be supplying Him with oil, an interpretation which is quite untenable. The other possible antecedent is 3:9, which gives the translation, 'These seven are the springs of the Lord; they flow out over the whole earth'.[1] The two visions are interconnected and both look towards a future renewal of God's people that will bring the water of life first to God's people (3:9), and through them to the world (4:10).

11,12. The question in verse 11 is repeated to make it more specific, and in framing it the second time a new detail is introduced. There are *two branches of the olive trees* and *two golden pipes,* not mentioned before. The word translated 'pipes' is used nowhere else in the Old Testament, and so it is not possible to be sure of its meaning, but together with the lamps found at Gezer were terracotta tubes which 'sprout' into a kind of spout or opening. These may have been used as a means of keeping the lamps supplied with oil, and may explain the 'pipes' of verse 12. If they transferred oil from the olive trees to the golden bowl of the lamp, or if the oil was collected in vessels used for refilling the lamps,[2] the lamp cannot stand for

[1] The verb translated 'range through' (Heb. *šûṭ*) means 'go about', 'run to and fro' (*e.g.* Nu. 11:8; Am. 8:12; Dn. 12:4), for which 'springs of water' is a more likely subject than 'eyes'.
[2] D. R. Jones, *TBC,* p. 76.

the Lord, for He is the source of supplies, not their recipient. *From which the oil is poured out* interprets the Hebrew, which reads 'which empty the gold out of themselves'. The 'gold' could be interpreted as the self-giving of Joshua and Zerubbabel on behalf of the community, but this is nearer to twentieth-century thinking than to biblical teaching. Probably RSV is correct in taking it to mean golden oil.

13,14. *These are the two anointed* (Heb. 'sons of oil'). By analogy with other uses of the idiom 'son of', the meaning is 'full of oil'; the reference is to the anointing of kings and priests, using imagery suggested by the vision. The two 'anointed' were Joshua and Zerubbabel. It is doubtful whether Zerubbabel would ever have undergone the ceremony of anointing, but he was the Davidic prince by ancestral right. These two *stand by* or 'wait upon' (*'al*) *the Lord of the whole earth*, which is a title that appears as an official designation of Nebuchadrezzar in Judith 2:5. Nebuchadrezzar and his empire had gone for ever, but for Israel's God it was a title appropriate for all time.

Having worked through the text of the chapter, we now return to its interpretation. The lampstand represents not the Lord but the witness of the Temple and the Jewish community to Him. In this way the vision is interpreted simply and coherently. Joshua and Zerubbabel wait on the unseen Lord, who is the source of their authority and power. They in turn give themselves to build both the Temple and the community; by daily life and worship the whole people is to be a light to others. The city set on a hill cannot be hid (Mt. 5:14). If we ask how such a thing could be true of people who had so recently been exiled for their failures, the answer lies in the supply of oil through the 'anointed ones' which kept the lights burning. It was 'by my Spirit, says the Lord of hosts' (verse 6). In the Revelation to John the seven golden lampstands represent churches (Rev. 1:20), just as Zechariah's lamp stood for the worshipping community of the post-exilic period. Ultimately the only true light was the Lord Himself (Jn. 8:1), but He saw fit to give light to the world through the church of both Old and New Testament times, and in particular through its leaders. They do their part to the best of their ability, but the factor that counts is their receptivity to the oil that flows from the olive trees into their branches, and through them to give light to others. For the operation of God's Spirit there can be no substitute, however able the leaders may be. The key verse of the whole passage proves to be verse 6. Far from being separate from the vision, the oracle to Zerubbabel is indispensable to an understanding of it. The completion of God's kingdom is as certain as the completion of the Temple. God's Spirit flows through His servants who wait on Him to turn the day of small things into the day of world-wide rejoicing, as the last living stone is added to the structure of which Jesus Christ Himself is the chief cornerstone (Eph. 2:20).

Chapters 3 and 4 clearly have Messianic import. Though in the first place they referred to the reconstruction taking place in Jerusalem in 519 BC, the rock (3:9), the stone (4:7), the Branch (3:8) and the Temple all had a significance beyond themselves. Though it is not defined, that significance is connected with the two 'sons of oil', Joshua and Zerubbabel, priest and Davidic prince, who together are the means of bringing new hope to the community. Through the high priest acquittal is pronounced and access to God's presence made possible; through the prince the Temple is completed and the lampstand allowed to shine out to the world. Two 'messiahs' or anointed ones have their roles co-ordinated; neither is adequate without the other. They are equal in dignity and importance. After the death of Zerubbabel the high priest was to increase in temporal power, for the governors in Jerusalem declined in importance, but the promises to the house of David were not forgotten. The people of Qumran expected two messiahs, one priestly and one Davidic,[1] but the two functions were to be brought together in the person and work of Christ.

b². Vision 6. Evil meets retribution (5:1-4)

The next two visions are concerned with continuing lawlessness in the land. One essential function of the ruler was to administer justice (3:7; cf. Dt. 17:9, where it was the task of the priest, and 2 Sa. 15:2,3, where the king was judge). Whoever undertook to enforce justice, it was an arduous duty, never adequately fulfilled, as the prophets indicated when they foretold a righteous rule (Is. 11:3-5; 32:1; Je. 23:5, etc.). No judge, however just, could prevent wickedness from proliferating in the land, hence the message of these two visions, which by

[1] 1 QSb, II, 12-14, translated by G. Vermes, *The Dead Sea Scrolls in English* (Penguin Books, 1962), 'The Messianic Rule', p. 121.

their brevity and relative simplicity correspond to visions two and three.

1. The introductory formula is identical with that of the second and third visions. The prophet now sees *a scroll*, not rolled up in its case and stacked in the archives for the use of the priests and scribes, but *flying*, open like a banner for all to read. The post-exilic period was to see a serious concern for religious education, and especially for the teaching of the law.

2. This scroll was of unusual dimensions, being only twice as long as it was broad, and it was of giant proportions. The cubit measured 18 inches, so it was 10 yards by 5, the size of a huge placard. In attempting to see significance in the measurements reference has been made to the dimensions of the Tabernacle, which can be calculated from the data given in Exodus 26:15–28.[1] If, as used to be thought, the boards were set edge to edge to form a solid wall, the holy place would measure 20 by 10 cubits, but more recently this assumption has been questioned. The boards formed an open framework rather than a solid wall[2] and so the resulting structure would be larger than used to be thought. It has also been pointed out that the porch of Solomon's Temple was built to these measurements (1 Ki. 6:3), but no acceptable reason has been suggested for connecting the porch with the scroll.

3. Previous visions had promised God's intervention to Judah's benefit, but there were moral conditions to be fulfilled, as there had been when the covenant was inaugurated. *This is the curse* (Heb. *'ālâ*) or 'oath'. The word is used several times in connection with covenant (Gn. 24:41; 26:28; Dt. 29:12; Ezk. 16:59, *etc.*). Implicit in the giving of the law was the teaching that those who kept it would prosper, while those who broke it would meet with disaster (hence the 'blessings' and the 'curses' of Dt. 28). The scroll represented the law, with its specific curses on law-breakers, operative in *the whole land* (Heb. *hā'āreṣ*). Though the word also means 'earth' (AV), it is reasonable to infer that the primary reference is to those

---

[1] H. G. Mitchell (*ICC*, p. 169) and C. H. H. Wright (p. 107) are two who think the holy place in the Tabernacle suggested the figures.
[2] A diagram of an Egyptian framework for a curtained tent is given in *NBD*, 'Tabernacle', p. 1231. See also the article.

who had entered into the covenant. It was vitally important that the Jews should not again fail to be a light to the nations. *Every one who steals* is a pithy way of saying 'every one who wrongs his neighbour', and *every one who swears falsely* (invoking the divine name) sums up blatant disregard for God's holiness. The seventh and the third commandments represent the two 'tables' of the law, dealing with duty to one's neighbour and duty to God. *Shall be cut off* (Heb. *niqqâ*). The verb means 'purged out' (RV), or 'exempted from obligation' imposed by the covenant oath. The covenant-breakers will no longer be within the covenant, and so will be 'cut off' from the community; *according to it* probably refers to the writing on the scroll.

4. God's words are often personified and said to go forth on His errands (Ps. 147:15; Is. 55:11). Because they go with His authority they have inherent power to accomplish His purposes, so that, even if there are insufficient human agents to see that wrong is punished, God's word will work its own retribution on the homes of the guilty, imperceptibly but surely bringing about their downfall. Whether the family dies out or moves away in disgrace, its evil influence is removed from Judah.

There is no specific mention of the appointment of judges in post-exilic Jerusalem until the time of Ezra (Ezr. 7:25). The vision brought encouragement to those who had to administer justice as one of many duties, and were aware of the disruptive elements in the community without being able effectively to deal with them. God's word had its ancient power; no-one would persist in disobedience and go unpunished. God's word also found its way where the judicial machinery could not go, to punish wrong committed in the privacy of the home. None could plead ignorance, for the scroll was large enough for all to see, and none could escape its judgment.

b³. Vision 7. Jerusalem is purified (5:5–11)

There was, however, another persistent aspect of the problem of evil in the land. The returned exiles lived alongside other settlers, who had different moral standards. Inevitably their way of life presented a less demanding alternative to the self-discipline required by the law. Moreover, the prophet may have been musing that there would be few homes which the curse (verse 3) would not consume. His call for repentance (1:2–6) is proof that he was aware that all needed forgiveness.

Though the sixth and seventh visions have a complementary meaning the imagery bears no resemblance as it did in the second and third visions.

5,6. The *ephah* was a large barrel used for measuring out grain (*cf.* Ru. 2:17; 1 Sa. 1:24, *etc.*). It was therefore a common household measure with a capacity of about 5 gallons.[1] Even if this should prove an underestimation, a 10-gallon measure would still not contain a human being. In the vision, however, it may have been enlarged, as the scroll was. *This is the iniquity* represents a widely-accepted emendation of the Hebrew, which reads 'this is their eye', AV *resemblance*. Granted that 'eye' can be applied to a wide variety of concepts in Hebrew (see note on 3:9), it seems best on three grounds to accept the emendation here. (*a*) It is supported by the Greek and Syriac versions. (*b*) The consonantal text requires only the substitution of a *wāw* for a *yôḏ*, letters which easily become interchanged. (*c*) The sense is greatly improved. The ephah, named by Amos in his invective on short measure given by the merchants (Am. 8:5), symbolized injustice *in all the land*. The life of the community was vitiated by iniquity that infected it in every part (*cf.* Hg. 2:14). The meanness that prompted the making of false measures was a symptom of an underlying perversity that was at the root of perverse actions and relationships.

7. This perversity becomes personified, but it is more than a literary personification. 'It is the presentiment that Evil has a face',[2] a presentiment which the New Testament was to endorse. The woman, made visible by the lifting of the lead cover, is still, like the evil she represents, mostly hidden from sight.

8. *This is Wickedness* (Heb. *rišʻâ*), a comprehensive word, often used as the antithesis of righteousness (Pr. 11:5; 13:6;

[1] 4 gallons 6¾ pints (*NBD*, p. 1323); 5½ gallons (*IDB* iv, p. 834). The ephah was approximately the equivalent of the bath (Ezk. 45:11,14), and estimations of capacity based on incomplete remains of two such measures have varied between 4.6 and 10.25 gallons.

[2] Th. Chary, p. 103, 'C'est le pressentiment que le Mal a un visage'.

Ezk. 18:20; 33:12), and including civil, ethical and religious evil. Because the Hebrew word is feminine, wickedness is personified as a woman. She attempts to escape from captivity, but the angel with superior strength is able to confine her to the ephah, though the verbs indicate a struggle involved. The power of evil was to be taken seriously.

9. Not only had Wickedness proved powerless before the angel, but she was now to be carried right away by two women with *wings like the wings of a stork*. The huge wings of the stork are a fitting simile, but it may be that the Hebrew name, *ḥasîdâ*, meaning 'faithful one' gave it an added significance. The removal of Wickedness, like the removal of Joshua's filthy garments (3:4), was an act of free grace on the part of the covenant-keeping (*ḥasîd*) God. Moreover, *the wind (rûaḥ)* was in their wings. In view of the double meaning of the Hebrew word (see note on 4:6), the meaning could be 'the Spirit was in their wings', so emphasizing that the removal of Wickedness was God's doing.

10,11. There is irony in the reply of the angel to the prophet's question. *Shinar* was the ancient name for the district in which the cities of Babylon, Erech and Akkad were situated (Gn. 10:10), from the earliest times regarded as opposed to God's way (Gn. 11:1–9). There in the land of Judah's recent captivity they are going *to build a house for it*. Another temple will be erected, perhaps a ziggurat like the tower of Babel, as the reference to Shinar (Gn. 11:2) suggests, but Wickedness will have to wait until it is prepared. *They will set the ephah down.* The verb has an unusual form, an intensified passive, which emphasizes her helplessness. Such were the other gods of Babylon (Is. 46:1,2). Once set there *on its base*, an idol to be worshipped, there it will stay. In the prophet's view there could be nothing in common between worship of the true God and the idolatry of Babylon. They were poles apart, for the idols were powerlessness personified.

If the prophet was concerned about the persistence of evil in the community and in the individual, here was God's answer. He in His covenant faithfulness removed it as far as the east is from the west (Ps. 103:11,12). Jeremiah had taught the same message, using the imagery of a new heart that would be responsive (Je. 32:39,40). Ezekiel the priest spoke in terms of washing away uncleanness (Ezk. 36:25), and

Zechariah's fourth vision had shown filthy garments being replaced by clean ones. Thus the truth of God's justification of the sinner was made known to men of the old covenant. At the same time the vision suggested that evil was a force to be reckoned with, that had its temple and its worshippers, but was firmly in God's control. If, as H. Frey suggests,[1] the removal of Wickedness to Babylon is in preparation for the final onslaught between good and evil, the vision leaves no doubt about the outcome. God has evil in His power.

a[1]. Vision 8. God's patrols compass the earth (6:1–15)

This concluding vision clearly corresponds to the first, though it differs from it in details. In the first there were horses but no chariots. There they were coming in to report, whereas here the steeds are anxious to be off. The former was set in a valley, shut in by trees; in the latter two mountains form the landscape. In both the first horses to be mentioned are the red ones, which in each case are apparently apart from the rest. Otherwise there are puzzling differences between the order and colours of the horses (see Additional Note, p. 138).

An attractive suggestion made by several Continental scholars[2] is that the first of the visions takes place in the evening, whereas the last comes at sunrise. A new era is dawning for Judah and the world, for God's purposes as set out in the visions are about to be fulfilled.

The oracle concerning the Branch (6:9–14) was not originally part of the vision, but it supplements the mention of the Branch in 3:8, and is relevant at the conclusion of the series of visions because Zechariah sees in him the key figure of the glorious future Temple, in the building of which men from the ends of the earth will take part (verse 15).

1. The *two mountains* represent the gateway of heaven (*cf.* verse 5). Various suggestions have been made to account for their being *of bronze*. (*a*) The rising sun gave them the colour of bronze. (*b*) Babylonian mythology, which depicted the sun-god rising between two mountains,[3] lay behind the imagery.

[1] *BAT*, p. 90.

[2] *E.g.* H. Frey, *BAT*, pp. 52, 91; F. Horst, *HAT*, pp. 218, 236; G. von Rad, *Old Testament Theology*, II, p. 287.

[3] Illustrated in H. Frankfort, *Cylinder Seals* (London, 1939), pl. XIXa, and *ANEP*, numbers 683, 685.

(c) The two bronze pillars, which stood on either side of the entrance to the Temple (1 Ki. 7:13–22), grew in the vision to the fabulous size of mountains, guarding the presence of God. Bronze was used together with iron for defence against attack (Je. 1:18), and in Jeremiah's vision symbolized that he was impregnable. This is probably the significance of bronze in this vision. None could take God's heavenly dwelling by storm.

2,3. The four chariots are distinguished by the colour of the horses harnessed to them: the first are red, and yet no red horses are among those sent out (verse 6); black and white occasion no comment, but in the fourth chariot are horses of two colours, 'grey' and 'bay' (RSV *dappled grey*), which each attach themselves to a chariot, according to the Hebrew text of verses 6,7 (so RV; RSV emends the text). The various translations of the last phrase, such as JB '(vigorous) piebald horses' and NEB 'dappled', with the footnote '*Heb. adds* roan' are accounted for in the Additional Note on Zechariah's horses, p. 138. The word 'chariots' is not used again in the original but only the colour of their horses. Chariots formed the storm troops in ancient warfare. They symbolize therefore God's initiative in international affairs.

4,5. The prophet needs a specific interpretation, and is told, literally, 'These are the four winds/spirits (Heb. *rûḥôt*) of heaven, going forth after presenting themselves before the Lord of all the earth'. The steeds are, like the winds, God's messengers (Ps. 104:4), and like the winds they travel over the face of the whole earth. All the earth belongs to the Lord whether the inhabitants acknowledge Him or not, and He gives orders concerning it all.

6. A word or phrase is missing from the Hebrew at the beginning of the verse, for it begins with 'which'. Since neither the red horses nor the east are mentioned, it could be that the missing clause was 'The red horses went towards the east country'.[1] It is appropriate that the black horses go to the north, with its sinister associations (Je. 1:14; 4:6; 6:22; Ezk. 1:4, *etc.*). *The white ones go toward the west country* is more likely to be the meaning than the Hebrew 'after them'. It involves the addition of only one consonant, which gives 'after the sea',

---

[1] JB, NEB incorporate this emendation in the text, following W. Hertzberg, F. Horst, K. Elliger and others.

that is 'to the west'. With the *dappled* allocated to the south, all four points of the compass are thus included.

7. *When the steeds* (translated 'grey' in verse 3) *came out.* The meaning of the word is in doubt, but RSV probably gives the sense. The adjective applies to all the horses, for no points of the compass are singled out. The horses paw the ground until the word of command is given. It is this command *Go, patrol the earth* that sums up the definitive message of the vision. From first to last (*cf.* 1:10) the affairs of the nations are under God's direction, not man's. It is this certainty that makes prophecy possible.

8. The word of the angel is unusually introduced. *He cried* indicates that an important proclamation is about to be made (*cf.* Jon. 3:7); indeed the angel reveals his identity, for he speaks as the Lord of the whole earth (*cf.* 4:14). Victory is proclaimed in the turbulent *north country*, and if there, then by inference victory has been achieved over every foe. Nothing can impede the completion of promised salvation. Recent events had been the work of God's Spirit, but now that work is finished, and the messengers to the north have set God's *Spirit at rest.* No more remains to be done.

The sequel is in verse 15, but the climax of history is to be a person, not a building, and the inclusion of verses 9–15 with the last of the visions points to the One for whom the Temple was intended (Mal. 3:1).

9. The introductory formula, which is found in 4:8; 7:4; 8:1,18, indicates that a prophetic oracle is to follow. Instead of the mysterious figures of the visions which required supernatural interpretation, the prophet is among people he can identify in a place well known to him.

10. New arrivals from Babylon, probably in a caravan led by those whose names are given, had come with gifts for the needy community in Jerusalem. From the position of the verb *have arrived* at the end of the sentence in Hebrew, the inference is that all four men had come together. *Josiah, the son of Zephaniah* is apparently the most distinguished of the four, to judge by the mention of his lineage, and of his dwelling house. The names of at least three of the four express a relationship to the Lord, as E. B. Pusey points out.[1] So faith expressed

[1] Pusey, p. 134: 'Tobiah, "the Lord is my good;" Yedaiah, "God

itself during the exile. *Take* is used elliptically, the object
'offerings' being understood. The writer is not likely to have
meant 'take ... Heldai ... ' and the others as witnesses,
because the Hebrew repeats 'from' before each name.

11. Zechariah is to ask explicitly for a share of the silver and
gold sent from Babylon by them. *Make a crown* (Heb. 'crowns',
'aṭārôt). There are three possible explanations of the plural,
and they are not mutually exclusive. (*a*) Eastern crowns were
circlets, which could be worn singly or fitted together to make
a composite crown (*cf.* Rev. 19:12, and the hymn 'Crown Him
with many crowns'). The mention of two different metals
indicates that there were at least two circlets. (*b*) In the
absence of a superlative form, Hebrew used the plural as one
way of denoting excellence (*cf.* Elohim 'God', a plural form
followed by a verb in the singular). In verse 14 the word
'crowns' is followed by a singular verb. (*c*) There is an *ôt*
ending distinct from the plural (*cf. ḥokmôt*, 'wisdom', in Pr.
1:20; 9:1; 14:1). F. D. Kidner[1] cites evidence that it is either
a Phoenician form of the singular or a Hebrew plural. 'If it
is the latter, it is to express intensity and fullness; and like the
plural Elohim (God), it uses a singular verb (*cf.* 9:1).' E.
Lipinski[2] thinks that the *ôt* is archaic, and that it gives an
'antique', 'sacred', 'mythical' flavour. The crown belongs to
this sacred realm. It was to be as magnificent as possible.
Though the Greek and Latin versions had the plural, the
Syriac translated with the singular noun, so conveying that
there was one crown. In verse 14 the Greek used the singular.

Set it upon the head of Joshua. That Joshua rather than
Zerubbabel should be crowned is thought by most commentators to be intrinsically unlikely, hence the popularity of a
conjecture which originated with J. Wellhausen, that the
primitive text named Zerubbabel as the one crowned. Two
main arguments support this view. (*a*) The word *'aṭārâ* is
exclusively the crown of royalty, or, in figurative contexts, a
crown of splendour or honour. It is never used of the head-
dress of the priests,[3] for which the usual word was *nēzer*,
meaning 'crown of consecration' (*cf.* Nazirite, 'consecrated

---

knoweth or careth for;" Josiah, "the Lord supporteth;" Zephaniah, "the
Lord hideth," and perhaps Cheldai, "the Lord's world." '
[1] *Proverbs* (*TOTC*), p. 60, footnote 2.
[2] *VT*, XX, 1, 1970, p. 34¹⁵.
[3] This can be verified from BDB, p. 742.

one'). In 3:5 yet another word was used which was applicable to king or priest, but it signified a turban rather than a crown. (*b*) It is claimed that the substitution of the priest's name for that of the prince can be explained by subsequent history. The Davidic line sank into oblivion after Zerubbabel's death, while the high priest flourished. A scribe, taking account of reality, is thought to have replaced Zerubbabel's name by that of Joshua, and so made the prophecy more credible.[1] If it could be demonstrated that scribes were in the habit of adjusting the texts they copied in this way, the argument would be more weighty, but the evidence is all in the other direction.[2] W. Eichrodt considers that the interpretation of this passage in terms of Zerubbabel, 'which can only be secured at the cost of hazardous conjecture, is mistaken'.[3] None of the ancient versions has Zerubbabel's name in this verse. Moreover, supposing that the scribe meant to delete all reference to the Davidic prince, he did not do so in verse 13. It is best to allow the text to stand, and to regard Joshua as the one who was crowned.

Another interpretation, adopted by P. R. Ackroyd and D. R. Jones, is that both Joshua and Zerubbabel were crowned.[4] Either two crowns were made, or the one crown was placed first on the head of Joshua, then on Zerubbabel (see below, verse 13).

12. The message from the Lord of hosts, the God of power, *Behold, the man whose name is the Branch* (Heb. *ṣemaḥ*), is addressed to Joshua and yet appears to apply to Zerubbabel. In Hebrew this is a cryptic four word phrase without articles: 'Lo, a man, Shoot by name.' There seems to be an allusion to Zerubbabel's name, which means 'Shoot of Babylon', and without question he was the Temple builder (4:9).

---

[1] Among commentators who take this view are H. G. Mitchell, *ICC*, pp. 185, 186; D. Winton Thomas, *IB*, 6, p. 1080; F. Horst, *HAT*, p. 237; K. Elliger, *ATD*, p. 128; Th. Chary, p. 110. See also JB, p. 1535, footnote (i): 'It is evident from vv. 12–13 that the original text read "Zerubbabel"....'

[2] K. A. Kitchen, *Ancient Orient and Old Testament* (Tyndale Press, 1966), p. 140, cites an example of the accuracy with which Egyptian scribes 'copied, revised, compared and verified sign by sign'. He comments that there is no reason to assume that the Hebrews would be less careful with their literary products.

[3] *Theology of the Old Testament*, II (SCM Press, 1967), p. 343 footnote.

[4] *PCB*², p. 649; *TBC*, p. 92. See also P. R. Ackroyd, *Exile and Restoration* (SCM Press, 1968), pp. 196f.

'Branch of the Lord' in Isaiah 4:2 is used in parallelism with 'the fruit of the land'. It is a highly figurative section which goes on to speak of cleansing, and of cloud and fire to protect Jerusalem. Jeremiah's use of the term (23:5; 33:15) is in connection with the coming Davidic king, whose name will be 'The Lord is our righteousness'. Again sin has been removed. The second of the two references follows the announcement of the Davidic Branch with the statement that neither David nor the Levitical priests will lack descendants. Already in Jeremiah's usage the term combines priestly and kingly functions. The priestly aspect is to the fore in Zechariah's first use of the term (3:8), yet even here Joshua, having been supplied with clean garments, is commissioned to 'rule my house'. The removal of sin is the *motif* of the passage (*cf.* 3:9b). In chapter 6 the prophet can assume some understanding of the metaphor. His hearers had been prepared for the Branch to fulfil priestly and kingly functions and therefore would realize that both Joshua and Zerubbabel contributed to the work of the coming Branch, while neither alone adequately represented him.[1] (When Isaiah referred to the Davidic king as the Branch (11:1), he chose the word *nēṣer*, 'shoot', and attributed to him all the qualities required of the righteous judge.)

He shall grow up in his place is a pun on the word 'Branch'; 'the shoot will shoot up from beneath'. He will come where there is little promise of new life, unexpectedly, like the root out of a dry ground (Is. 53:2).

13. The repetition of the statement *he shall build the temple of the Lord* has been thought by some to represent a scribal error. Indeed the Syriac omits the last clause of verse 12, and the Greek the first clause of verse 13, but this difference indicates that they both followed an identical Hebrew text. Each has corrected an apparent mistake in the Hebrew ms, which evidently included the repetition. A. Petitjean postulates that two distinct literary units, 10–12 and 13, 14 have been combined, hence the double statement.[2] Insufficient weight has been given to the possibility that the repetition was deliberate, a device to distinguish between 'he' Joshua and 'he' the

[1] J. G. Baldwin, '*Ṣemaḥ* as a Technical Term in the Prophets', *VT*, XIV, 1964, pp. 93–97.
[2] Petitjean, p. 289.

Branch, as well as between the contemporary Temple and one to come.

And he shall bear royal honour (Heb. *hôḏ*). The adjective 'royal' is a justifiable addition to clarify the meaning of *hôḏ*, a word often signifying the majesty of the king (Ps. 45:4; Je. 22:18), and the majesty of God (Pss. 96:6; 104:1; Is. 30:30, *etc.*), but also the beauty of the olive (Ho. 14:6), the vigour of a man (Pr. 5:9; Dn. 10:8) and the strength of a horse (Zc. 10:3). The Branch is to be invested with royal splendour, *and shall sit and rule upon his throne* (Heb. *kissē'*). The word 'throne' is repeated in the next clause, *a priest by his throne*. 'By' is not the usual translation of *'al*, 'upon' (AV, RV), but the allocation of a throne to the high priest is so unusual as to make the translator hesitate.[1] The plain meaning of the Hebrew is 'a priest on his throne'.

A suggestion which has met with considerable support is that both Joshua and Zerubbabel were present on the occasion, just as both were depicted in the vision of the lamp and the two olive trees. As the prophet makes the statements in verse 13 he turns first to Zerubbabel who will build the Temple, then to Joshua who will bear the glorious priestly honour, then back to Zerubbabel who will rule on his throne, and finally back to Joshua who will also rule from his throne. The last clause announces that they will work together in perfect harmony.[2] There is no necessity in this case to emend the text, and the interpretation takes into account the interplay of references to both king and priest. On the other hand it is doubtful whether *hôḏ*, 'royal honour' can be interpreted as 'sacral glory' (D. R. Jones); it is more natural to take 'and shall bear royal honour' as referring to the prince, so that all the first three clauses seem to be speaking of a king, and only the last about a priest. Moreover, the Hebrew does not repeat the pronoun 'he' in the third and fourth clauses. It is unlikely, therefore, that a distinction of subject is intended.

Attractive as Rignell's suggestion is, it does not find support in the text. The symbolic coronation and the enigmatic term 'Branch' referred to a future leader, who would fulfil to per-

---

[1] The early Greek translators substituted 'on his right hand' for 'on his throne'.

[2] This interpretation, which originated with L. G. Rignell, *Die Nachtgesichte des Sacharja* (Lund, 1950), pp. 231, 232, has been adopted by P. R. Ackroyd, *PCB²*, p. 649; D. R. Jones, *TBC*, p. 92; A. Petitjean, pp. 293ff.

fection the offices of priest and king, and build the future Temple with all appropriate splendour (Hg. 2:6–9). In this way the priestly and royal offices will be unified. The old interpretation that Messiah is meant[1] has not been displaced. Nowhere else in the Old Testament is it made so plain that the coming Davidic king will also be a priest. It is for this reason that the passage has occasioned so much questioning.

14. Future generations needed a permanent reminder of such an important sign as the coronation of the high priest. The placing of the symbolic crown in the Temple was (a) a memorial for those who represented the donors of the gold and silver, the exiles in Babylon, and (b) a visual aid for the priests in their teaching. It may be that the names were inscribed on it. *Helem*, not *Heldai*, is the form of the first in the Hebrew. Among the early versions Syriac harmonized with the names in verse 10 and preferred Heldai, a rationalization which has been followed by RSV, JB, NEB. The unexpected change of name is likely to have been original. It may be that Heldai, 'mole' preferred to use his more dignified name Helem, 'strength' for official purposes, or the names may have been interchangeable (*cf.* Heled in 1 Ch. 11:30, spelt Heleb in 2 Sa. 23:29 and Heldai in 1 Ch. 27:15). The Hebrew *Ḥēn* (see AV, RV) instead of Joshua is more difficult, but the clue may lie in its meaning 'grace', seen in connection with 'Joshua', 'saviour'. A less likely possibility is that the original read 'The crown shall be . . . for grace/beauty and for a memorial' but became altered by a scribe to '*Ḥēn* (grace), son of Zephaniah' because his eye fell momentarily on verse 10.

15. This verse looks like a sequel to verse 8, but because there was good reason for placing the oracle with the vision, it becomes the concluding summary of the whole chapter. *Those who are far off shall come and help to build the temple of the Lord.* The building of Zerubbabel's Temple can hardly have been meant because it was already well on the way to completion, and those 'far off' are not necessarily confined to Jews of the dispersion (*cf.* 2:11; 8:22). The 'Book of Visions' looked farther afield than the rebuilding in Jerusalem, and embraced all nations. Like many other prophetic passages it was concerned with the focal point of all history, the coming of the

---

[1] The Targum translated the word 'Branch' by 'Messiah'.

Davidic king, who would transform the concepts of Temple and of leadership.

The prophet ends with one of his characteristic phrases (*cf.* 2:9; 4:9), and a warning that, though the fulfilment of the prophecy is certain, moral integrity in the community is essential. This ethical emphasis is in keeping with the whole salvation story (Ex. 15:26; Dt. 7:12–16; 28:1–14). How the prophecy will be fulfilled if moral obedience falls short he does not say.

Additional Note on Zechariah's horses

There are three puzzling features connected with the horses in the first and eighth visions. (*a*) The meaning of the adjectives which describe them. (*b*) Why the colours are not the same in each of the three lists (1:8; 6:2,6,7). (*c*) Why all four points of the compass are not mentioned in 6:6. In view of the emendations which have been incorporated into RSV, JB, NEB, it is necessary to use RV or the Hebrew itself if the Hebrew text is to be given primary consideration.

(*a*) In 1:8 the only adjective difficult to translate is *šᵉruqîm*, 'sorrel' (reddish brown) RV; AV 'speckled' follows the early Latin and Syriac Versions. Greek used two adjectives meaning 'dappled' and 'many coloured'. In 6:3 there is hesitation over *bᵉruddîm*, 'grey' (RV 'grisled', *cf.* French *gris*), and the accompanying word *'ᵃmuṣṣîm*, 'bay', apparently from the root meaning 'be strong'. For *bᵉruddîm*, which means 'mottled' in Genesis 31:10, the Versions have 'many coloured' and 'livid'. The second adjective 'bay' is omitted in the Syriac, hence the one adjective in NEB, and the brackets round 'vigorous' in JB. The meaning 'strong' given to *'ᵃmuṣṣîm* in the Latin and by Aquila is not likely to be right. There is no reason why one group of horses should be singled out as strong. A colour is much more likely, but no satisfactory meaning has so far been suggested. The Greek 'dappled' or Aramaic 'light coloured' are the nearest.

(*b*) Those who think of the first as a sunset vision and the eighth as a dawn vision[1] explain the differences between 1:8 and 6:2 in terms of the colours connected with sunset and dawn. In 1:8 the red, sorrel and white are the colours of the sunset, whereas the black, white and grey of 6:2 are the colours

[1] See commentary on 6:1–15, p. 130.

of early dawn. (The first chariot, like the first horse in 1:8, is in a category apart.) Other commentators assume that originally the colours in the three lists would have been identical, and therefore aim at reconciling the differences. W. D. McHardy[1] follows up a suggestion of G. R. Driver that abbreviations may have been used in the ancient texts, in much the same way as we use initials, to save repeating expressions that were well known, or that occurred frequently in any given book. Originally the colours in this instance may have been represented by initials, which later copyists in varying degrees misunderstood. W. D. McHardy works on this supposition and succeeds in reconstructing a text in which the same four colours occur each time the horses are mentioned.

In 1:8 his order is red, yellow, black, white; in 6:2 red, black, white, yellow; in 6:6,7 black, white, yellow, red. Yellow replaces the unsatisfactory translations of *'ᵃmuṣṣîm* noted above. If only the consonants *'m* represented this adjective in the text they could have stood for *'ᵃmānâ*, the Greek for which is *chrysorroas*, 'golden'. According to R. H. Charles[2] 'pale yellow' is the colour required by *chlōros* in Revelation 6:8 and probably by Zechariah 1:8. Here the second adjective had the same initial letter *'āleph*, hence the substitution of 'yellow' for 'red'. The other changes are accounted for on similar grounds. Black (initial *š*) replaces sorrel (initial *s*) in 1:8.

The reconstruction is ingenious but involved. Though a consistent pattern satisfies the western mind we need to beware of assuming that the ancient writer had to have every detail co-ordinated as if for a scientific thesis. We have no means of knowing whether the colours of the horses stood for particular countries, as many ancient commentators thought,[3] or, as seems likely, whether the details were merely background. The text builds nothing on the colours of the horses, and though it is essential to endeavour to discover the exact meaning of the text, we may be wrong in assuming that consistency was intended by the prophet.

(c) One way of reconstructing the text to include all four points of the compass has already been given in the commentary

---

[1] *BZAW*, 'The Horses in Zechariah' in *In Memoriam Paul Kahle* (Alfred Töpelmann, 1968), pp. 174–179.

[2] *Revelation of St. John*, I (*ICC*, 1920), p. 169.

[3] J. Calvin, *op. cit.*, p. 140; the editor in a footnote cites Jerome, Cyril, Kimchi among others who take an allegorical view. Calvin himself took a similar view (pp. 142, 143).

on 6:6. Another method is that adopted by NEB. Instead of insert-
ing the clause about the red horses in the supposed *lacuna* at
the beginning of verse 6, the black are left as the first named,
the white go to the west as in JB, the dappled to the south, and
the roan to the east. The last clause has been filled out with
a probable reconstruction. W. D. McHardy follows this order,
though he substitutes 'yellow' for 'dappled'. There are variant
readings of the text at the beginning of verse 7, which render
the present text suspect and make possible the guess that
originally the reading was 'to the east country'.

These reconstructions must be regarded as tentative. So far
as the prophet's message is concerned the only group of importance is that which goes to the north (north and east, understood), where the struggle for world domination had for
centuries been concentrated. Egypt was still an important
power, hence the mention of the south also, but to the west
there was nothing of importance going on to warrant special
mention. From a stylistic point of view the prophet gains by
leaving the two other directions vague. It is enough to know
that the Lord is triumphant over the dominant world powers.
The lesser are included with the greater.

III. MESSAGES PROMPTED BY THE QUESTION ON FASTING (7:1 – 8:19)

The last main section of the first part of the book is introduced
by a new date, that of the arrival in Jerusalem of a delegation
with a question about the liturgical calendar. The keeping of
holy days was a matter in which Jews in Babylon wished to
keep in line with the Jerusalem community. The answer is
found in 8:18,19, but the sermon material and collected sayings in the intervening sections all have a bearing on the
subject, though they were not necessarily all composed on this
occasion. The first sermon (7:5–14) brought the debate before
the nation. The collection of sayings (8:1–8), perhaps already
well known because often repeated by the prophet, look at the
present and future, while in the second sermon the fact that
God has already begun to give His blessing predominates.
Therefore fasts are inappropriate and feasts must take their
place.

a. The question (7:1-3)

1. The date, 7 December 518 BC (see the table on p. 29), formed the heading for the whole section. To judge by the use of the third person, it was added by the editor, who avoids an exact repetition of the order adopted in the other dates (1:1,7). On the ground that Babylonian names for the months were not in common use till the time of Nehemiah (445 BC), the phrase *which is Chislev* is often said to be a later explanatory gloss.[1] JB therefore brackets it together with *the word of Yahweh was addressed to Zechariah*, reckoned also to be a later interpolation.

2. The correct way to translate this verse is far from evident, as a comparison of the standard English versions will indicate. Problems centre round (*a*) the subject of the verb 'sent', (*b*) the object of the verb.

(*a*) In Hebrew the word order is 'Sent Bethel Sharezer and Regem Melech and his men'. There is no sign to indicate that 'Sharezer' is the object of the verb, and so it could be part of the subject. Three possible subjects have been suggested: Bethel, he, referring to Darius (verse 1), and Bethel-Sharezer.

(i) *Bethel* is the subject in RV, RSV, JB. This town, 12 miles north of Jerusalem, had been the centre of worship for the northern kingdom from the time of Jeroboam I (1 Ki. 12:29). Though it escaped destruction at the time of the Babylonian conquest, it was destroyed 'by a mighty conflagration during the latter part of the Neo-Babylonian period or possibly the beginning of the Persian'.[2] Associated throughout its history with a syncretistic cult, the struggling new Bethel may have found its religious affinities with the Samaritans. D. Winton Thomas thinks that Zechariah rebuffed the delegation for this reason.[3] But 223 loyal Jews belonging to Bethel had returned from Babylon (Ezr. 2:28); their influence would be considerable in a small community. Bethel, Lydda and Ono are the most northerly towns mentioned in the Ezra lists. Those who returned would be more likely to look towards Jerusalem as their focal point than to Samaria. All the same there are good reasons for thinking that the delegation did not come from Bethel.

[1] H. G. Mitchell, *ICC*, and numerous Continental theologians.
[2] W. F. Albright, *Archaeology and the Religion of Israel*[4] (Johns Hopkins Press, 1956), p. 172.   [3] *IB*, p. 1083.

(ii) King Darius, named in verse 1, has been suggested as the one who sent the deputation. E. Lipinski[1] arrives at this by omitting as a gloss 'the word of the Lord came to Zechariah', and so making 'he sent' refer back to Darius as the antecedent. The supposed motive of Darius would be to satisfy himself that his contributions to the Temple were being used to best advantage. It is unlikely that Darius was responsible for sending the delegation and furthermore there is no ground for omitting the clause in verse 1 which, unless it is omitted, alters the sense required by this interpretation.

(iii) The most probable solution is to take *Bethel-Sharezer* as a personal name and make it the subject of the verb, as does NEB. A similar compound, Nergal-Sharezer, is recorded in Jeremiah 39:3, while names compounded with Bethel are known from the fifth-century BC Elephantiné papyri and from Neo-Babylonian cuneiform texts.[2] The Babylonian equivalent to Bethel-Sharezer occurs in a text dating from the years 541–540, close enough to the date of Zechariah to be the very person named there.[3] This translation involves omitting one 'and', but otherwise follows the Hebrew text. It is very likely that the delegation came from Babylon, if only because there was a delay of three and a half months between the fast and their arrival. This was the approximate length of time required for the journey from Babylon to Jerusalem (Ezr. 7:7–9). The delay would be inexplicable if the men had come only from Bethel, and moreover there would be nothing remarkable about a delegation arriving from so short a distance to cause the date to be remembered. On the other hand a delegation which had taken the arduous journey from Babylon, and was setting the precedent of consulting the prophets and priests in Jerusalem before making any liturgical changes, might well be recorded in the annals.

(*b*) The object, *Regem-melech*, is usually taken to be a proper noun. Similar names in the Old Testament (*e.g.* Nathan-melech, 2 Ki. 23:11; Regem, 1 Ch. 2:47; Ebed-melech, Je. 38:7) may be cited in support. The expression does, however, occur at Ugarit as the title of the king's spokesman,[4] and in

---

[1] 'Recherches sur le livre de Zacharie', *VT*, XX, I, 1970, p. 37.
[2] The evidence is conveniently collected by W. F. Albright, *ob. cit.*, p. 169.
[3] J. P. Hyatt, 'A Neo-Babylonian Parallel to BETHEL-SAR-EZER, Zech 7, 2', *JBL*, 56, 1937, pp. 387–394.
[4] C. H. Gordon, *Ugaritic Textbook* (Rome, 1965), 1010, lines 1,2.

the Syriac translation the form Rab-Mag (Je. 39:3,13) is probably borrowed from an Assyrian expression for a royal officer sent on a military or diplomatic mission. The Greek versions also support the title of a royal functionary. If this is correct the leader of the delegation came with royal authority. His arrival would be a state occasion, and *his men* (not 'their men', RV, RSV) would be official retainers. No wonder the occasion was remembered.

The setting now becomes clearer. Jews who have risen to positions of leadership in Babylon, or possibly Persian leaders who have become proselytes, have been questioning the need, now that the Temple is almost rebuilt, to keep the fasts which commemorated the fall of Jerusalem. Changes in religious observances can be made only by the authority of the divinely-appointed priests and prophets in Jerusalem, so an outstanding man at court is chosen to lead the delegation. The hope may have been that, by reducing the number of Jewish holy days by four (8:19), one of the problems of integration with Persian employers and employees, namely the compulsory holidays required by Jews, might be lessened. So they came *to entreat the favour of the Lord* (*cf.* 8:21,22), a current expression for the sacrifice and worship offered in the Temple. The liturgical setting is clear in Malachi 1:9, and is probably implied in other contexts (2 Ch. 33:12; Je. 26:19; Dn. 9:13).

3. The question is put in the first person because the one who asks it represents the community. The fast of *the fifth month* marked the tragic destruction of the Temple on the seventeenth day (2 Ki. 25:8). The other subsidiary events were included under the greater (*cf.* 8:19): the ninth day of the fourth month is recorded as the date when the city wall was breached (Je. 39:2); the fast of the seventh month commemorated the murder of Gedaliah (2 Ki. 25:25; Je. 41:1f.), and the tenth day of the tenth month marked the beginning of Nebuchadrezzar's siege of the city (2 Ki. 25:1,2; Je. 39:1). These special days had become hallowed by observance for over sixty years.

The address of the prophet's words in verse 5 shows that what follows was not a direct answer to the delegation. In fact no direct answer is recorded, for even when the subject is resumed in 8:19, the message is for the house of Judah. No doubt it was the arrival of the delegation that raised the question. The words of Zechariah recorded here give his spiritual teaching on the subject, appropriate for all time.

b. The first sermon (7:4-14)

Though at first sight the division at verse 8 might suggest that two sermons have been combined, the two parts belong together. The one aim is to bring home the purpose of fasting.

4. The introductory formula in the first person bears Zechariah's 'autograph' (*cf*. 4:8; 6:9; 8:18).

5. When he is told to speak to *all the people of the land*, Jews living in and around Jerusalem and Judah are meant (*cf*. Hg. 2:4), and not the hostile elements as in Ezra 4:4. Zechariah also addresses *the priests*, who, though they taught the law and pronounced decisions on ritual matters (Hg. 2:11), were dependent on the prophet for the word of the Lord in new situations. No ready-made answer is given, for Zechariah believed in group involvement as an educational method. What had been their motive in fasting? His question is skilfully worded, and repeats the key words. Was their fast for the Lord, the Lord alone? A comment on *these seventy years* is given on 1:12. In view of the fact that the events commemorated in the fast did not take place before 587 BC, Zechariah must be reckoning the seventy years from that date in this verse.

6. This second question implies that, just as they normally ate and drank to satisfy their own needs, so self-interest prompted their fasting. It amounted to no more than self-pity. A similar accusation occurs in Isaiah 58:3, followed by teaching that fasting should result in renewed concern for and generosity towards the needy. Could it be to this passage that Zechariah refers in verse 7? The theme scarcely occurs in the prophets generally acknowledged to be pre-exilic (but *cf*. Ps. 34:18; Joel 1:14; 2:12).

7. Zechariah assumed in his hearers a knowledge of the ethical teaching of earlier prophets (*cf*. 1:4). If only Judah had listened then, before it was too late. The cities and countryside would then have been pulsing with life and enjoying prosperity. Empty, ruined buildings were everywhere a reminder of depopulation. The *South* (Heb. *negeb*, dry) designates an area south of a line from Gaza through Beersheba to the Dead Sea, and forming a triangle with Kadesh-barnea at its southern apex. In spite of its Hebrew name the area was not a desert in biblical times, except when it was devastated by war. The *lowlands* (Heb. *šᵉp̄ēlâ*) were the foothills between the hills of Judah and the coast. The higher slopes produced olive and sycamore trees, while the valleys provided a high yield of grain, given farmers to till the soil. The third geographical division, the mountains, were uncultivated in peace or war, and therefore are not mentioned. What is abundantly clear is that the country was desperate for people to rebuild the cities and restore the farms. No mention is made of the territory of the northern kingdom.

The contrast between verses 7 and 14, accounted for by the moral insensitivity of previous generations which called down on them God's chastisement, raised the question of the spiritual responsiveness of the prophet's contemporaries. How did they measure up to the standards set by the pre-exilic prophets? The free quotations which follow verse 8 sum up prophetic teaching.

8. This verse breaks the sense and is hard to justify in this context. An editor appears to have thought that the words 'Thus says the Lord of hosts' introduced a new oracle, and to have inserted his heading accordingly.

9. Four precepts are singled out by the prophet to sum up the standards which had been meant to characterize Israel's social life.

The positive command *Render true judgments* sums up the importance which had always been attached to justice in the community since the time of Moses (Ex. 18:19–23). The verb 'judge' (*šāp̄aṭ*) includes passing judicial sentence, but is used in the wider meaning of restoring harmony and peace where there has been conflict and injustice. Every member of the community in his social relationships, and not the judges only, had this responsibility towards others. Similarly the cognate noun (*mišpāṭ*) 'justice' indicates the principles which are to regulate relationships between people and bind society together, as they bind a man to God (Pss. 9:8b; 76:9; Is. 30:18), especially in the covenant relationship (Ho. 2:19). The adjective 'true' adds a reminder that it is only too possible to judge according to the letter of the law, and fail entirely to vindicate the right. True justice involved concern for the individual, especially the downtrodden righteous man (Is. 42:3; 59:14,15), generosity (Ezk. 18:8), humility (Ps. 25:9,10). It derived from God Himself.

The second positive precept fills out the first, with which it is closely related. *Kindness* (Heb. *ḥeseḏ*) was an attitude of love and loyalty that was expected to mark certain human relationships: those within the family, especially marriage (Gn. 20:13); those between friends (1 Sa. 20:15; 2 Sa. 16:17) and between allies (2 Sa. 10:2). It was the expected response to kindness rendered (Gn. 40:14; Jos. 2:12). Where a covenant had been made *ḥeseḏ* between the parties was binding (Gn. 20:13; 1 Sa. 20:15), hence the use of the word in connection with the divine covenants. Former prophets had attributed the breakdown of order in society to lack of truth and *ḥeseḏ* and knowledge of God (Ho. 4:1–3), while by contrast God kept covenant (Ho. 2:19), and required His people to 'hold fast to love (*ḥeseḏ*) and justice' (Ho. 12:6). Zechariah probably had in mind also Micah 6:8, with its plea that men would 'do justly, love mercy (*ḥeseḏ*) and walk humbly with thy God'. The generosity and warmth that characterize true friendship were to permeate all relationships.

10. Exploitation of weakness is out of keeping with justice, kindness and mercy. This fact, made clear in Exodus 22:21–24, is frequently driven home by the prophets (Is. 1:17,23; Je. 7:6; 22:3; 49:11; Ezk. 22:12). The *widow* and *fatherless*, having lost their breadwinner and defender, were in a weak position financially and socially, and were therefore liable to be defrauded and grossly wronged by the unscrupulous (Mi. 2:9). The *sojourner*, or temporary resident, was at a disadvantage simply because he was 'different'. The *poor* had no bargaining power and were at the mercy of the rich (Am. 4:1). Human clannishness and love of gain were to give place among God's people to generosity, friendliness and practical help. This was 'justice' in His sight.

The fourth precept of Zechariah's summary is negative in form, and forbids the very thought of wronging others. In 8:16,17 Zechariah uses the same phrase *devise evil* in a legal context, suggesting that it may also imply 'bring false accusation in law'. If so there is a chiastic pattern in verses 9,10: the first and fourth precepts correspond, and the second and third balance one another.

It was these moral standards which should occupy those who fasted, because the fall of Judah had been caused by a breakdown of these standards.

11. Their predecessors had refused to give such teaching a hearing (Is. 6:10), though *hearken* (Heb. *qāšaḇ*) means more than to hear. It means to take the words so seriously that one subjects them to such tests as history and experience provide. In this way a man learns that they are words of truth and wisdom. Instead, Israel had *turned a stubborn shoulder*, like an animal that stiffened every muscle in its effort to refuse the yoke (Ex. 32:9; Dt. 9:6,13,27; 2 Ki. 17:14; Je. 7:26, *etc.*). The word came by hearing and so they deliberately plugged their ears (literally 'made them heavy').

12. The word was meant to penetrate the heart, but nothing could penetrate *adamant*. Zechariah's originality avoided cliché in so likening their hardened heart (Je. 7:24; 9:14; Ezk. 36:26) to diamond, a simile used in another connection in Ezekiel 3:8 but nowhere else.

It is a matter of debate whether *the law* (Heb. *tôrâ*) is used here in its technical sense as part of 'the Law and the Prophets' or whether the word means simply 'instruction'. The prophet's basic injunctions (verses 9,10) found their origin in the law, and it is likely that he was referring to the Pentateuch. *The words which the Lord of hosts had sent by his spirit through the former prophets.* This remarkable doctrine of the Holy Spirit as mediator of God's word to the prophets, who were themselves its mediators, has no parallels in the prophetic books. In Isaiah 42:1 and 61:1 God's Spirit is given to someone other than the prophet. The closest parallel is Nehemiah 9:30, a passage which may have been part of the pre-exilic liturgy for days of national mourning.[1] A well-known psalm may underlie both Nehemiah 9:30 and Zechariah 7:12, in which case resemblances between the two passages would be explained. The fact remains, however, that Zechariah is the first to record this aspect of the doctrine of the Spirit.

Having summarized God's requirements and Israel's refusal to obey, divine *wrath* follows. The theme needed no elaboration,

---

[1] A. Petitjean, pp. 348, 349, takes this view, and in support cites among others, whose works are less easily accessible, Y. Kaufmann, *The Religion of Israel*. Trans. M. Greenberg (Allen and Unwin, 1960), p. 210, note 17.

because its out-working in the year 587 and in all the suffering that followed had written it large for even the nations to see.

13. The chiastic form *I* (he), *they, they, I* well expresses the idea of just retribution. RSV and NEB emend the Hebrew, and follow the Syriac version *As I called*; contrast RV and Hebrew 'as he cried'. The change of person from 'he' at the beginning to 'I' at the end of the sentence is not uncommon in the prophets. The prophet has been using the third person in the previous verses and he continues to do so until suddenly he finds himself using the very words of the Lord, so vivid is the message in his mind. This also explains the future tense (RV, Hebrew Imperfect). When the judgment was formulated the situation was still future.

14. In the event the tragedy was twofold. The population was *scattered*, 'blown to the four winds' as if by a typhoon, which left *the pleasant land . . . desolate*. The *nations which they had not known*, primarily Babylon and Egypt, but including the lands of the wider dispersion, were outside the covenant, dedicated to a way of life abhorrent to Israel (Ps. 137:4). Meanwhile the 'pleasant land', promised as part of God's covenant gift (Gn. 15:18; Dt. 34:4), and intended to be abundantly fruitful (Ex. 3:8), was devastated, empty. God's apparent withdrawal of the love-gifts of His covenant was the hardest part of the punishment.

No mention of the fast-days is made in the sermon, but Zechariah has gone to the heart of the problem. It was easy to spend fast-days mourning their losses, but harder to face up to God's continuing demands. Were they any more prepared than their fathers to work out in everyday life the spirit of God's law? The purpose of fast-days was to give them renewed incentive to do so through renewed experience of confession, forgiveness and future hope.

c. Relevant sayings (8:1–8)

Without any transition the prophet switches from the out-working of God's wrath to reassurance of His loving concern. The rhythmic sayings, short and memorable, which follow could have been the 'texts' of different sermons, put together deliberately to produce their cumulative effect. Destruction and desolation was not the end of the story.

1. The introductory formula lacks the words *to me* in the original, a fact which suggests that Zechariah was repeating words he had often spoken rather than expressing a new revelation.

2. The divine *jealousy* for Jerusalem had been stated in 1:14, and Old Testament usage shows that God's jealousy is to be understood in relation to the covenant (see Additional Note on The divine jealousy, p. 101). The argument is borne out by this passage (*cf.* verse 8). It is as though God can no longer bear the estrangement from His people brought about by their obstinacy. Though they are not truly seeking Him now, even in their fasts, His depth of feeling for them wells up into action on their behalf. As Ezekiel saw so clearly, restoration was totally due to God's initiative and grace (Ezk. 36:21,22,32). In the same chapter (36:6) Ezekiel links together God's jealousy and His *wrath* (*cf.* 5:13; 16:38,42; 23:25 and Is. 59:17, 18; Na. 1:2) in a passage which, like Zechariah 8, proclaims a new start for the people and land of Israel. But whereas the divine jealousy and wrath elsewhere oppose Israel, in Zechariah they work on her behalf, and the word 'wrath' would be better translated 'ardour'. In the original Hebrew the word order forms a chiasmus:

> I am jealous for Zion with a great jealousy,
> with a great ardour am I jealous for her.

The zeal with which God had carried through His chastisement of Israel and then of the nations (1:15,21) was now burning to restore the covenant bond.

3. The second 'memorable saying' also recalls 1:14b–16, and has a connection with 2:10. All three passages expect the coming of the Lord to Jerusalem to inaugurate a new era. His dwelling will be the Temple, and His continuing presence will ensure that this time Israel will be faithful to the covenant. Jerusalem will be called *the faithful city* (*cf.* Is. 1:26, where 'city of righteousness' and 'faithful city' are synonymous). In this way the recurring cycle of apostasy followed by punishment will be broken. In the light of verse 8 it is perhaps not too much to claim that the righteousness and faithfulness are God's, imputed by Him to His people, and then worked out in their lives. *The holy mountain*, crowned again by the Temple, is called 'holy' because the Lord has chosen again to dwell there. His presence is the key to the blessings which are to follow.

4. The elderly suffered acutely in the disasters of 587, together with the youth and fighting men (La. 2:21). It is likely that few elderly people had felt equal to the three-month journey back to Jerusalem from Babylon, and their wise advice and the stability they gave to the community were missed in the *streets* or rather 'squares' (Heb. *rᵉḥōḇōṯ*) of Jerusalem. The blessing of long life will restore the age balance when the new day dawns.

5. Children are an essential part of the prophet's picture of an abundant population. He wants to see the squares of the city *full of boys and girls*, not because they can work and contribute to the national prosperity, but for their own sakes, for he pictures them at play. Family life will not be diminished by poverty or war.

6. The fourth saying warns against allowing human reason to decide what God is likely to do. Two similar verses (Gn. 18:14; Je. 32:25) record incredulity in the face of marvellous promises. It is as difficult to believe the promises as it is to take seriously the threats of judgment. Evidently the population was so depleted that the thought of an abundance of people of all ages seemed too good to be true. Natural increase was inadequate. Only the Lord's intervention would replenish their numbers.

7. I *will save my people*. The verb *save* (Heb. *hôšiaʻ*) means here to 'deliver from captivity', as it does in Jeremiah 30:7-11; 31:7, and in Isaiah 43:1-7 (*cf.* 10:6). This is how the population problem will be solved, for people will come from *east* and *west*. Again two directions represent the four (*cf.* 6:6, RV). Zechariah avoids a laboured style.

8. Those who have been far off are to be brought right into the city of Jerusalem where the Lord Himself has chosen to dwell (verse 3), and, greatest privilege of all, the covenant promise is renewed to them (Ex. 19:5; 29:45; Lv. 26:12; Je. 31:33). Thus liberation and restoration to the land of Judah depend on election and covenant promises, as the original Exodus did. When He calls them 'my people' and they claim Him as their God, Israel's *righteousness* will prove the *faithfulness* of His statements.

b¹. The second sermon (8:9-17)

While the first sermon drew its lesson from the past, in the second the prophet contrasts past and present. In both there is a strong ethical emphasis (*cf.* 7:9,10 with 8:16,17).

This sermon falls into two parts, verses 9-13 and 14-17. Each part begins with a reference to the unhappy past, first the immediate past, and secondly the more distant past (verse 14). Each time the intention is to lay stress on the change that has taken place. 'But now' (verse 11) and 'so again' (verse 15) are the pivotal expressions.

9. The idiom *let your hands be strong*, often used as an exhortation to fight (Jdg. 7:11; 2 Sa. 2:7; 16:21), here indicates that courage is needed to undertake some demanding task, or rather, continue it until it is finished. Haggai's corresponding expression is 'be strong' (2:4, RV). The ground for encouragement was the teaching of the prophets, but which prophets? Zechariah is usually specific (1:4; 7:7,12), and here he defines them as those who were preaching when repair of the Temple began (RSV, NEB, JB follow the Greek in translating 'since the day . . . '). No mention is made of prophets in Ezra 3, the record of the first attempt to start work on the Temple. Only Haggai and Zechariah himself are known to have been at work in 520/519 BC, and therefore the reference seems to be to the words of Haggai (1:6-11; 2:15-19).

10. *Those days* indicates the period before work on the Temple began in earnest. It was important to recall the poverty and insecurity they had known to enable them to appreciate the improvements they had witnessed. Just as both *man* and *beast* had suffered in the destruction under the Babylonians (Je. 7:20; Ezk. 14:13), so the whole of nature continued to be bound up in the experiences of humanity (Hg. 1:11). Agricultural prosperity depended on right relationships between men and God, as did peace and stability. Who was *the foe* in years between 537 and 520? The Samaritans became foes once their offer of help was rejected (Ezr. 4:1-5) if they were not before, but A. Petitjean points out[1] that the word *ṣār* in the prophets applies to foreign nations hostile to Israel, especially those who profaned and destroyed the sanctuary, and exiled the Jews (Is. 63:18; Je. 30:16; 50:7; Ezk. 39:23). They harassed *him who went out or came in*, an idiom which often has

[1] Petitjean, pp. 392, 393.

a military significance (*e.g.* Nu. 27:17; Jos. 14:11; 1 Sa. 29:6), but which in this verse refers to ordinary social comings and goings (*cf.* La. 4:18). It was probably not so much the occupying powers who were responsible for the attacks as old enemies who had become accustomed to regard Judah's territory as their own (Ezr. 3:1). Misunderstandings, resentments, animosity, characterized even Jewish society, according to the last clause of this verse. When God withholds His blessing the symptoms are poverty, insecurity, broken relationships.

11. *But now* that era has passed, the turning-point having been whole-hearted commitment to God's cause in rebuilding the Temple. On this ground alone God is dealing with them altogether differently. How utterly basic is repentance!

12. The promised inheritance is expressed in terms of *the seed, the vine, the ground* and *the heavens.* As for the seed-sowing, it will be in peace (Heb. *šālôm*), that is favourable circumstances. RSV, JB, by interpreting the first part of the promise figuratively,[1] set it out of line with the other three. Haggai had promised that prosperity would be theirs from one particular seed-sowing onwards (2:19), so showing that the days of God's disapproval had ended once the Temple building began. For the rest of the verse Zechariah gives his version of the covenant blessings promised in the Pentateuch (Lv. 26:3–13; Dt. 28:11, 12) and in the prophets, especially Ezekiel 34:25–27. His primary reference, however, may be assumed to have been to his contemporary Haggai, who noted the withholding of dew (1:10) and of rain (1:11) as the cause of the poor crops, and who later announced that the vine and all fruit trees would bear good crops (2:19).

As the land was promised to Joshua to possess as God's gift (Jos. 1:11), so God promises to *cause the remnant . . . to possess* it. The prophet's needy contemporaries were the spiritual descendants of Joshua, who was repeatedly told to 'be strong' (Jos. 1:6,7,9,18; *cf.* Zc. 8:13b), and who triumphed.

13. The contrast between the past and the future, which has been the subject of the passage, is repeated in miniature in its final verse. The 'as . . . so' construction, used in 1:6 and 7:13

---

[1] So also H. G. Mitchell, *ICC*, p. 214. He gives a summary of the suggested emendations and translations, and accepts that of J. Wellhausen, *Die Kleinen Propheten*, pp. 45, 187.

to make a comparison, is used here and in the following two verses to express a strong antithesis. 'Whereas in the past you were a curse, from now on you will be a blessing.' *A byword of cursing*. Having been cast off, 'cursed' by their God, the Jews became an object of scorn and execration to the nations. It was Jeremiah who had seen the impending exile as a curse on them from God (24:9; 25:18; 29:22). *So will I save you* from the nations (*cf.* verse 7) *and you shall be a blessing*, that is, blessed by God (*cf.* verse 12) and actively a blessing to the nations (verses 20f.). Zechariah includes both Judah and Israel in this promise, but unlike Jeremiah who, when he mentions both kingdoms, puts Israel first (5:11; 11:10,17), Zechariah is in no doubt about the priority of Judah in the restoration. Like Ezekiel (37:15-22), he saw that reunion of the two kingdoms was essential, and that Jerusalem would be their one capital. Ezekiel does not name his city, except in 48:35, but Zechariah does (1:17; 2:2, *etc.*), and exalts it as the religious centre of all nations (2:10-12; 6:15; 8:20-23).

Fear not is no mere morale booster, for in the security of the renewed covenant there is positively no occasion for fear. Instead all *hands* are to be *strong*; energies are to be concentrated on working to turn the promises into facts of history (*cf.* Phil. 2:12,13).

The second part of the sermon reiterates what God undertakes to do (verses 14,15), and then what He expects of His people (verses 16,17).

14. It was Jeremiah who had seen the exile as something which God purposed (Je 4:28; 51:12; La. 2:17). Zechariah is equally sure that God directs the history of His people according to unchangeable decrees.

15. Now that He has *purposed . . . to do good* (and Zechariah has just defined this 'good', verses 12,13; *cf.* Je. 32:40,41; Ezk. 36:11), the fulfilment of that purpose is certain. Hence the repetition of *fear not*.

16. By beginning with what God has done, and only then turning to human obligations in the light of God's great goodness, Zechariah is keeping the order of biblical revelation. First God delivered the Israelites from slavery in Egypt, then He gave them His law (Ex. 20:2,3); first grace, then law, for the law is a means of grace. The precepts that follow sum up the character of those who are in covenant relation with the Lord of hosts.

The short code of law resembles that in 7:9,10. The structure is similar: two positive injunctions are followed by two negative ones, and there is similarity of content: true judgments are demanded, and evil thoughts about others condemned. In the forefront is the command to *speak the truth to one another* (*cf.* 8:3,8 where *truth*, AV, RV, NEB, Heb. *'emet*, characterizes both Jerusalem and God's dealings with her). Straightforward dealings and reliability are the foundation of a stable society.

At the law courts *in the gates* (Dt. 21:19; Ru. 4:1–12; Is. 29:21; Am. 5:10f.) judgments are to be passed *that are true and make for peace*. The prophet goes out of his way to express the need to follow not the letter but the spirit of the law, so that decisions reached commend themselves to all as just and right, and so make for peace and stability. This in turn leads to the prosperity God promises, which is part of the content of peace (Heb. *šālôm*).

17. Equally vindictiveness, hatred, falsified evidence lead to a breakdown of mutual trust. The Lord says not only that they are wrong but that He hates them (*cf.* Mal. 2:16). It is for this reason that God's law is to be kept. It is an expression of His character and of His wish, and His people fulfil it to please Him (Jn. 8:29). Here is the theological basis of ethics.

a¹. The answer (8:18,19)

After all that the prophet has said of the past and of the present, the original question of 7:3 answers itself. In the light of the new things that God was about to do, all of which proved that the time of mourning was over, what point was there in dwelling on the past? The delegation had raised a question which enabled the prophet to convey to exiles and repatriates alike that a new day had dawned. It was time to begin again, with new attitudes and new hopes.

19. All four fast-days (for the significance of each date see the commentary on 7:3) are to become times of *joy and gladness, and cheerful feasts*. Jeremiah had foretold that it would be so (31:10–14), and he saw that the rejoicing would not be in passing pleasures, 'My people shall be satisfied with my goodness, says the Lord' (Je. 31:14b). This well of joy cannot turn bitter or dry up because the Lord Himself is its source. Hence the reminder to *love truth and peace*, the qualities that He loves (*cf.* verse 17). The command to love does not occur frequently in the Old Testament,[1] but it underlies the whole covenant relationship and therefore also the ethics set out under the covenant as the condition of blessing.

IV. CONCLUSION:
UNIVERSAL LONGING FOR GOD (8:20–23)

The announcement made in 2:11, that many nations will join themselves to the Lord, is taken up and expanded to form the conclusion of this part of the book. Jerusalem will be the rallying-point for huge processions, intent on finding the secret of joy and gladness, truth and peace, that the Jews enjoy. Similar prophetic passages are Isaiah 2:2–4 (*cf.* Mi. 4:1–5) and Isaiah 66:18–21.

This vision of the nations seeking God completes the purpose of the call of Abraham (Gn. 12:3), that in him all the nations of the earth should be blessed. Though the divine anger had turned against the devastators of Judah and Jerusalem (1:15, 21), the prophet sees that God purposes their salvation.

20. The *peoples* are other races and nationalities, as the subsequent verses show.

21. The inhabitants of distant cities encourage one another to find God, and so serve as evangelists. They sense the urgency of their journey, *let us go at once*, and they set an example, *I am going*. *To entreat the favour of the Lord* indicates that the nations are to enter into the Temple liturgy and so approach the Lord (*cf.* the commentary on 7:2). They enter the new covenant (2:11).

22. The response is in inverse order to the invitation, so forming a chiasmus, and avoiding monotony of style.

Though originally Zechariah had a message of condemnation for the nations (1:15,21; 2:9), even for them God's intention was their salvation (2:11). The return of Israel to

---

[1] Apart from the two great commandments (Lv. 19:18, 34; Dt. 6:5, and repeated elsewhere in Dt.), only in Amos 5:15 is there a command to love, though in Psalm 31:23 there is an exhortation to love the Lord. The frequency or infrequency with which a truth occurs in Scripture is no guide to its importance.

Jerusalem sets all eyes on that city and paves the way for *many peoples and strong nations* to follow eagerly in their search for God. Though Jerusalem is depicted as the centre of the world, this is no mere nationalistic self-glory on Judah's part. If the Lord has chosen to make Jerusalem His dwelling-place, it is to Jerusalem that the nations must come if they are to find Him. This much the wise men from the East knew (Mt. 2:1).

23. *In those days* is less usual than 'in that day', but the expression contrasts with 'in these days' (verses 9,15). This world-view, including in God's kingdom people from *the nations of every tongue* (*cf.* Acts 2:5), could not be more comprehensive. *Ten men* to every Jew anticipates the thousands of thousands of Revelation 5:11. The number ten is used regularly in the Bible as the number of completeness (*e.g.* Gn. 31:7; Lv. 26:26; dg. 17:10; Ru. 4:2; 1 Sa. 1:8; Je. 41:8). The intensity of their desire for God is indicated by the verb *take hold of*, which occurs twice in the Hebrew (*cf.* AV, RV, NEB). It is used of Moses snatching the serpents by the tail (Ex. 4:4), and of David taking the lion by the beard (1 Sa. 17:35). They could not afford to let go! The spread *robe* was a symbol of the protection of marriage (Ru. 3:9; Ezk. 16:8), while to clutch the robe of Samuel was for Saul a bid for reconciliation (1 Sa. 15:27). Evidently their intention was to be accepted in the covenant alongside the Jew. The word *Jew*, used in apposition to all other nations, occurs first in Jeremiah 34:9, and only for the second time here. It is frequent in Ezra-Nehemiah.

These people of other nationalities ask the favour of being allowed to accompany the Jews and so find God. Their eagerness demonstrates their faith. *God is with you* recalls Abimelech's words to Abraham (Gn. 21:22), the divine promise to Isaac (Gn. 26:3,24), Moses (Ex. 3:12), Joshua (Jos. 1:5) and the conclusion reached by other nations in Isaiah 45:14, 'Surely God is in thee'. The renewed covenant of the post-exilic period (8:13) includes the nations, who, as Ezekiel saw (36:23), would recognize the Lord as God when, through the renewed Israel, He vindicated His holiness. True godliness draws others to Him (1 Cor. 14:25), and is a factor used of God in completing the number of His people.

PART II

I. TRIUMPHANT INTERVENTION OF THE LORD: HIS SHEPHERD REJECTED (9:1 – 11:17)

a. The Lord triumphs from the north (9:1–8)

Whereas earlier prophets had foreseen enemies invading from the north (Is. 41:25; Je. 1:14f.; Ezk. 26:7), now it is the Lord who conquers every city and people as He makes His way south to set up camp in Jerusalem. The familiar imagery of the holy war depicts the humiliation of each opposing power by the superior might of the Lord, as He takes control in His land. Originally the Mediterranean coast had been designated Israel's territory (Nu. 34:5,6) and yet it had never been possessed by Israel. Now at last the Lord will claim it.

The historical setting of the passage has been allocated to widely differing periods. In the last century an eighth- or seventh-century BC date was favoured for chapters 9–11; since then a post-exilic date has been preferred (*cf.* Introduction, p. 63). During the last decade small units have been studied independently, on the assumption that they originated independently, and some of the verses under review have again been assigned to the pre-exilic period.[1]

Renewed interest in a possible eighth-century date has centred round 2 Kings 14:28, where Jeroboam II is said to have 'recovered for Israel Damascus and Hamath, which had belonged to Judah'. Sargon II (722–705 BC) conquered both these cities, but Hamath was still of importance in the Greek period and was a war zone in the time of the Maccabees (1 Macc. 12:25). Damascus was certainly much more important in the tenth to eighth centuries BC than it was in the Persian and Greek periods. Tyre flourished from the time of Solomon, and survived capture by four great powers, but after the defeat by the Greeks never quite recovered. The Tyre depicted in this passage could be that of any period between

---

[1] *E.g.* H. Tadmor ('Azriyau of Yaudi', *Studies in the Bible* (Scripta Hierosolymitana VIII), Jerusalem, 1961, pp. 269–270) contends that verses 1–6, 10, belong to the time of Uzziah, about 739 BC. B. Otzen (*Studien über Deuterosacharje* (Acta Theologica Danica VI), Copenhagen, 1964, pp. 62–113) dates 9:1–8 in the time of Josiah. E. Lipinski ('Recherches sur le livre de Zacharie', *VT*, XX, 1, 1970, pp. 46–50) attributes verses 1, 2 to the reign of Uzziah.

1000 and 332 BC. As for the Philistine cities, they lost their independence and distinctive culture after they were captured by Nebuchadrezzar, and the predictions of verses 5 and 6 suggest therefore a pre-exilic date.

The most satisfactory conclusion is that the writer is not taking any particular historical standpoint, but rather, in the manner characteristic of apocalyptic, is using past events to typify a supremely important future event. Just as successive alien armies swept through Syria and Palestine and claimed a right to each territory, so finally the Lord will see every proud city capitulate to Him.

The question of the unity of this passage has already been raised.[1] E. Lipinski points out that the rhythm of verses 1,2, is 2+2, whereas in verses 3–8 it is 3+3. On this ground he distinguishes two sections.[2] The literary structure of verses 1–8 strongly supports their unity, however, as P. Lamarche shows.[3] The two halves of the poem are exactly balanced, verses 1–4 dealing with the north, verses 5–8 with the south. Again, verses 1,2 and 7b,8 speak of salvation, whereas the middle sections proclaim judgment, so that the pattern is *a b b a*. A small point which confirms the chiastic structure is the use of the 'eye of the Lord' *motif* in verse 1 (see commentary below), and at the end of verse 8.

1. *An oracle.* This translation of the Hebrew *maśśā'*, 'burden', is chosen also in JB and NEB, although it does not capture the full sense of the original. Moreover, the accents in the Hebrew text connect *maśśā'* with what follows, *the burden of the word of the Lord* (AV, RV), and so do not support the use of the word 'oracle' as a heading. This particular phrase occurs only three times in the Old Testament, here and in 12:1 and in Malachi 1:1. For a brief account of its possible significance see Additional Note, p. 162.

The land of Hadrach is the northernmost of the places listed. Though it is not mentioned elsewhere in the Old Testament, the name is known from Assyrian cuneiform inscriptions as Hatarikka, a city and country against which the Assyrians fought in the mid-eighth century BC.[4] It lies to the north of Hamath. The Hebrew has no verb and could read 'The

---

[1] See p. 157, n.1.
[2] *VT*, XX, 1, 1970, p. 46.
[3] Lamarche, p. 42.
[4] *ANET*, pp. 282, 283.

burden of the word of the Lord in Hadrach, and Damascus its resting place', as though the prophet were watching its progress until it came to rest in Damascus, where it paused on its journey. *Damascus* was the capital of Syria, one of Israel's traditional enemies, and had been the source of much cruel suffering (Am. 1:3). Whether the 'word' is one of rebuke or encouragement is not clear. The main point is that Syria will submit to the Lord.

The remainder of the verse is explanatory, and its meaning has been much disputed. *Aram* (Syria) and Adam (man) are very similar in Hebrew, and were sometimes confused in the transmission of the text. This accounts for one of the differences between AV/RV and RSV. The other major difference is the substitution of the words 'cities of' (Heb. *'ārê*) for 'eye of' (Heb. *'ēyn*), a change for which there is no textual warrant. It would be possible to accept 'Aram' but reject 'cities of', so translating, 'For the Lord has an eye on Syria', or 'The eye of Syria is toward the Lord'. It has been suggested that the 'eye of Syria' might be a popular name for Damascus.[1] On the whole it is probably better to keep the more difficult reading and translate, 'For the Lord has his eye on all men as on the tribes of Israel' (*cf.* 1:8d). The alternative, 'The eye of man and of all the tribes of Israel is toward the Lord' is less likely because (*a*) only the prophet saw this vision; (*b*) it is a constant human failing to refuse to look to the Lord;[2] at the very beginning the Lord's purpose is shown to be universal in its scope.

2. *Hamath* on the Orontes river had featured in some accounts of the limits of the promised land (*e.g.* Nu. 13:21; Jos. 13:5; Jdg. 3:3). It was remembered as a great city in the time of Amos (Am. 6:2), and survives even today as Hama on the main road between Aleppo and Damascus. *Tyre and Sidon*, cities of Phoenicia, are also claimed as the Lord's. There is a discrepancy between the plural subject and the singular verb 'is wise'. The sense is preserved without emending the text if the word 'Sidon' is followed by a full stop and *Because she is very wise* is made the beginning of a new sentence, which continues into the next verse.[3] Tyre was famed for practical

[1] R. C. Dentan, *IB*, VI, p. 1093.
[2] *Cf.* E. Zolli, ' 'EIN 'ADAM', *VT*, V, 1955, pp. 90–92.
[3] *Cf.* Lamarche, p. 37.

shrewdness in driving a bargain, both in business and in politics.

3. In her wisdom *Tyre has built herself a rampart.* The succinct paronomasia or word-play of the Hebrew, *ṣôr māṣôr* (Tyre rampart), expresses intense scorn. The 'rampart' was a break-water, 820 yards long and nine yards thick, built in the time of Hiram, king of Tyre, and friend of David and Solomon, to defend the island fortress. Israel had greatly benefited from the skills of Tyrian builders and seamen, whose technological and commercial superiority, described in Ezekiel 27, resulted in fabulous wealth and power. It was, however, Tyre's arrogance that caused the prophets to declare its doom (Is. 23:8, 9; Ezk. 28:2ff.).

4. Powerful and impregnable as she appears, Tyre's destruction is coming. *And hurl her wealth into the sea.* The Hebrew is capable of bearing more than one interpretation because 'wealth' (*ḥayil*) has many other meanings, including 'strength', 'efficiency', 'army', and the preposition means both 'into' and 'in'. Thus the other English translations (*e.g.* AV, RV, *he will smite her power in the sea*) do not represent any emendation in the text. In the violent overthrow what does not become the victim of the sea will be *devoured by fire* (*cf.* Am. 1:10).

The Assyrians subdued Tyre in 722 BC after a five-year siege, and Nebuchadrezzar besieged it for thirteen years before withdrawing, unrewarded, in 572 BC (Ezk. 29:18). The Persians in their turn took the city, but it was Alexander the Great who broke Tyre's resistance by building a mole from the mainland. When the city capitulated he dealt cruelly with the population, putting to death its leaders, and enslaving large numbers. Though Tyre survived even this treatment it never flourished again as it had done before the defeat by Nebuchadrezzar.

5–7. The Philistines, hearing the news of Tyre's destruction, are understandably alarmed, especially *Ekron*, the northern-most of the four cities, which would be the first to suffer. The prophet seems to have had Amos 1:8 in mind, though he freely adapts the phraseology to suit his own needs. This time it is *Gaza* and not Ashkelon that will lose its king, and *Ashkelon* rather than Ashdod whose inhabitants will perish. The names in verse 5 provide a chiastic pattern, *a b c b a*. *Ashdod* will find itself with a mixed population, as it began to have from the exile onwards (cf. Ne. 13:24). During the Persian period the city gave its name to a division of the fifth satrapy, neighbouring divisions being Samaria, Yehud and Idumea.

In the middle of verse 6 there is a change from the third to the first person. Now the Lord explains what He will do. He is going to transform the Philistines by breaking down their stubborn pride, removing repulsive ritual, and making them part of the 'remnant' of His people. Just as blood was forbidden as food to Israelites, so it will be to them. Those who offered unlawful sacrifices and ate forbidden meat in a kind of magic brew (Is. 65:4; 66:3,17) could never share a meal with God's people; but the Lord would take away such practices and the guilt they incurred, hence the incorporation of the Philistines into the people of Judah. The cities of Ekron, Ashdod and Gaza had originally been allocated to Judah (Jos. 15:45–47). *Ekron shall be like the Jebusites* refers to the fact that when David took Jerusalem he did not wipe out the Jebusite inhabitants, but allowed them to be absorbed into Judah.

The Assyrians attacked the Philistine cities several times between 734 and 701 BC; Nebuchadrezzar deported both rulers and people, so breaking Philistine independence once and for all. During the post-exilic period the cities acquired a very mixed population, which could scarcely be described as Philistine (see introductory paragraph, p. 158). An outworking of Zechariah's prophecy is seen in Acts 8:26–40, where Philip went not only to the Ethiopian but also to the cities of the Philistine plain. Azotus (Acts 8:40) was the Roman name of Ashdod.

8. Finally the word of the Lord on its triumphant march reaches Jerusalem. *My house* may refer to the Temple, but it probably has the wider connotation of the land, as in Jeremiah 12:7ff. and Hosea 8:1; 9:15. No longer will alien armies tramp their way through Judah's territory, because the Lord will guard it (cf. Zc. 2:5), nor will great powers occupy it, because His eyes keep watch (cf. note on verse 1).

Two links between this verse and chapters 1–8 are worth noting. *So that none shall march to and fro* is identical in Hebrew with 'so that no one went to and fro' in 7:14, and mention of the *eyes* of the Lord takes up the expression 'the eyes of the Lord, which range through the whole earth' (4:10b). In both contexts the Lord's all-seeing eye purposes to defend and provide for His people.

The first section of this second part of the book establishes from the start two important facts: the Lord's victory is certain, and He intends to bring back to Himself peoples long alienated from Him. These truths underlie all that follows and culminate in the universal worship of the King, the Lord of hosts, in 14:16–19.

Additional Note on 9:1
The burden of the word of the Lord

One problem which faces every translator is the impossibility of finding in the new language exact equivalents for some of the words he has to translate. Hebrew *maśśā'* is one of these. It comes from the root *nāśā'*, which means 'to lift up', 'to bear a burden', hence the meaning given to the word in the AV/RV 'burden', 'the burden of the word of the Lord'. Isaiah used the word as a heading to his prophecies concerning the nations (Is. 13–23), where the RV text 'The burden of Babylon', 'the burden of Moab', *etc.* is puzzling. The margin 'oracle concerning' is readily accepted as being much more meaningful. Similarly in Zechariah 9:1 'oracle' has become the accepted translation in RSV, JB, NEB. In this context, however, a difficulty arises because to say 'the oracle of the "word" of the Lord' is tautology, because *dābār*, 'word', can also mean 'oracle'. For this reason, despite the accents which have traditionally bound the words together, *maśśā'* has been separated from the rest of the phrase to form a heading 'An Oracle', and 'the word of the Lord' becomes part of the message.

A detailed study of the word *maśśā'* has been made by P. A. H. de Boer,[1] who examines its sixty-odd occurrences in the Old Testament, consults the ancient versions to see how early translators understood it, and finally, after considering examples of modern exegesis, he reaches his conclusions. In spite of the fact that lexica and translators have distinguished two words, one meaning 'load' and the other 'oracle', de Boer fails to find any evidence for such a distinction. He finds that its etymology and use in the Old Testament, as well as its rendering in the ancient versions, indicate a single meaning. *Maśśā'* is a burden, 'imposed by a master, a despot or a deity

[1] *An Inquiry into the Meaning of the Term Maśśā'* (Brill, Leiden, 1948).

on their subjects, beasts, men or things'.[1] It can apply to leadership of God's people, to a cultic duty and to a judgment of God. As used in prophecy it acquires an ominous sense linked up with the catastrophic nature of so many prophecies. In the headings of prophetic oracles *maśśā'* means 'burden imposed on . . . '. As a technical term it introduces the theme of the following passage, indicating the character of the prophecy.

Though the word 'oracle' persists for want of a more accurate term, if de Boer's thesis is accepted there is more to this heading than that word would suggest. It lays stress on the prophet's sense of constraint in giving the message that follows. He would not have chosen to give it but he finds he has no option (*cf.* Je. 20:9; Lk. 12:49,50). It has been placed on him, and like the loadbearer, he has to accept it and discharge his duty. Like an ambassador he is given his message, and however unacceptable it may be he cannot alter it; hence the burdensome aspect of his calling.

To the rather neutral term 'oracle', therefore, must be added the idea of compulsion, urgency, dread; the prophet would escape if he could from what may understandably be called his 'burden'.

b. Arrival of the king (9:9,10)

Shouts of joy are to greet Jerusalem's king. The prophet outlines first his character and then his achievements. Who is this king? Although the king-theme is a dominant note of pre-exilic rather than of post-exilic prophecy, and is characteristic of the eighth century in particular (Is. 9:6,7; 11:1–5; 32:1–8; Ho. 3:4,5; Am. 9:11,12; Mi. 5:2–4), most commentators agree that the Messianic king is foreshadowed here. The twelve-line poem could stand alone in its own right, but it follows not only the triumphant theme but also the poetic structure of the preceding section, reverting to the 2+2 rhythm with which the chapter opened.

Reminiscences of earlier biblical literature abound. R. C. Dentan is no doubt right in seeing a reference to 'the mysterious figure pictured in Genesis 49:10–11'.[2] Others see a preoccupation with David, and evidence that God's dealings with David

[1] *Op. cit.*, p. 214.
[2] *IB*, VI, p. 1096.

teach God's plan for His people.[1] As might be expected this is a particularly fruitful theme, for David was supremely the prototype of the Messiah. In the description of his kingly deeds there are echoes of Micah 5:10, and the extent of his kingdom 'from sea to sea, and from the River to the ends of the earth' is a quotation from Psalm 72:8, to mention only the most obvious references.

Both Matthew and John refer to these verses in their accounts of Jesus' triumphal entry into Jerusalem, but neither quotes precisely the prophet's words. Matthew (21:5) borrows his first words from Isaiah 62:11, and then follows the Hebrew, whereas John (12:15) writes a very free summary, introduced by 'fear not'. The fact that Passover crowds recognized the fulfilment of prophecy in a man's journey into Jerusalem on a donkey proves that the passage was well known by the ordinary Jew of Jesus' day. This was, of course, an everyday sight. The verses may have been among 'Testimonia' collected and popularly taught to provide information about the coming king.[2] Even though the Evangelists saw fulfilment of verse 9, they did not go on to quote verse 10, which may indicate that they were conscious of having witnessed only a partial fulfilment. Even the victory was scarcely obvious at the time, which may account for John's omitting reference to it. It is still only too evident that the disarmament of Jerusalem and peace among the nations are features yet to be fulfilled.

9. *Rejoice greatly, . . . shout.* A similar call to exult in Zephaniah 3:14 is linked with a proclamation of the presence of 'the King of Israel, the Lord' (3:15) in the city. In Zechariah 2:10 there is a call to sing and rejoice because the Lord has promised to come to reside in Jerusalem, and now His arrival is to be accompanied with wild joy. 'Daughter Zion . . . daughter Jerusalem' may be nearer the original than the usual English translation.[3] Since the names of towns are feminine in Hebrew,

[1] *E.g.* D. R. Jones, *TBC*, pp. 130f.

[2] The hypothesis was first put forward by Rendel Harris and published in book form under the title *Testimonies* (1916, 1920). It was later taken up and examined by C. H. Dodd in *According to the Scriptures* (Nisbet, 1952). There is a possible reference to Zechariah 9:9 in the Qumran literature, 1 QM 12.12, translated by Y. Yadin: 'Zion, rejoice exceedingly and shine forth in songs of joy, O Jerusalem, and be joyful, all ye cities of Judah.' This reference tends to support the view that the prediction was well known.

[3] See N. H. Snaith, *Study Notes on Bible Books. Amos II* (Epworth, 1946), p. 82, who believes the words are in apposition and not in a construct relation as used to be thought.

'daughter' is appropriate. The turn of phrase, which is frequent in Lamentations and Isaiah, and occurs in Psalms, Jeremiah, Micah, Zephaniah, draws attention to the personal relationship between the Lord and His people. The idiom is used even of Tyre (Ps. 45:12), Tarshish (Is. 23:10), Sidon (Is. 23:12), Babylon (Ps. 137:8; Zc. 2:7), cities over which the Lord claims 'parental' rights. Usually 'daughter' occurs in contexts which speak of a broken relationship (*e.g.* Is. 1:8; Je. 4:31; 6:2; La. 2:1); the contrast in this verse is striking.

The focus now switches to the character of the king. He is 'righteous' (Heb. *ṣaddîq*), as Isaiah's descriptions had insisted (Is. 9:7; 11:4,5; 32:1), but this is no static quality. In each passage righteousness is seen in the activity of the King, governing, administering justice, encouraging right. When rogues continually succeed in getting away with their crimes, while innocent people suffer and find no redress, to be promised that right will triumph, that the righteous will be vindicated, is a cause for deep joy. The use of *ṣedeq* in the sense of 'vindication' in Isaiah 40–55 underlies the RSV *triumphant*. Several times in these chapters in Isaiah the twin ideas of righteousness and salvation occur together (*e.g.* Is. 45:8; 46:13, AV, RV; 51:4,5), and vindication is to be granted to the Lord's Servant (49:4; 50:8; 53:12). This link with the Servant points towards an interpretation of the second adjective *nôšāʿ*, 'saved', 'delivered'. The king has been through some ordeal in which he has experienced the Lord's deliverance, and so is *victorious*, but 'He is victorious, not in himself or anything that he personally commands, but by the grace, and in the might, of the God of Israel. . . . His triumph, therefore, is the triumph of the faith of the Servant of Yahweh.'[1]

With that in mind it is no surprise to read that the king is *humble* (Heb. *ʿānî*). This word is more often used in the sense of 'poor' (*cf.* Zc. 7:10; 11:7,11, RV) or 'afflicted' (Is. 14:32; 51:21; 54:11), and though when the Servant is described as 'afflicted' (Is. 53:7) another word is used, there is a correspondence of idea here also between the Servant and the King.

Riding on an ass. There was nothing remarkable about princes riding in state on asses in the Judges' period (Jdg. 5:10; 10:4; 12:14), for they were the usual mount. When David fled from

---

[1] H. G. Mitchell, *ICC*, p. 273. The salvation of men through the righteous life and vicarious death of Christ, vindicated by the resurrection, is, of course, the theme of Paul's Epistle to the Romans.

Jerusalem asses were provided for him (2 Sa. 16:2). E. Lipinski goes so far as to claim that the ass was the royal mount *par excellence* in the Near East, and this may well have been so, though the evidence on which he draws belongs to the second millennium BC from Ur and Mari.[1] The horse was the usual mount for princes, according to the Barkal stela erected by Thut-mose III (*c.* 1490–1437 BC), who wrote of 330 princes taken prisoner near Megiddo, 'They all went on donkey (back), so that I might take their horses.'[2] In the Persian period we know that a horse was mount for the Persian king, Ahasuerus (Est. 6:8), but prophetic scorn of trust in war-horses (verse 10, *cf.* Is. 2:7; 31:1; Mi. 5:10; Hg. 2:22) may have favoured the use of asses in Israel. The ass was an appropriate mount for one who came on a mission of peace. *On a colt the foal of an ass.* The parallelism is suggested by Genesis 49:11, part of the mysterious deathbed pronouncement of Jacob on Judah, in which Judah's ruler binds 'his foal to the vine and his ass's colt to the choice vine'. The expression 'ass's colt' is attested at Mari,[3] where its significance is 'purebred', that is, an adult ass, born, not of a mule, but of a female ass. It thus qualified to be a royal mount. Only one animal is intended, despite Matthew 21:7.

10. Three lines dealing with complete disarmament are balanced by three lines about the coming kingdom. The change to the first person makes clear that the Lord takes the initiative and not the king.[4] Mention of *Ephraim* and *Jerusalem* is a reminder that the northern and southern kingdoms will again be united, but they will not be the only ones to benefit, for peace is to be declared to all nations, and ensured by the presence of the righteous king ruling over a world-wide empire. The *chariot*, the *war horse* and the *battle bow* and their modern equivalents will be 'banished' (NEB), for they will be entirely incongruous when there is a ruler competent to 'care for the true welfare' of all the nations.[5] The quotation in the last two lines of the poem from Psalm 72:8 is reminiscent of the territory ideally allotted to Israel (but rarely in her

[1] 'Recherches sur le livre de Zacharie', *VT*, XX, 1, 1970, p. 51.
[2] *ANET*, p. 238.
[3] *ANET*, p. 482 note 6: 'I caused the foal of an ass to be slaughtered.'
[4] JB and NEB, which have the third person of the verb, 'he will banish', follow the Greek versions.
[5] For a note on *peace* (Heb. *šālôm*), see comment on Haggai 2:9.

possession), from the Red Sea to the Mediterranean, and from the wilderness of Sinai to the Euphrates (Ex. 23:31; 1 Ki. 4:21). The psalmist had omitted the boundaries because the king of whom he wrote was the one for whom all men were subconsciously longing, and to whom all would give their allegiance. Moreover, his coming was sure, as the emphatic statements of both psalmist and prophet indicate. The only realistic hopes of world peace still centre in this king.

On this note of triumph it might have seemed appropriate for the prophet to bring his book to an end, but he was burdened with other less palatable truths which were an equally integral part of his charge, and to which he was to come in 11:4-17.

c. Jubilation and prosperity (9:11 – 10:1)

There are differences of opinion as to where this section should end, but as 10:2b leads into the 'shepherd' theme the break has been made at the end of 10:1. The historical setting now becomes clearer. Exiles are languishing in desert conditions when they might be enjoying the full provisions of a prosperous land, their future security assured. Hence the enthusiastic promises and exhortations, and the highly colourful language borrowed from warfare, to describe the Lord's dramatic intervention. Partly on account of the unusual allusions and metaphors RSV, JB and NEB have made corrections in the Hebrew to make the English run more smoothly. These corrections, which are usually noted in the margin, are sometimes based on one of the ancient versions.

11. The particle *also* connects closely the new theme with what has just gone before. The Lord enlarges on the new era as it will affect the people of His covenant. *The blood of my covenant with you.* The covenant was ratified by blood sacrifice at its initiation with Abraham (Gn. 15:9-11), at its extension under Moses (Ex. 24:5-8), and in its continual renewal through the daily offerings in the Temple (Ex. 29:38-46). Only in Exodus 24:8 is the 'blood of the covenant' expressly mentioned in the Old Testament, apart from this passage. The association of the two words has become familiar through Jesus' use of them at the institution of the last supper (Mk. 14:24), and in His death they took on their full meaning.

I will set your captives free. The Hebrew has the perfect tense, as often in prophecy, so indicating the imminence of God's action, which had an application beyond the return of exiles (Rom. 6:16f.). The words *from the waterless pit* (Heb. *bôr*) are omitted from NEB and bracketed in JB. They have long been considered to be a gloss,[1] but none of the early versions omits them, and they make good sense. To be delivered from a pit in which there was no drinking water was life from death.

12. First the prisoners are exhorted, *return to your stronghold*, 'fenced city' (*cf.* Zc. 2:5), *O prisoners of hope*, that is, those who believe in the promised king and therefore are expectant. NEB treats this line as a gloss, probably because there is difficulty in the Hebrew, and because many emendations have been suggested by different commentators. Moreover, the Greek versions have a different sense, and mean, 'You will stay in your strongholds, O prisoners of the congregation', presumably implying to await deliverance.[2] The RSV satisfactorily represents the meaning of the Hebrew. *I will restore to you double*. Now Zion is addressed again. A double share of joy is to compensate for a past sorrow (Is. 61:7, a double share being the privilege of the firstborn, Dt. 21:17), or maybe a doubling of the population is implied.

13. In bold metaphor the prophet depicts the Lord's weapons. He has not been disarmed. Despite the dispersion both northern and southern kingdoms are His *bow* and *arrow*, each essential to the usefulness of the other. Moreover, He will use them *like a warrior's sword*, which came into action once victory had been gained. These weapons are not, however, to be interpreted in terms of war, any more than similar imagery applied to the Servant implied literal fighting (Is. 49:2). We are to picture the Lord so in command of the affairs of Israel and Judah that He can handle them as effectively as an experienced soldier does his weapons. *Over your sons, O Greece*. These words, omitted from the text in NEB, and bracketed as a gloss in JB, are said to overload the metre, because the first two lines form a couplet, which should be balanced by a couplet

---

[1] See H. G. Mitchell, *ICC*, p. 282. The reasons given are: '(1) It disturbs the measure. (2) It adds a thought unnatural in this connection. (3) It is easily explained as a reminiscence of Gn. 37:24 or Je. 38:6, probably, since the Jews interpreted *bôr* as meaning Egypt, the former. It is merely an example of misapplied rabbinical learning.'

[2] T. Jansma regards the Greek as a mistranslation of the Hebrew (p. 73).

and not by three lines.[1] It is usually assumed that the 'sons of Greece' are enemies to be overcome, and that the gloss was inserted in Maccabean times to give the prophecy contemporary relevance. But the term *Javan* is applied in Genesis 10:2,4 and in Isaiah 66:19 to distant, unknown peoples on the edge of civilization, and it is probably used in the same sense in this eschatological context.[2] The fact that the Greek includes the words is proof that they were part of the text when that version was made.[3] RSV represents the meaning of the Hebrew text. God's people are to share exultantly in the world-wide victory of the Lord.

14. The language now becomes clearly that of theophany (*cf.* 2 Sa. 22:8–18; Ps. 29; Hab. 3:3,11), described in terms of a storm. The thunder is the Lord's *trumpet* (Heb. *šôpār*), an instrument used to sound all signals, not only of war but also of ritual and religious occasions, such as the beginning of the Sabbath. In apocalyptic passages such as this (*cf.* Is. 27:13) the trumpet is used by the Lord to call His people to worship. *Whirlwinds of the south.* Because Sinai to the south had been the scene of theophany (Ex. 24:9,10,15,18) and the place of God's revelation in the Covenant ceremony, Old Testament poetry often depicts the south as the place of the Lord's abode (Jdg. 5:4,5; Hab. 3:3). Dust storms are a feature of the weather in this desert area (Is. 21:1).[4]

15. At first sight this verse seems to conflict with the interpretation given thus far, and to demand a battle scene.[5] On the other hand the next verse, far from continuing a war scene, is idyllic. The prophet is expressing in vivid metaphor the exuberant abandon of a victorious Israel. *They shall devour and tread down the slingers*, better 'slingstones' as in the Hebrew (RSV mg.). The verb *devour* (Heb. *'ākal*) is the common word 'to eat', and so the sense can equally well be, 'They shall eat' –

---

[1] So H. G. Mitchell, *ICC*, p. 279. For a contrary opinion see R. C. Dentan, *IB*, VI, p. 1097.

[2] See D. R. Jones, 'A Fresh Interpretation of Zechariah IX–XI', *VT*, XII, 1962, p. 248. 'In rhetoric of this kind Jawan is appropriately set over against Zion, as a symbol of the nations. The picture is similar to that of Is. xlix 22, where Yahweh calls to the nations . . . (*cf.* Is. lx 4, 9).'

[3] *I.e.* probably by the middle, and certainly by the end, of the second century BC, according to J. W. Wevers (*IDB*, IV, p. 276).

[4] D. Baly, *The Geography of the Bible* (Lutterworth, 1957), pp. 65, 66.

[5] For such an interpretation see H. G. Mitchell, *ICC*, p. 280.

the victory banquet, understood. The slingstones that have come their way as missiles will be as useless then as all other weapons of war. rsv continues its bloodthirsty interpretation, borrowed from the Greek translations, *and they shall drink their blood like wine,* whereas the Hebrew means, 'they shall make a noise as though drunk'. At this victory banquet, however, the exuberance is not a sign of drunkenness but has a totally different explanation (*cf.* Eph. 5:18), and knows no limit, for it will be 'full to the brim', like the bowls full of sacrificial blood, which was poured out at the base of the altar (Lv. 4:7, etc.).

16. The metaphor now changes. The Lord's *flock* are safe in His land, and so precious are they to Him that they seem to Him to shine *like the jewels of a crown,* as they circle the hills.

17. The prospect satisfies the prophet as he contemplates young men and women growing up in a land of peace and full harvests.

10:1. Such a transformation of nature was bound up with rainfall, a gift to *men,* that is, mankind in general, *from the Lord,* who is in control of the welcome rain-bearing *storm-clouds.* Today man can make rain, at least on a small scale, and at a price. But quite apart from that fact a verse like this too easily leads our thoughts on to weather-forecasting and away from the writer's meaning. His subject is still salvation (9:16) depicted in terms appropriate for a farming community, concerned about sheep, crops, and above all rain, on which everyone depended. We might ask whether all modern knowledge has really made men any less dependent on rain, and therefore on God. When it comes to deeper, spiritual needs of which the rain is a symbol, again there is no help but in God.[1]

The poetic section opened with a reference to the 'waterless pit' (9:11), which may represent the exile. The contrasting plenty that is promised stands for spiritual fulfilment in God's kingdom. But the prophet was not thinking in 'other-worldly' terms. He really believed God's victory extended to practical farming. He saw famine as a thing of the past (*cf.* Dt. 11:13, 14), and problems of food distribution non-existent because everyone would have abundant supplies from his own fields.

---

[1] K. Elliger (*ATD,* p. 154) interprets the prophet's use of 'rain' as a picture of salvation.

Human utopias concentrate on material equality; God's promise is abundance for all, and, more deeply satisfying still, abundance of joy, transforming human personality.

d. Rebuke for sham leaders (10:2,3a)

With a sudden transition the prophet is in the present, aware of the contrast between the ideal future and the contemporary situation.

2. The introductory *for* (Heb. *kî*) is better translated here 'because'. The first four lines so introduced look to the result, introduced by *therefore*. Because the leaders looked in the wrong direction for their advice they failed to give an effective lead, and the people drifted aimlessly. *Teraphim* were household gods (Gn. 31:19), used in the Judges' period for divination (Jdg. 17:5; 18:5), condemned by the time of Saul (1 Sa. 15:23), but still in use in the eighth century (Ho. 3:4). *Diviners* interpreted omens as a means of foretelling the future, but in Israel they were banned, together with a whole list of dubious practitioners, whom the prophets were to replace (Dt. 18:10ff.). *Dreamers.* Though God sometimes spoke through dreams, as for instance to Jacob (Gn. 28:12), Joseph (Gn. 37:5–9), Nebuchadrezzar (Dn. 2), there were spurious prophets who claimed to have had authoritative dreams and misled many with their lies (Je. 23:32; 27:9,10). By the post-exilic period Israel should have left behind unlawful and inadequate methods of decision making, but they were the alternative to accepting God's way as revealed through the prophets. A modern parallel is the renewed interest in magic, spiritism and other survivals of primitive times. The more widespread modern equivalent is to ignore God altogether and tacitly to assume that no problem is beyond man's unaided power to solve.

The people wander like sheep. The verb means 'set off on a journey', but since they have been misdirected they get lost and are *afflicted*; they suffer because they are at the mercy of powerful and unscrupulous men. The wording is strongly reminiscent of Ezekiel 34:6–8. *For want of a shepherd.* 'Shepherd' was used as a symbol for ruler in the Near East before it was so used in the Bible. An Egyptian text, 'The Admonitions of IPU-WER', dated before 2000 BC, describes a god-king who will deliver Egypt: 'Men shall say, "He is the herdsman of all men".'[1] Hammurabi identified himself in the prologue to his

[1] *ANET*, p. 443.

laws, 'Hammurabi the shepherd, called by Enlil, am I'.[1] So
when Jacob called God 'Shepherd' (Gn. 49:24) and when
Moses prayed for a successor, 'that the congregation of the
Lord may not be as sheep without a shepherd' (Nu. 27:17),
they were both making use of a familiar figure of speech. In
the poetry of a psalmist and several of the prophets it was
developed to express longings after God (Ps. 23; Is. 40:11)
and deep desires for a just king (Is. 44:28; Je. 23:2–4; Mi.
5:4). Ezekiel, with his great gift for extended metaphor and
allegory, built a whole chapter on the theme, in the course of
which he brought together the coming Davidic king and the
ideal shepherd (Ezk. 34:23,24). When Zechariah used the
term 'shepherd' the word had thus acquired a significance
which the western reader might easily fail to appreciate.

3a. The expected judgment is pronounced. In Hebrew the
emphatic words of the sentence are *against the shepherds*, so-
called, and *the leaders*, literally 'he-goats', an uncomplimentary
extension of the same pastoral metaphor (Ezk. 34:10,17).
These leaders take advantage of the weakness of others, and
get their own way by bullying. While 'shepherd' usually
denoted 'king', it included all in positions of authority, whether
Israelites or foreigners occupying the land. The Lord *will visit
with punishment the leaders of the flock* (NEB, following closely the
Hebrew idiom).

Lamarche divides these eight lines into two stanzas, the
former giving reasons for the condemnation, and the second
pronouncing judgment. The structure suggests the exact
correspondence between the outworking of retribution and the
wrong done.[2]

c¹. Jubilation and restoration (10:3b – 11:3)

The prophet now resumes the victory theme of 9:11 – 10:1.
Identical imagery occurs: battle, elation as if through wine,
and by contrast flock and shepherd, but whereas in the earlier
passage the emphasis is on the transformation of circumstances, now it is on strengthening Israel for action. There is
also a certain narrowing from a world setting to a Near
Eastern one. NEB captures extremely well the mood of the
poetry here.

[1] *ANET*, p. 164.
[2] Lamarche, p. 54.

The poem divides into two equal parts at the end of verse 9. The first half deals with the restoration of the two kingdoms, with verse 6 as the pivotal verse; the second half introduces the other nations involved, with verse 12 as the pivotal verse. Twice the verb 'strengthen' (Heb. *gibbēr*) is used (6a,12a), and though the translation cannot bring out the connection, 'mighty men' (verse 5) and 'mighty warrior' (verse 7) come from the same root. Other stylistic features are the chiastic pattern in verses 10,11 (Egypt, Assyria, Assyria, Egypt) and the repetitive sentence structure in 10:4 and 11:2,3.[1]

3b. *For the Lord of hosts cares for his flock.* The one equipped with all power to strengthen His people *will visit his flock* (NEB). By translating the Hebrew literally here NEB keeps the connection in the original with 'I will visit with punishment' in 3a, though this time the meaning is 'visit with deliverance'.

This verse draws attention to the polarity of meaning in the Hebrew verb *pāqad* as it is used of the Lord's activity among His people. Basically it expresses the conviction that He closely observes them and *cares for* them, to the extent of intervening in history on their behalf. Joseph was convinced that God would 'visit' the Israelites in Egypt to deliver them (Gn. 50:24). Under Moses this hope was fulfilled. The Lord 'visited' them in mercy and redeemed them from slavery to Pharaoh (Ex. 3:16; 4:31; 13:19), but when, having experienced that deliverance, they flouted His commands, He visited them in judgment (Ex. 32:34. Heb. *pāqad 'al*). The same order of events is observable in Amos 3:2. The Lord had made Israel His own privileged, covenant nation, but the privilege had been abused, hence the inevitable alienation. In our text the order is reversed. Having visited the irresponsible leaders with punishment (*pāqad 'al*, 3a) the Lord is visiting His people to demonstrate by their victory that they are His. The metaphor resumes the salvation theme of 9:16.

The house of Judah. These words are said by H. G. Mitchell to be 'clearly a mistaken gloss, being inconsistent with vv. [6f], where Ephraim is the object of Yahweh's favour as well as Judah'.[2] Once the literary structure of the poem is recognized the words are seen to be an essential part of the text, for they make clear that Judah is the subject of the first stanza (verses 3b–5). Ephraim is to be the subject of the second stanza

---

[1] P. Lamarche sets out the stylistic pattern in detail on pages 62, 63.
[2] H. G. Mitchell, *ICC*, p. 288.

(verses 7–9). In a rapid succession of metaphors the role of Judah is described. First, having referred to Judah as 'his flock', unexpectedly they are likened to *royal war-horses* (NEB). Those who in their submission to the Lord are like sheep become invincible as war-horses in His service.

4. The metaphors pile up, emphasizing initiative and yet stability in leadership: *war horse, cornerstone, tent peg, battle bow*, all of them figures of speech from earlier writers. The introductory words in each line *out of them* represent the repetition in the original, though the Hebrew has 'out of him', referring probably to Judah, but just possibly to the Lord. *Cornerstone* (Jb. 38:6; Is. 28:16) symbolizes the steadfast strength on which a whole edifice can depend. It is used figuratively for 'ruler' in Judges 20:2 (Heb.); 1 Samuel 14:38 (Heb.); Isaiah 19:13, while in Psalm 118:22, which speaks of the rejected stone becoming the chief cornerstone, the rejection of the ruler is implied. This is a theme to be developed by the prophet in the next section. *Tent peg.* Probably this is the meaning here, though the Hebrew *yāṭēḏ* also means 'a peg on which to hang things', like Isaiah's 'peg in a sure place' (Is. 22:23), applied to a coming leader in Judah. In both cases the figure aptly depicts endurance under the strains implicit in leadership. The *battle bow*, the figure representing conquest, had already been pronounced obsolete in the universal kingdom, but it serves to symbolize fearless initiative in the Lord's cause (2 Ki. 13:17; Rev. 6:2). The last line plainly states *out of them every ruler*; Judah will be the tribe to supply future leadership. The Targum interprets this verse as referring to the Messiah. 'Ruler' (Heb. *nôḡēś*) had the meaning 'oppressor' in 9:8, but it is used in a good sense here; it implies a man of action, determined to achieve his goal.

The contention of many commentators that this verse is a scribal gloss[1] has no textual support.

5. The modern English translators transfer the word *together* from verse 4 to verse 5, with the slight textual support of the Syriac version. The whole house of Judah will be like *mighty men* (Heb. *gibbôrîm*), valiant fighters, *trampling the foe in the mud of the streets*. RSV gives no indication of the fact that the words 'the foe' have been added to complete the sense, following

---

[1] *E.g.* H. G. Mitchell (*ICC*, p. 289). K. Elliger (*ATD*, p. 155) and F Horst (*HAT*, p. 248) regard only the last line as a gloss.

Micah 7:10. No army can avoid trampling over the dead if it is to press the battle to victory, but such carnage may not be in the mind of the writer here. The Greek and Latin have no preposition 'in', hence the NEB, *who tramp the muddy ways in battle.* The simile is intended to describe triumphant conquest in the face of overwhelming odds, footmen against cavalry. The fact that they have fought at all and not fled in retreat admits of only one explanation, *the Lord is with them.*

6. Now the Lord Himself proclaims what He intends to do (*cf.* 9:6). This key verse opens with a double promise arranged chiastically in the Hebrew word order:

> 'I will strengthen the house of Judah
> And the house of Joseph I will save.'

Judah and *Joseph* stand for the southern and northern king-doms as a whole; all who were still living far from 'the land' would be made mighty and be delivered, and be brought back home.[1] *I will answer them* implies prayer for deliverance, which has been heard and is about to be answered, because the period of discipline is over.

7. Just as Judah will become like mighty men (verse 5), so will Ephraim be *like a mighty warrior* (Heb. *gibbôr*), and find conscious delight in such strength. Whole families and genera-tions will see God's deeds and exult with joy. In the Lord their history makes sense and finds its goal.

8,9. Whereas in Judah's case the main thrust of the message concerned the leadership, in Ephraim's case the return of her exiles is the dominant theme. The earlier collapse of the northern kingdom (722 as opposed to 587 BC), and the more ruthless scattering of the population as a deliberate policy on the part of the Assyrians (2 Ki. 17:6), made any hope of re-assembling their descendants remote. But the Lord says, 'I will signal for them'. Here RSV follows the Greek rather than the more picturesque Hebrew, 'I will whistle for them'. This is the shepherd, who knows just where his sheep are because he scattered them, calling them back with his own characteris-tic call. *I have redeemed them,* or 'ransomed them'. The thought

---

[1] The Hebrew verb is a composite one, combining 'to return' and 'to reinstate'. It is possible that the Hebrew has a conflate text to perpetuate two traditions, one of which is supported by the Greek version, and the other by the Syriac, while the Latin and Targum may presuppose the conflate text of the Hebrew. See Jansma, p. 87.

is that they have been brought out of bondage (*cf.* Mi. 6:4), a figure that is pregnant with meaning in the light of New Testament usage (*e.g.* 1 Pet. 1:18). *They shall be as many as of old* (literally, 'they shall increase as they have increased', RV). Probably the thought is that so many will respond to God's summons that the population will be as great as ever.

Though I scattered them. Two slight emendations underlie the RSV here: the future (Heb. imperfect) is changed to the perfect, as the sense requires, and the unexpected word 'sowed' is changed by one letter to give 'scattered'. Though the Targum supports this, and the sense is unambiguous, the vigour of the original is lost, for sowing implies a harvest and so conveys hope. *They shall remember me*, recognizing from afar after many years the shepherd's call, *and (together) with their children they shall live*, that is, find in responding and returning, not mere survival, but life.[1]

10. In the second half of the poem the prophet turns his attention to other nations necessarily involved, symbolized by Egypt and Assyria, which have to let them go, and by Gilead and Lebanon which have to provide them with territory. *Egypt* is an obvious choice because of the complex of associations that had grown out of the Exodus experience (*e.g.* Is. 11:11–16; Ho. 11:1,11; Mi. 7:15). *Assyria* summed up all those lands to the north and east where captives were living, including Babylon and Persia.[2] Verses 10 and 11 belong together as the chiastic arrangement of Egypt, Assyria, at the beginning, and Assyria, Egypt at the end, shows. So great will Ephraim's population be that even when Gilead, which stands for all the territory east of Jordan, is theirs it will still not be sufficient for them.

11. Many corrections have been suggested for the opening words, which read in Hebrew as RV, *And he shall pass through*

---

[1] Greek has 'they will rear their children', and this is followed by NEB. JB emends the Greek, and translates 'they will teach their sons'.

[2] Those who date the writing of these chapters in the Greek period lay stress on the rise of Jews to posts of importance in Egypt in the Greek period. They point out that fortunes changed under Ptolemy III (247–222 BC), and 'this is the period to which belongs the prophecy here recorded' (H. G. Mitchell, *ICC*, p. 293). Mention of Assyria does not necessarily contradict a date in the Greek period, because the name frequently stands for powers which subsequently took over territory that once belonged to Assyria. In the third century it could stand for the Seleucids. So H. G. Mitchell, *ibid.*, p. 294.

the sea of affliction. Since in the previous verses Ephraim had been referred to in the plural, the singular 'he' is unexpected, and RSV adopts from the Greek the plural subject 'they'. An alternative would be to understand 'he' as the Lord, the sentence being interposed by the prophet in the third person, but there is understandable reluctance to accept that the Lord passes through affliction, hence the Greek, which translates 'sea of affliction' as 'the narrow sea'. A popular emendation, adopted by JB and RSV, is 'sea of Egypt', which makes good sense but has no textual foundation. On balance it is better to retain the more difficult but suggestive Hebrew text. In figurative language the prophet declares that Ephraimites will follow along the way opened to them by the Lord as He goes ahead through all the barriers between them and their land. Triumphs like those of the Exodus will be theirs also. In the last two lines assonance between *Assyria* (*'aššûr*) and *shall depart* (*yāsûr*) skilfully conveys the prophet's scorn of Assyria and Egypt, which stand for all the nations that oppose God's rule.

12. This verse, central to the second half of the poem as verse 6 was to the first half, repeats the promise *I will strengthen*. Four Hebrew words in succinct chiastic arrangement constitute the message: a. *I will strengthen them;* b. *in the Lord;* b[1]. *in his name;* a[1]. *they will march.*[1]

11:1–3. This short lyric poem, addressed to Lebanon and Bashan, representing the nations with which the second half of the poem began (10:10), concludes the section. Prophets had often linked together these two lands (Is. 2:13; Je. 22:20; Ezk. 27:5,6), and the imagery in Zechariah is drawn from earlier prophecy.

Cedars. The cedar was used as a symbol of the royal house of Judah in Ezekiel (17:3,4,12f.). As the king of trees it sometimes stood for pride (Is. 2:13), which could be reduced to nothing with a few blows of the axe (Is. 10:33,34). It was a particularly apt symbol for alien powers which had the effrontery to reckon themselves independent of God (*cf.* Ezk. 31, AV/RV, where the kings of Egypt and Assyria come into that category). The lesser forests of *cypress* and *oaks* may well lament once the cedars have fallen. All the same the imagery is difficult to interpret because if, as seems likely, the cedars

---

[1] JB, RSV adopt the Greek, 'they will glory'.

stand for the great powers, what of Lebanon itself, where the cedars grew? Probably the metaphor is not to be applied to specific nations; the different types of tree represent nations large and small. Mention of *thick forest* in *Bashan*, the famous cattle-rearing table-land to the north and east of the Sea of Galilee, is surprising. According to D. Baly, the trees 'would have been in clumps of woodland rather than continuous forest'.[1] AV *forest of the vintage* follows the margin of the Hebrew text (*bāṣîr*), but the meaning is obscure. The adjective 'thick' (*bāṣûr*) really means 'fortified'; perhaps it was suggested by the cities for which the trees stood. There is further inconsistency in the imagery; destruction by fire is mixed with loss by felling, one consideration among several which lead H. G. Mitchell to doubt the genuineness of verse 2.[2] But the mixed metaphor does not obscure the sense.

Verse 3, inspired by Jeremiah 25:34–37, refers to alien kings as *shepherds*, lamenting the ruin of their *glory*, but whereas Jeremiah sustained the metaphor, 'the Lord is despoiling their pasture' (verse 36), in Zechariah the imagery is interpreted. The poem becomes even more ominous, *Hark, the roaring of the lions*; the metaphor is applied to kings by Jeremiah (50:44) and by Ezekiel (19:1–9). The lions have lost their lairs and are dangerously at large, threatening life. They have emerged from the *jungle of Jordan*, the dense confusion of tamarisks and other shrubs extending on either side of the meandering river, and covering the area inundated by flood waters when the snows of Hermon melt in spring.[3] 'Jungle' (Heb. *gā'ôn*) is more accurately 'majesty'; the prophet continues to lay stress on the downfall of the arrogant. There is irony in this lament of trees, shepherds, lions, over the devastation that affects them all. The bold mixture of metaphors is possible because all are drawn from geographical features common to the Jordan valley and Transjordan.

At this point the poetry ends, to be resumed again twice only, and then in brief sections (11:17; 13:7–9). The unifying theme has been the coming triumph of the Lord, which will be shared by His people in exultant joy. The climax is the

---

[1] D. Baly, *The Geography of the Bible*, p. 220.

[2] *ICC*, pp. 296, 297.

[3] For a photograph of the undergrowth see D. Baly, *op. cit.*, p. 200. The extent of the jungle, which still harbours wild boar, is illustrated in L. H. Grollenberg, *Atlas of the Bible* (Nelson, 1956), p. 17.

arrival of the king to set up his universal kingdom, but first there is opposition to be overcome, hence the darker side of the picture.

b¹. The fate of the good shepherd (11:4–17)

Without passing premature judgment on this difficult passage, it is possible to say at the outset that the central subject is leadership. It is often assumed that if a country were to find a ruler totally dedicated to the good of his people, who would rid the land of injustice and encourage all that makes for harmony, peace and happiness would prevail. One insight of this prophet is that such a ruler would not only not be welcomed, but he would be positively hated and rejected.

The imagery of shepherd and flock has already permeated the poetry (9:16; 10:2,3,8f.; 11:3), much as the Servant theme recurs in Isaiah 40–55. Now, however, as in the Servant Songs, the prophet highlights his theme, concentrating on it to elucidate the implications of godly leadership.

The flock in question is undoubtedly Israel, and the shepherd belongs to Israel. Temporarily the world-view is lost, and there is a focus on one people, one land, except for the hint of universal cataclysm in verse 6.

There are three clear divisions: (a) The Lord gives one last chance (verses 4–6). (b) The good shepherd is rejected (verses 7–14). (c) A worthless shepherd replaces him (verses 15–17). There is no chiastic pattern here. Instead a simple alternative is outlined in verses 4–6, and each of the two possibilities is developed in turn in the second and third paragraphs.

4. *The Lord my God.* Now the prophet is speaking.[1] He makes plain at the outset that he is in the closest possible relationship with the Lord. As His representative he is to *become shepherd of the flock.* Was the prophet meant to act out this scene as other prophets did? It seems likely that we are dealing here with an allegory rather than with an acted parable, if only because of all the other people involved as the chapter continues. *Doomed to slaughter.* These sheep are being raised to provide meat, and are soon to be sold in the market before being taken to the slaughter-house. But the sheep are men and women, suffering

[1] D. R. Jones ('A Fresh Interpretation of Zechariah IX–XI', *VT*, XII, 1962, p. 252) argues for an autobiographical framework of these three chapters, found in 9:1,8; 11:4,7,8,13,15.

under oppression. Even those who feed them help to fill the pockets of the traders, who get a better price for well-fattened sheep. NEB *Fatten the flock for slaughter* captures the sense but by omitting the key word 'shepherd' abbreviates too much.

5. *Those who buy them* are occupying powers, who expected to benefit financially from their captives. 'Them' is feminine, indicating that the sheep are ewes, intended for breeding and not for slaughter. *Those who sell them* are *their own shepherds*, Jewish leaders, who ingratiated themselves with the authorities to their own material advantage, regardless of the suffering they caused. We know that bribery had corrupted Israel's law courts for centuries; kings from Solomon onwards had taxed the poor and enriched themselves, and in the Maccabean era money was to buy the office of high priest from Seleucid rulers in Antioch. *Blessed be the Lord, I have become rich* is bitterly ironical. Riches are no proof of the Lord's favour (Mk. 10:23), least of all when they are obtained by fraud.

6. From the outset it becomes clear that the shepherd's effort to save the flock will be a failure. Did Jesus meditate on this passage as He considered His mission? The time has come for self-seeking to reap its just recompense, as it did at the fall of Jerusalem (Je. 13:10,14). *Each into the hand of his shepherd.* *Shepherd* (RSV) represents a small emendation in the Hebrew, which reads 'neighbour'. NEB rejects the emendation and reads, *I will put every man in the power of his neighbour and his king*, which avoids tautology, if 'shepherd' stands for king. *They shall crush the earth*; Heb. *hā'āreṣ* can also mean 'the land', and therefore it is not certain that there is a reference to all nations here.

7. The second paragraph opens with the prophet obediently taking up his role as shepherd *for those who trafficked in the sheep*, not as in the older versions, *the poor of the flock*. The Greek took the Hebrew consonants to mean 'traders', literally 'Canaanites', but the word probably meant originally a class of merchants, rather than a race of people.[1] This reading has found general acceptance. The *two staffs* indicate the principle of the shepherd's leadership. *Grace* (Heb. *nō'am*), or perhaps better 'graciousness', 'beauty', 'favour', is a characteristic of God (*e.g.* Ps. 27:4; 90:17); *Union* is the intended outcome of gracious leadership. The idea of two staffs is reminiscent of

[1] *IDB*, I, p. 494, 'Canaanites'.

Ezekiel's two sticks, which he joined together to represent the coming reunion of the northern and southern kingdoms (Ezk. 37:15–23).

8. *In one month I destroyed the three shepherds.* These words are probably the most enigmatic in the whole Old Testament. The shepherds have been identified in at least forty different ways,[1] ranging over all the known leaders of Israel from Moses, Aaron and Miriam to the Pharisees, Sadducees and Essenes of the Roman period. *I destroyed* may be a little strong for a verb which can mean 'deposed'. *One month* is interpreted freely by most commentators to mean (*a*) a short time, (*b*) thirty years, each day representing a year, or (*c*) an extended period, so adding greatly to the possible number of identifications. Emphasis on *the* three shepherds, which is true to the Hebrew, encourages speculation as to who these leaders were.

Those who consider the passage to be pre-exilic tend to favour the last three kings of Judah, Jehoiakim, Jehoiachin, Zedekiah.[2] The Seleucid period was the choice of the majority of scholars from about 1870 onwards, and this view still has its advocates. The tables below include the kings and high priests of the time, whose names appear in the various theories.

THE SELEUCID PERIOD IN JUDEA 198–140 BC

Kings in Antioch

Antiochus III (the Great)	223–187 BC
Seleucus IV (Philopator)	187–175 BC
Heliodorus, murderer of Seleucus, deposed	175 BC
Demetrius, son of Seleucus, hostage in Rome	175 BC
Antiochus IV (Epiphanes)	175–163 BC
Antiochus V (Eupator)	163–162 BC
Demetrius I	162–150 BC
Alexander Ballas	152–145 BC[3]
Demetrius II (Nicator)	147–139 BC[3]

[1] See, *e.g.*, H. G. Mitchell, *ICC*, p. 306. Since there are so many different views reference in footnotes will be confined to works written this century and available in English, the only exception being the commentary by C. H. H. Wright, which was written in 1879.

[2] *E.g.* W. E. Barnes, *CB* (1917 edition), p. 86.

[3] The overlap in dates is correct, and represents the period of hostility between the two rulers.

The three Seleucid kings most popularly thought to be the three shepherds who were deposed are Seleucus IV, Heliodorus, Demetrius, because all these disappeared from power within a year.[1] A second possibility, considered by H. G. Mitchell to be slightly less likely, is Antiochus III, Seleucus IV and Heliodorus. Some favour Antiochus IV, Antiochus V and Demetrius.[2]

The 'shepherds' could equally well be high priests, who were the local rulers in Jerusalem during the second century BC.

High Priests in Jerusalem

Onias III (lawful Zadokite)	*c.* 198–174 BC
Jason (Zadokite but ousted his brother Onias. Appointed by Seleucids)	174–171 BC
Menelaus (non-Zadokite; used bribes)	171–161 BC
Lysimachus (his brother and deputy, killed in a riot)	briefly in 161 BC
Alcimus (Aaronite, appointed by Seleucids)	161–159 BC
Interregnum	159–152 BC
Jonathan the Hasmonean	152–143 BC
Simon the Hasmonean	143–140 BC

One interpretation is that the good shepherd is Onias III (*cf.* 2 Macc. 4:1ff.), and the three who were removed would be those who obtained office through bribery, Jason, Menelaus and Alcimus.[3] Another view is that the three shepherds are Jason, Menelaus and Lysimachus. M. Trèves[4] has recently supported a Maccabean date and contended that Judas Maccabaeus is the good shepherd, who, when he liberated Jerusalem, may be assumed to have deposed apostate priests,

---

[1] H. G. Mitchell (*ICC*, p. 307) thinks this to be the most likely identification.

[2] *E.g.* C. H. H. Wright, *Zechariah and his Prophecies* (Hodder and Stoughton, 1879), p. 313.

[3] So W. O. E. Oesterley, *A History of Israel*, II (Oxford, 1932), pp. 258f. R. H. Kennett ('Zechariah', *PCB*, 1919 edn., p. 581) identifies the good shepherd with Onias III, but explains how the three shepherds may be shown to be the sons of Tobias, referred to by Josephus (*Wars,* I. i).

[4] 'Conjectures Concerning the Date and Authorship of Zechariah IX–XIV', *VT*, XIII, 1963 pp. 196–207.

and some officials loyal to the Greeks (1 Macc. 4:42; *cf.* 7:24). He thinks it plausible that the worthless shepherd should be identified with Alcimus. Judas was the leader of loyal Jews, and might well be thought to qualify for the role of good shepherd.

Confidence in a second-century date for this passage has not, however, been maintained. There is a lack of any decisive evidence, as the multiplicity of identification proves, and in the light of recent studies caution has been recommended in classifying biblical literature as Maccabean.[1] It is possible that the verse is a gloss inserted into the text, perhaps in the Maccabean period, to give the prophecy contemporary relevance,[2] but that is only a guess. The fact that we know practically nothing about the history of the Jews between the years 350 and 200 BC leaves open the possibility that the 'shepherds' referred to lived during this period.[3] Other commentators are more cautious and admit the impossibility of recognizing the historical situation.[4]

In the face of such a diversity of opinions certainty about the identity of the three shepherds is impossible, and, since no one suggestion has proved convincing, further speculation over possible candidates is likely to be unprofitable. There is, however, one further consideration. Apocalyptic uses numbers symbolically. Is the number three used in that way here (*cf.* Dn. 7:8,24) to signify completion? If so, the good shepherd would be removing from power all the unworthy leaders who frustrated his work.

I became impatient with them. In the allegory the shepherd came to the end of his endurance; much the same reaction is attributed to the Lord by Isaiah (1:13f.). *They also detested me.* The people as a whole did not appreciate the best of shepherds. The Hebrew verb, which occurs only here in the Old Testa-

---

[1] P. R. Ackroyd, 'Criteria for the Maccabean dating of the Old Testament Literature', *VT*, III, 1953, pp. 113–132.

[2] So R. C. Dentan, *IB*, VI, p. 1104. H. G. Mitchell also regards this verse as a gloss (p. 306), and thinks that in the original context the 'shepherd' represented Ptolemy III (247–221 BC), and the worthless shepherd Ptolemy IV (221–203 BC).

[3] R. C. Dentan (*IB*, VI, p. 1102) writes: 'It is tempting to follow many commentators in referring the allegory to the time of the Maccabean wars, but it is hardly likely that the passage can be so late in date. It is more probable that the situation is that of the Ptolemaic perod.'

[4] *E.g.* P. R. Ackroyd, *PCB²*, p. 653.

ment, expresses loathing. Darkness resented and loathed the light.[1]

9. By withholding his leadership the shepherd abandoned the people to the consequences of their rejection of him: death, and mutual destruction. He simply let things take their course.

10. The breaking of the staff 'Graciousness' symbolized the end of a gracious rule. This king, in company with all the best of Judah's kings, had entered into covenant with the people, so accepting responsibilities towards them (*cf*. Dt. 17:14–20; 2 Sa. 5:3; 2 Ki. 11:17). *With all the peoples* evidently applies to the Jewish colonies scattered among the nations, as in 1 Kings 22:28; Joel 2:6, though more usually gentile nations are meant.

11. As in verse 7, *the traffickers in the sheep* follows the Greek version (Heb. 'the poor of the flock'). The merchants, keenly interested, took in what was going on, and *knew that it was the word of the Lord*. What the prophet had done at the Lord's command was just what the merchants wanted to be done. They wanted to be rid of the shepherd. Once again God's providence seemed to be favouring them (*cf*. verse 5).

12. In the allegory the shepherd was responsible to the merchants, who in turn paid him wages, but having renounced his task the shepherd could no longer demand as of right his final payment. *And they weighed out*. Stamped coinage of guaranteed value was not in general use, or it would not have been necessary to weigh the money (see commentary on Hg. 1:6). Since coins were common during the Greek period in Palestine, this is circumstantial evidence for a date during the Persian era. *Thirty shekels of silver*. This was no mean sum. Persian governors before Nehemiah had exacted forty shekels in tax (presumably *per annum*), and the amount is quoted as burdensome (Ne. 5:15). The fact that in the Mosaic law (Ex. 21:32) thirty shekels was demanded in compensation for the death of a slave indicates the high value set on human life.[2]

---

[1] Commentators who identify the good shepherd with a historical king or high priest take this verse to indicate a change of policy on his part. He would be guilty of neglect and be rightly loathed and rejected by the people.

[2] The Law of Hammurabi distinguished the status of the dead man and compensated accordingly. If an ox gored to death a member of the aristocracy the owner was to pay a half-mina of silver, but if a slave the payment was one-third of a mina. A mina was probably fifty shekels. *DOTT*, p. 35; *ANET*, p. 175.

Presumably the merchants could offer no less. Matthew clearly referred to this incident by using the word 'weighed' (Mt. 26:15), though RSV obscures the allusion by translating 'paid'.

13. *Cast it into the treasury* (AV, RV, following the Hebrew, *unto the potter*). The two words have a similar sound in Hebrew, 'treasury' is *'ôṣār*, 'potter' is *yôṣēr*, and both meanings feature in Matthew 27:6–9. The Temple treasury stored not only the tithes and precious things dedicated to the Lord (Jos. 6:24; Ezr. 2:69; Ne. 7:70), but also served as a 'bank' for the private individual (2 Macc. 3:10ff.). Potters were connected with the Temple because the sacrificial ritual needed a continual supply of new vessels (Lv. 6:28). A guild of potters may have been minor officials at the Temple. Certainly Jeremiah seems to have been able to point to the potter at work as he preached (Je. 18:6), and to buy an earthenware bottle close to the Temple (19:1). Both readings can therefore be meaningful, but neither captures the irony which the context demands, with its reference to *the lordly price at which I was paid off by them.*

The versions have a variety of meanings. The reading 'treasury' comes from the Syriac, but this seems to be the result of a scribe's ingenuity, accommodating the reading to what he took to be the sense.[1] Jerome's Latin version suggests 'sculptor', but this would be a rare use of the Hebrew word. The Greek understands 'founder', a meaning explored by C. C. Torrey,[2] and adopted by K. Elliger.[3] M. Delcor links the verse with Judges 17:4, where two hundred shekels of silver were made into a molten image. By comparison thirty shekels would make only a figurine, and in this detail, he thinks, lies the irony. If they will not have the Lord's shepherd to rule them the only alternative is to have a little god made from the silver pieces (*cf.* Ezk. 16:17; Ho. 2:8). The explanation rings true and makes good sense of an otherwise difficult text. Since *yôṣēr* means 'shaper' it applies equally well to a worker in metal as to a potter. It is true still that, unless a man is allowing God the direction of his affairs, he will depend on financial expediency to guide him.

[1] So M. Delcor, 'Deux Passages Difficiles: Zacharie 12:11 et 11:13', *VT*, III, 1953, p. 74. 'En outre, *'ôṣār* paraît bien être une leçon facilitante.'
[2] 'The Foundry of the Second Temple', *JBL*, LV, 1936, p. 256.
[3] *ATD*, p. 160.

In the house of the Lord. If there was a foundry in the Temple C. C. Torrey assumed that it would be for the purpose of melting down gifts of gold and silver with a view to storing the metal in earthenware jars, as the Persians did.[1]

14. Another inevitable outcome of rejecting the Lord's shepherd was disunity, hence the breaking of the second staff. It should be mentioned that K. Elliger[2] sees in this act a reference to the Samaritan schism, so called because about 325 BC the Samaritans, who inhabited the territory of the old northern kingdom, broke away from the Jerusalem community, and established their own rival temple on Mount Gerizim. Some two hundred of their descendants still live on the slopes of that mountain. K. Elliger's theory is, however, highly conjectural.

15. In the third part of the allegory the prophet is told by the Lord to impersonate a worthless shepherd, that is, one who is morally corrupt and indifferent to God's claims. We are not intended to attempt to identify this person. 'This time the Shepherd role does not refer to Yahweh, but points to the moral that, if Yahweh is not received as a Shepherd, then another will be, and that other will be a shepherd of doom.'[3]

16. The failings of this shepherd are expressed in pastoral imagery and recall Ezekiel 34:3,4. Negatively he lacks concern. NEB has an expressive translation here: he will *neither miss any that are lost nor search for those that have gone astray*. The second clause differs widely from AV *neither shall seek the young one*. Hebrew manuscripts have four different readings, but 'strayed' is attested by the versions and is now generally accepted. This shepherd will fail to fulfil his obvious duties by neglecting the sick and injured. He will be taken up with his 'perks', the choicest meat, and he will *throw away their broken bones* (NEB). This last clause is an attractive interpretation of *tearing off even their hoofs*, which is a more literal rendering.

17. A short poem concludes the section, and brings to an

---

[1] Herodotus III. 96.
[2] *ATD*, p. 163. The editors of JB accept this interpretation. See marginal note (m), p. 1541.
[3] S. B. Frost, *Old Testament Apocalyptic* (Epworth, 1952), p. 132.

end the first half of the second part of the book.[1] *Woe to . . .*, or better, *trouble is coming to the worthless shepherd* (JB), both predicts and at the same time effectively pronounces judgment on the incompetent shepherd who neglects his flock. Rhythm and assonance in the original intensify the message. With arm and right eye out of action the leader will be powerless to fight, or even to take aim, against his enemies.

In spite of the textual difficulties and the impossibility of anchoring the incident historically, the message of this chapter is plain. Responsibility for human chaos lies squarely on human shoulders. God has offered men His shepherd, but they have rejected Him, to their own irreparable loss. The cost of this rejection to the shepherd is depicted later (13:7). Behind Jesus' designation of Himself as the good shepherd (Jn. 10:11–18) lies this deep prophetic understanding both of human nature and of history.

II. FINAL INTERVENTION OF THE LORD AND SUFFERING INVOLVED (12:1 – 14:21)

A glance at the analysis (pp. 85f.) will show that the themes dealt with in chapters 9–11 recur in chapters 12–14, but with increasing intensity as they progress towards 'that day'. The expression 'on that day' is repeated sixteen times by way of reminder in the three chapters. Finally in chapter 14 the events of 'that day' are graphically described in picture language, typical of apocalyptic, and they lead up to the establishment of God's universal kingdom, when all the nations will worship Him.

c². Jubilation in Jerusalem (12:1–9)

The war and victory theme with which the prophet begins is localized in Jerusalem, for the scattered exiles have now returned. The city is besieged by all nations, and therefore its population is hopelessly outnumbered. Even Judah has

---

[1] H. G. A. Ewald's suggestion that 13:7–9 should follow 11:17 (see Introduction, p. 66) has not been adopted, despite its wide acceptance and the fact that NEB has even rearranged the text accordingly. Not only is there no textual justification for moving the poetry from chapter 13, but, as the analysis (p. 86) shows, the prophet placed it where he did with good reason. Moreover, as D. R. Jones argues cogently (*VT*, XII, 1962, p. 251), 13:7–9 'belongs inextricably and demonstrably to its context'.

deserted the capital in its unequal struggle, unequal that is until the Lord intervenes. The reversal of the enemy is so decisive that everyone acknowledges God's defence of the city, and knows it will be victorious. The universal scope, God's intervention miraculously to save Jerusalem, and the sense of finality are characteristics of apocalyptic; interpretation must be in keeping with the *genre*.

Though all the translations rightly adopt a prose form, what we have in this chapter is poetic prose. P. Lamarche distinguishes little logical and literary unities, which he calls strophes.[1] These he finds arrange themselves in pairs, verses 2,3; 4+5,6; 7,8. Verse 1 forms the introduction, and verse 9 the conclusion.

1. A note on the heading was included in the comment on 9:1. See also Additional Note, p. 162. *Concerning Israel* is unexpected in view of the concentration of interest on Judah and Jerusalem, but there is no difficulty if 'Israel' is taken to refer to the whole people, and not merely to the northern kingdom as it is in 11:14. The conflict between Israel and Judah does not feature in chapters 12–14. *The Lord, who stretched out the heavens. . . .* This reference to the mighty Creator of the universe as well as of the earth and of man, reminiscent of Isaiah 42:5, is a fitting introduction to these chapters, which look towards the consummation of all things in the Lord, the King (14:17).

2,3. The parallel phrases in these two verses show that they belong together: 'Jerusalem a cup of reeling' corresponds to 'Jerusalem a heavy stone'; the words 'all the peoples' are repeated; the siege idea is repeated. For some reason all the nations desire to capture Jerusalem,[2] as in 14:2, but they have taken on more than they bargained for. *Jerusalem a cup of reeling.* The 'cup' symbolized the life experience which God purposed for man. This might be a 'cup of salvation' (Ps. 116:13), a cup overflowing with blessing (Ps. 23:5), but more often, in view of man's perverse unbelief, it had to be a cup of the Lord's wrath. This Jerusalem had had to drink to the

---

[1] Lamarche. p. 74. R. C. Dentan (*IB*, VI, p. 1106) describes verses 2ff. as 'a brief hymn in liturgical style'.

[2] The prophet assumes that Jerusalem is the centre of the earth (Ezk. 5:5; 38:12). See S. Terrien, 'The Omphalos Myth and Hebrew Religion', *VT*, XX, 1970, pp. 315–338.

dregs (Is. 51:17; *cf.* Je. 25:17,28), but now it has been removed (Is. 51:22), and the turn of the nations has come to drink it. Their intoxication will reduce them to helplessness. NEB takes the word *saþ*, 'cup', in its other sense of 'threshold', hence the very different reading.

It will be against Judah also. The Hebrew does not make easy sense in the second half of verse 2, and the ancient versions give no help. JB omits, but the sense is probably captured by NEB, *Judah will be caught up in the siege of Jerusalem.* Judah was opposing Jerusalem, either by choice or by the compulsion of the enemy's superior strength.

Jerusalem a heavy stone. The picture is of a team of porters, working together to lift a rock. In spite of their manpower (all the nations) they injure themselves in the process, and so are forced to give up the attempt.

4,5. Again the picture changes. Now there is a cavalry charge against the city, which seems to be paralysed and helpless. Whereas in the previous couplet the nations suffered as it were the consequences of their own decision, in this verse the Lord actively intervenes. Again there is repetition, 'I will strike every horse'; *with panic*, as happened in Barak's battle against Sisera (Jdg. 5:22), *and its rider with madness*. Madness was linked with blindness in the catalogue of disasters which would follow apostasy (Dt. 28:28). *Upon the house of Judah I will open my eyes.* Again for the fourth time there is reference to the 'eyes of the Lord' (3:9; 4:10; 9:8), and they plan to spare and save in a day of judgment. The fact that God has intervened on Jerusalem's behalf causes Judah to throw in her lot on His side.

6. Again the agent is the Lord, *I will make the clans of Judah like a blazing pot in the midst of wood....* The very fact that Judah is among the enemy is turned to advantage. As instantaneously as fire ignites dry tinder and ripe sheaves, so will Judah inflict devastation on the enemy while Jerusalem watches.

7,8. Rivalry between the house of David in Jerusalem and the rest of Judah is to be resolved by God's promise of victory to Judah first. Each needs the other and neither is to lord it over the other. The Lord's *shield* over Jerusalem's inhabitants will protect them, and His might will give to the weakling the calibre of David. Hopes are still centred on the *house of David*, which shall be *like God*, a bold assertion, modified in the next phrase, *like the angel of the Lord*. Suppliants had addressed David saying he was 'like the angel of God' (1 Sa. 29:9; 2 Sa. 14:17,20; 19:27). This was an honorific, consciously exaggerated. The fulfilment in Jesus proved to be an understatement.

9. The concluding verse sums up in unambiguous words the main point of the passage: *the Lord will seek to destroy all the nations that come against Jerusalem*. The fact of a world conflict is assumed and final victory for Jerusalem, whether literal or figurative, is assured.

b². Mourning for the pierced one (12:10 – 13:1)

There is a striking contrast between this section and what has gone before. The elation of victory is now tempered by mourning. The house of David and the inhabitants of Jerusalem, who had just been given a reassuring word of the Lord, are not to presume. They need a new spirit (12:10) and a new cleansing (13:1), that are somehow connected with profound mourning for a man put to death in the city.

10. *A spirit of compassion and supplication*. The source of this new attitude of heart is the Lord, *I will pour out*. Compassion (Heb. *ḥēn*) is literally 'grace', but in this context the particular grace demonstrated is repentance for a murder committed, and so the free rendering is justified. NEB has *a spirit of pity and compassion*, so keeping the free translation of *ḥēn*; 'compassion' is from the Greek *oiktirmou*, but the Hebrew *taḥᵃnûnîm* means 'seeking for grace', hence 'supplication'. *When they look on him whom they have pierced*. The early translators evidently found this verse an embarrassment, for their versions show marked variations on the Hebrew.

Pierced in the Greek becomes 'treated despitefully', 'insulted', and in Aramaic 'spurned'. *On him* is the reading in some Hebrew MSS, but they are not the most reliable. Greek, Syriac Aramaic and Latin follow the better Hebrew MSS and read *to me* (*cf.* AV *upon me*, RV *unto me*). Evidently some early copyist(s) felt that the prophet could not have intended to put into the mouth of the Lord the apparent contradiction that He had been put to death, and therefore changed the pronoun. The more difficult reading is likely to have been the original, and should be retained. NEB keeps both pronouns and reads, *They*

shall look on me, on him whom they have pierced. This involves slight
alterations to Hebrew consonants and vowels, the only support
for which is a late Greek version (Theodotion, second century
AD), which may have been influenced by John 19:37. John's
use of the verse cannot be taken as evidence because the New
Testament writers used the Old Testament text very freely
(*cf.* the comment on Zc. 9:9 as used by the Gospel writers);
he may not have been intending to do more than give the
general sense.

If we accept that the original probably read 'on me', what
is implied? Three typical interpretations will show how widely
commentators differ. Many think that the prophet had in mind
some historical individual such as Onias III, assassinated in
170 BC, or Simon the Maccabee, assassinated in 134 BC;[1] but
no known historical individual quite satisfies, even if it were
feasible to date the passage so late. A contrasting view is that
of A. E. Kirkpatrick: 'It is Jehovah who has been thrust
through in the person of His representative.'[2] But how can
two distinct people die in the death of only one? Kirkpatrick
himself admits that 'the passage is an unsolved enigma'.
J. Calvin took the death as metaphorical: 'Now God speaks . . .
after the manner of men, declaring that He is wounded by the
sins of His people, and especially by their obstinate contempt
of His word, in the same manner as a mortal man receives a
deadly wound, when his heart is pierced.'[3]

Before giving further suggestions it is advisable to consider
the total context. The remainder of the chapter concentrates
on the mourning that follows the death of the pierced one,
mourning as bitter as for *an only child.* In Genesis 22:2; Jeremiah
6:26; Amos 8:10 the Greek translates the adjective 'only' as
'beloved' (*agapētos*), whether the reference is to an individual
(Isaac) or to the whole people, as in the Jeremiah and Amos
references. Similarly the *first-born* was the specially precious
son in every Jewish family. As early as the Exodus period
Israel was described as the Lord's first-born (Ex. 4:22). There
is therefore some ground for the collective interpretation of the
pierced one in D. R. Jones' translation: 'And they shall look
unto me (Yahweh) touching (those) whom they (the nations)

---

[1] So W. O. E. Oesterley, *A History of Israel*, II, p. 269.
[2] A. F. Kirkpatrick, *The Doctrine of the Prophets* (Macmillan, 1906), p. 472.
[3] J. Calvin, *Commentary on the Gospel According to John*, II (Calvin Translation Society, 1847), p. 242.

have slain' or 'killed in war.'[1] He thinks the reference is to the martyrs of Judah, whose death in the final battle is the price of Jerusalem's salvation. He also draws attention to the closely related theme in Isaiah 52:13 – 53:12[2] where he interprets the Servant also as a 'collective' noun. While it is just possible to see the vicarious suffering of individuals within the nation as redemptive, what connection is there between the death of these martyrs and the cleansing from sin that followed the mourning (13:1)? The interpretation is not convincing.

11. A puzzling simile follows: mourning *as great as the mourning for Hadad-rimmon in the plain of Megiddo.* RSV implies that Hadad-rimmon was a person, whereas AV, RV imply that it is a place name. The latter is the older interpretation, going back to Jerome, who identified it with a place he knew as Rummané, not far from Jezreel. Since he lived in Bethlehem for many years he may have had sound evidence for this identification, but other places have since been preferred. Rimmon is a place name in the Old Testament (Jos. 15:32; 19:7; Zc. 14:10) but also the name of a god (2 Ki. 5:18). Many modern commentators have abandoned the old interpretation in favour of a liturgical and mythological interpretation. Hadad-rimmon has been taken as another name for the Babylonian god Tammuz,[3] or as a fertility deity similar to Tammuz, with annual rites like the weeping for Tammuz denounced by Ezekiel (Ezk. 8:14).[4]

The Ras Shamra tablets have shed light on Canaanite religious practices, and possibly on this verse, as H. H. Rowley believed.[5] Hadad is the ancient Semitic storm god (*cf.* Hadadezer, meaning 'Hadad is my help', in 2 Sa. 8:3, *et al.*). In the ancient Canaanite myth Hadad, father of Aleyin, bewailed his son's death at the hand of Mot (whose name is connected with the Hebrew word for 'death'). Later the murder was avenged and both Aleyin and Mot were brought to life again. If this was the basis of a ritual enacted annually

[1] D. R. Jones, *TBC*, p. 161. He interprets the Hebrew sign of the accusative in the sense of 'concerning' (BDB, p. 85).
[2] Pointed out also by H. G. Mitchell, *ICC*, p. 331.
[3] The view of W. O. E. Oesterley and T. H. Robinson, *Introduction to the Old Testament* (SPCK, 1934), p. 424.
[4] Put forward by J. Pedersen, *Israel*, II (Oxford University Press, 1940), p. 475, and by F. F. Bruce, *This is That* (Paternoster Press, 1968), p. 111.
[5] H. H. Rowley, *The Re-discovery of the Old Testament* (James Clarke, 1945), p. 49. See also *DOTT*, p. 133.

it may have influenced popular ideas in Israel, and have provided a standard of comparison for the repentance of which the prophet speaks.

It is possible that some such ancient custom survived into the post-exilic period, combined with the commemoration of some historical event significant for Israel, such as the death of Josiah, as the mention of Megiddo suggests (2 Ki. 23:29). The English Christmas arose out of just such a synthesis of pagan and Christian festivals. We know that lamentation for Josiah was still an annual event when the books of Chronicles were edited (2 Ch. 35:25). Maybe the Jews conjectured that if the godly Josiah had not been killed the exile might have been averted.

Early difficulty over the verse is evident from the Aramaic, a translation of which is given by T. Jansma, 'like the mourning for Ahab the son of Omri whom Hadadrimmon the son of Thabrimmon killed and like the mourning for Josiah the son of Amon whom Pharaoh Hagira (the Lame) killed'.[1] This third interpretation of Hadadrimmon makes him a historical individual, responsible for the death of Ahab, and not otherwise known to us (1 Ki. 22:34), but the explanation is unsatisfactory because the mourning should be for Hadadrimmon and not for Ahaz. M. Delcor, who finds repugnant the idea that mourning for a pagan deity should be put on a level with mourning before the Lord, extracts from the Aramaic the word 'Amon', the consonants of which he thinks were confused with those of Rimmon. The resulting translation makes good sense: 'the mourning of that day will be like the mourning for the son of Amon (*i.e.* Josiah) in the plain of Megiddo.'[2] Yet, based as it is on an emendation of one version, the interpretation must be reckoned highly conjectural.

The names of the mourners in verses 12–14 draw attention again to David (*cf.* verse 10; 13:1), who lamented deeply the deaths of Saul and Jonathan and of Absalom (2 Sa. 1:19–27; 18:33). F. F. Bruce, noting the references to David, thinks the wording of the oracle 'could conceivably be drawn from the national liturgy, and more particularly from the part played in that liturgy by the king'.[3] Furthermore, P. R. Ackroyd asks

---

[1] T. Jansma, p. 118. (The English word order has been corrected.)
[2] M. Delcor, 'Deux passages difficiles: Zacharie 12:11 et 11:13', *VT*, III, 1953, pp. 67–73.
[3] F. F. Bruce, *This is That*, p. 112.

whether there was not perhaps at some time a cult of Absalom to which some features of this oracle may ultimately be attributed. This he connects with the excessive mourning of David for Absalom.[1] Evidence for such liturgies has yet to be discovered.

After such a confusion of viewpoints how are verses 10 and 11 to be interpreted? The murder has occurred in Jerusalem of a man, who is in some way identified with the Lord, and the inhabitants of the city have been responsible for his death. After the event they have been conscience-stricken, and in their deep grief have found within themselves the gift of a new spirit of repentance and supplication for forgiveness, which is closely followed by the promise of cleansing from a newly opened fountain (13:1; *cf.* Ezk. 36:25,26). Though the word for 'pierced' in Isaiah 53:5 is a different one from that in verse 10 here, Lamarche is surely right in finding significant the fact that both writers express the same idea: with the piercing and death of the messenger of the Lord is connected the forgiveness of sins. Zechariah, however, does not identify his pierced one with either the Servant or the king.

12-14. Though the prophet says *the land shall mourn*, his concern is with Jerusalem, and more particularly with the royal line, as David's mourning had been. When the royal family mourns all the citizens mourn with them. David had a son *Nathan* (2 Sa. 5:14; *cf.* Lk. 3:31), and Levi a son *Shimei* (Nu. 3:18). The royal and priestly families are singled out for their involvement in the crime; perhaps their ambition and jealousy had prompted it. The effect of the repetition, *every family by itself and their wives by themselves*,[2] is to lay stress on the genuineness of the repentance. None is merely being influenced by the tears of others, nor acting hypocritically, as the professional mourners did. True repentance remains a gift of God's Spirit (verse 10).

13:1. Whatever had been the motivation behind the crime, an aspect not touched on in the text, it had been deliberate and premeditated. All the more remarkable then that *there shall be a fountain opened . . . to cleanse them*. This was a cleansing

---

[1] P. R. Ackroyd, 'Criteria for the Maccabean Dating of the Old Testament Literature', *VT*, III, 1953, p. 130, footnote 4.
[2] The Mishna taught the separation of men and women in mourning: Sukkoth 51b, 52a.

unknown in the pre-Christian era, though it was promised by Ezekiel (Ezk. 36:25), and illustrated by Zechariah in the removal of Joshua's filthy robes (Zc. 3:4,9). This fountain was to cleanse even from the murder perpetrated on the Lord's representative; indeed the crime would be connected with the possibility of cleansing, as this little section teaches (*cf.* 'on that day . . . mourning', 12:11, with 'on that day . . . a fountain', 13:1).

Sin (Heb. *ḥaṭṭa'ṭ*) is the general term for human misconduct, while *uncleanness* (Heb. *niddâ*) covers ritual and sexual impurity; the latter is a favourite word with Ezekiel (*e.g.* Ezk. 36:17,25), who, in company with other prophets, included idolatry under the figure of adultery. For this reason the word may have prompted the prophet's next theme (verses 2–6). If Ezekiel's 'sprinkling with water' suggested the fountain for cleansing, Ezekiel's river (Ezk. 47), flowing out of the sanctuary and bringing healing, was to be referred to also (Zc. 14:8), to symbolize the wonder of forgiveness, cleansing, restoration, for a guilt-ridden world.

d¹. Rejection of sham leaders (13:2–6)

No-one in Israel escaped the Lord's condemnation through the prophets, not even the prophets themselves. Both Jeremiah and Ezekiel had the task of accusing fellow prophets of being rotten to the core (Je. 23:9ff.; Ezk. 13). Antagonism towards those who brought the unwelcome message was to be expected, but the word carried its own authority, which was to be established without question once Jerusalem fell. There continued to be counterfeit prophets after the exile; in fact the word 'prophet' is used in this chapter only in a derogatory sense. The message is that the day is coming when those who posed as prophets will so fear exposure that they will deny ever having made such a claim. To speak 'in the name of the Father and of the Son and of the Holy Ghost' words that encourage evil is the ultimate blasphemy.

2. The previous section dealing with sham leaders (10:2–3a) had announced the Lord's active opposition to them. Now they are to be unmasked and removed for ever. An important first step in God's self-disclosure is the unmasking of evil. *I will cut off the names of idols* means that men will no longer ascribe supernatural powers to mere things, nor worship them as divine. The 'name' implied existence and personality, attributed to idols by their devotees, much as a child invests a puppet with personality, whereas they were only 'shapes' formed by men's hands. Here was the basic illusion which lay behind the sham leadership. The 'power game' still has its names and its precious gods. *The prophets and the unclean spirit.* Any inspiration these prophets claimed encouraged unhealthy influences in the land that were clearly not of God's spirit. 'Thus you will know them by their fruits' (Mt. 7:20). The expression 'unclean spirit', so familiar from the Gospels, comes only here in the Old Testament.

3. The persistence of false prophecy to his own time leads Zechariah to envisage its possible recurrence, even after the Lord has dealt with it. The safeguard is that public opinion will not tolerate such a prophet. His own family will condemn him to death for blasphemy in accordance with Deuteronomy 13, though whereas stoning is the manner of death laid down in that chapter, here the parents are to 'pierce him through'. The verb is the same as in 12:10, a fact that alerts the reader to question whether the 'witch hunt' has overstepped the mark, and wiped out the true with the false.

4. The reaction of the professional prophet is predictable. In the face of unpopularity he disclaims any association with the prophetic movement. The *hairy mantle*, characteristic garb of Elijah (2 Ki. 1:8), and used to identify the prophets, he discards as an embarrassment.

5. Far from earning his living by prophecy, he says he has worked on the land from boyhood. While the general sense is plain the exact meaning of the Hebrew is not, as the variety of translations indicates: *man taught me to keep cattle* (AV), *I have been made a bondman* (RV), *the land has been my possession* (RSV). The last is an emendation that has been widely accepted, and appears in JB as 'the land has been my living'.

6. *What are these wounds on your back?* The literal translation would be 'between your hands', that is, on the body, whether on the chest or back (*cf.* 2 Ki. 9:24); 'hands' could stand for 'arms'.[1] As the farm hand is stripped for work his body reveals

[1] The expression occurs in *ANET*, p. 131, 'Ugaritic Myths and Legends', 2 III AB A: 'Strike the back of Prince Yamm, between the arms of Judge Nahar.'

scars which are taken to be the self-inflicted wounds of an ecstatic prophet (1 Ki. 18:28), but he explains them as the result of a brawl *in the house of my friends*. It is an unlikely story, not without its irony, and with sinister implications. The friends could be 'lovers', that is, associates in idolatrous worship, which is a usual connotation of the word (*e.g.* Ho. 2:7, 10ff.; Ezk. 23:5,9). In accordance with verse 2, the man makes no mention of the names of idols.

b³. The shepherd slaughtered, the people scattered (13:7-9)

This startling poem resumes the shepherd motif from chapter 11, though in chapters 12 and 13 the subject of leadership has never been far from the prophet's thoughts. The Lord calls on the sword to strike the shepherd. The leaderless flock flounders and undergoes severe testing and loss, which result in deeper assurance of their identity as the Lord's people. S. B. Frost sees this 'complete and self-contained little gem' as the climax of chapters 12 and 13.[1]

With regard to the position of this poem in relation to 13:2-6, D. R. Jones believes that it belongs here and should not be transferred to follow 11:17. 'It is in fact linked to XIII 1-6 in the following way. What God in His law (Deut. XIII) requires of his people in their inflexible severity towards false prophets (overriding claims of kith and kin and affection), this He Himself will practise in His relationship to His own shepherd. One might say that in XIII 7-9, as compared with XIII 1-6, the Lord God practises His own precept!'[2]

7. *Awake, O sword, against my shepherd*. These words are quoted in the Zadokite Covenant Document of Damascus[3] as Zechariah's, in a context dealing with the time when God visits the earth to judge the wicked. *My shepherd* indicates that this is no ordinary leader, but the Lord's gift to His people. With different vowels (for Hebrew was originally written with only the consonants) the word *rōʿî* would mean 'companion', but the context shows that the meaning here is 'shepherd'; all the same there may be a play on words here in view of the parallel *the man who stands next to me*. The expression 'who

---

[1] S. B. Frost, *Old Testament Apocalyptic*, pp. 135f.
[2] D. R. Jones, *VT*, XII, p. 251.
[3] CD 19.5-9 (MS B), quoted by F. F. Bruce, *This is That*, p. 103.

stands next to me' is used elsewhere only in Leviticus (*e.g.* 6:2; 18:20) to mean 'near neighbour'; similarly the shepherd is one who dwells side by side with the Lord, His equal. It is all the more remarkable that the Lord commands the sword, *strike the shepherd*, though there is a parallel in Isaiah 53:10, 'Yet it was the will of the Lord to bruise him'. The *sheep* are the Lord's people, as in Ezekiel 34. As at the time of the exile they are to be leaderless and therefore *scattered*, and the Lord's hand is to be against *the little ones*. NEB translates as *the shepherd boys*. The idea is that the humble and helpless will suffer, as indeed the faithful friends of the Lord suffered at the crucifixion (Lk. 2:35), and there are indications elsewhere that the church will suffer severely, even to apparent extinction, before the final intervention of the Lord (Mk. 13:19,24; Rev. 11:3–10). Certain commentators interpret the last line differently, taking it as a gesture of protection for the helpless.[1]

8. In some terrible catastrophe two-thirds of the population of the land of Israel is to be killed (*cf.* Ezk. 5:2,12), but that is not the end of the suffering.

9. The Lord will put the remaining third *into the fire* (*cf.* 3:2, 'a brand plucked from the fire'; and Ezk. 5:4; Mal. 3:3), a traditional metaphor for removal of impurities (Pr. 17:3; Is. 1:22,25; Je. 6:29f.; Ezk. 22:20–22). *Silver* and *gold* in a molten state precipitate any alloy or impurity, and so the fire is used to obtain the purest metal. Thus the suffering has a constructive purpose. *They will call on my name.* As a result of all they have experienced they find their true identity in relationship with the Lord, for they call on Him, and He claims them as His own. The last four lines of the verse have an appropriate chiastic structure – *they, I, I, they* – reflecting that there are two sides to any relationship, even when it is between God and man.

Who is the shepherd? The prophet is not explicit. Had he wished he could have drawn together the Davidic theme with that of the shepherd, but he did not do so. Nor did he identify the shepherd with the Servant of Isaiah 53, though it is likely that he had that passage in mind. The very fact that the passage is to a degree enigmatic is an invitation to meditate on it, and there are indications that it influenced the thinking of Jesus more than any other shepherd passage in the Old Testament[2]

---

[1] Lamarche, p. 92.
[2] *Cf.* R. T. France, *Jesus and the Old Testament* (Tyndale Press, 1971), pp. 103f., 107ff.

(*cf.* Jn. 10, with its repeated emphasis on the shepherd laying down his life for the sheep, and on the scattering of the sheep).

c³. Cataclysm in Jerusalem (14:1–15)

The 'war and victory' theme now reaches its final phase. The chapter opens with a defeated Jerusalem, stripped of possessions and honour, submitting to all the indignities inflicted by the conqueror. Since the enemy is 'all the nations' this defeat of the holy city makes possible the setting up of one world government, a league of nations opposed to God. The conquerors revel in their spoils, but leave half the population in the city, taking only half into exile. Those who remain suffer even further, but eventually they see the intervention of the Lord. The human drama is nearing its end. Earthquake is inadequate to account for the geographical changes in and around Jerusalem, for the city will rise to dominate the whole land, while the surrounding hills will sink to become a plain (verse 10). The very alternation of day and night and the characteristics of the seasons will disappear. God Himself will reign as king in Jerusalem. All His enemies will yield up their riches before succumbing to plague, panic and death. Their conversion is not envisaged.

The dramatic reversal from defeat to victory is well expressed in the chiastic structure of this section. Verses 1–6 begin with Jerusalem crushed in defeat. 'The day of the Lord . . . is darkness, and not light' (Am. 5:18), but, though awesome events continue to overtake the city, there is progression towards one particular day, known to the Lord (verse 7). This is the turning-point. From that day Jerusalem becomes the source of light and life. There the Lord sets up His world government, and whereas at the beginning Jerusalem was being despoiled, at the end all the nations are financing God's kingdom. Whereas at the beginning God's people suffer, at the end His enemies suffer and die. Unity in the Lord is the only unity that endures. His kingship is very greatly stressed, hence the fall of those who oppose Him.

The text is again obscure in places, and RSV does not necessarily represent the most likely reading.

1. *Behold, a day of the Lord is coming.* The Hebrew is more accurately translated, 'A day is coming for the Lord', which is the more arresting for being unusual, and it lays the emphasis on the Lord, not on the 'is coming'. A threat rather than a promise is implied (*cf.* Joel 1:15). Just as the prophets had taught that the fall of Jerusalem in 587 BC was God's doing, so now the first stage in the events of 'that day' is the city's utter defeat (*cf.* Rev. 11:3,7–10). God's people never deserve His favour, though they readily assume they do. Judgment begins with them (Je. 25:29; Ezk. 9:6; 1 Pet. 4:17). The defeated watch helplessly while their belongings are shared out among the enemy troops. The use of the second person, *from you, in the midst of you*, makes unavoidable the personal application to Jerusalem.

2. Only after laying stress on Jerusalem's defeat does the prophet reveal the extent of the conflict. It was ludicrous that *all the nations* should fight against one city. The material gain would be negligible, and in any case the numbers involved would make it impossible. The only explanation is that this is an ideological conflict to remove a non-co-operative element that blocked the way to an international world order. Victory would easily be gained with overwhelmingly superior resources; plunder and rape follow, and then half the inhabitants are deported. In view of 13:8, if this is meant to have happened earlier, only one-sixth of the original population would by now remain.

3. *The Lord will . . . fight against those nations*. There is ambiguity in the preposition 'against' (Heb. *b^e*), for it is the usual word for 'in', and so it could convey that the Lord was among the enemy, fighting against Israel. On the other hand, in combination with the verb 'fight' it usually means 'against'. The same construction occurs in verse 14, where the sense suggests that Judah is fighting in Jerusalem and not against it. The early Christian Fathers, Cyril, Theodoret and Eusebius, interpreted the verse to mean that the Lord fights against Jerusalem, but the great majority of modern commentators think of Him as intervening on Israel's side, against the nations. The argument is not conclusive that the construction should be the same both in this verse and in verse 14. The sense is all-important. Surely the city would have been overcome by the armies of the world without the Lord's presence amongst them. It is more likely therefore that the usual modern interpretation is correct. The Lord intervenes on behalf of His people, *as when he fights on a day of battle*. The simile is a reminder that this is apocalyptic picture language. The supreme example of such a day of battle was the crossing of the Red Sea, when the helpless Israelites watched the Lord fight for them; it was as they stood still that they 'saw the salvation of the Lord' (Ex. 14:13,14). They did not need to fight, nor did the Lord literally wield weapons.

4. Apocalyptic features are now prominent. The Lord descends, not on Mount Zion, because it is occupied by the enemy, but on *the Mount of Olives*, first mentioned by this name here in the Bible.[1] Referred to by Ezekiel as 'the mountain which is on the east side of the city' (Ezk. 11:23), it is in fact a ridge, two and a half miles long, running north to south on the east side of Jerusalem, and separated from the city by the deep Kidron valley. As it is higher than the Temple mount it completely blocks any view to the east, and it was inconveniently steep as an escape-route from the city. The opening of *a very wide valley* through this ridge removed the barrier and at the same time provided dramatic evidence of the arrival of the Lord in power. Jesus probably had this verse in mind when He spoke of the removal of 'this mountain' (Mk. 11:23).[2] The ascension of Jesus on the Mount of Olives, and in particular the promise of the angel concerning His return (Acts 1:11), draw attention to the significance of this prophecy and suggest a literal fulfilment.

5. Understanding of this verse is complicated by ambiguities in the text. The traditional Massoretic way of reading the first verb gives the meaning 'you shall flee' (AV, RV), whereas the Aramaic and Greek took the same consonants to mean 'shall be stopped' (RSV, JB, NEB). To add to the difficulties the same verb is repeated twice later in the verse. The Massoretic Text takes it to mean 'you shall flee' each time; the Greek takes it to mean 'shall be stopped' each time, while the Aramaic has for the first verb 'shall be stopped' but for the other two 'you shall flee'. This last makes best sense and is adopted by the translators of RSV: *and the valley of my mountains shall be stopped up*.[3] 'My mountains' are probably Mount Zion and the Mount of Olives, in which case the valley which is stopped up is the

[1] In 2 Sa. 15:30 the Hebrew is 'Ascent of the olive trees'.
[2] W. Manson (*Jesus the Messiah* (Hodder and Stoughton, 1943), pp. 29, 30) points out that the incident took place in the vicinity of the Mount of Olives, and suggests that Jesus was reminded of Zechariah 14:4.
[3] For further detail see Jansma, p. 131.

Kidron; and the mountains formed by the new valley through the Mount of Olives *touch the side of it*, so blocking it. On the other hand those who prefer to read the first verb as 'you shall flee' take 'my mountains' to be the ones formed by the new valley. There have been various suggested emendations, such as that of J. Wellhausen, 'And the valley of Hinnom shall be stopped up,'[1] a reading adopted by R. C. Dentan[2] and by JB. The fact that the valley of Hinnom is to the south and west of the city makes this unlikely to be correct. H. G. Mitchell[3] argues that the verb 'stop up' is used almost always of springs (*e.g.* Gn. 26:15,18) and urges that the same is true in this verse. The spring would be Gihon, in the Kidron valley. Gihon and the Hebrew for 'valley of my mountains' begin in the same way, so causing a scribe to confuse the text. Other commentators have not followed H. G. Mitchell here. *The side of it* is itself an emendation, for the Hebrew reads *Azel* (AV, RV). If a proper noun is intended the place is not otherwise known. It would be somewhere to the east of Jerusalem, marking the eastern end of the valley.

It is impossible to be sure how the text read originally, but the general meaning is clear. The earth movements which open a valley eastwards will also block up the Kidron valley, so providing a level escape route from Jerusalem. *The earthquake in the days of Uzziah*, by which the book of Amos is dated (Am. 1:1), must have taken place about the middle of the eighth century BC. It had evidently been so terrible as to become legendary.[4] Amos himself established the use of earthquake imagery in eschatology (Am. 6:11; 8:8; 9:1–5).

Then the Lord your God will come. RSV has followed the Greek text in translating 'your God'. The Hebrew has 'my God'. Similarly in the second clause *with him* is taken from the versions, whereas the Hebrew has 'with thee'. There is much to be said for retaining the Hebrew, for though the RSV appears to make better sense, this in itself is a warning sign, because scribes would have tended to rationalize the text in this way. There are many examples in the prophets of unexpected changes from the third to the second person of the verb (*cf.*

[1] *Die kleinen Propheten Übersetzt und Erklärt* (ed. 3, 1898).
[2] R. C. Dentan, *IB*, p. 1111.
[3] *ICC*, p. 343.
[4] 'Serious earthquakes occur about once every fifty years in Palestine, though minor earth tremors are very much more frequent' (D. Baly, *The Geography of the Bible*, p. 22).

2:8). The prophet sees the events vividly as though they were happening before his eyes, and he turns his descriptions into a prayer for the fulfilment of the vision. When the Lord God comes with His *holy ones*, His heavenly attendants (Ps. 89:5,7), history will have reached its goal.

6. The meaning of this verse is uncertain. The Hebrew begins, 'In that day there will not be light'. The last two words may mean 'the splendid ones (stars) congeal', that is, lose their brightness. RSV, JB, NEB, all adapt one or other of the early versions and convey that all extremes of temperature will cease. Whatever the true reading should be, cosmic changes are implied.

7. Time will no longer be measured in days, for night will never fall. 'That day' will be one continuous day (Is. 60:19,20; Rev. 21:25; 22:5), and so its light will not be dependent on sun, moon or stars. There is no contradiction between this verse and the Hebrew of verse 6 if the 'light' there is interpreted as sunlight.

8. The dream of an abundant water supply in Jerusalem will become fact. Instead of the spring Gihon, which supplied water that 'flowed gently' to become the Siloam brook (Is. 8:6), and was never really adequate for the city's needs, rivers independent of seasonal rainfall would rise in Jerusalem, to flow constantly to east and west until they reached the Dead Sea and the Mediterranean. Ezekiel's river flowed from the sanctuary in an easterly direction only (Ezk. 47:1-12). Ezekiel made much of the resulting fertility, whereas Zechariah leaves to the imagination the transformation which ever-flowing streams would make in a dry, stony land.

The reference of Jesus to a Scripture promising 'living water' (Jn. 7:38) may be mainly to this verse.[1]

9. Israelites for generations had been singing 'The Lord reigns' (Pss. 93; 97; 99), but it had been a declaration of faith. Once 'that day' comes He will be seen to be King over His world kingdom. Statements such as this explain the impact of Jesus' first preaching, 'The time is fulfilled, and the kingdom of God is at hand' (Mk. 1:15). *The Lord will be one* is an apparently superfluous message, for the Jews repeated in the *Shema*ʻ 'The Lord our God is one Lord' (Dt. 6:4). The new

[1] R. H. Lightfoot, *St. John's Gospel, A Commentary* (Oxford, 1956), p. 183.

factor will be that every man will acknowledge that He is the one and only God. *And his name one.* God's name Yahweh expressed all He had ever been and ever would be (Ex. 3:13–17). 'The Lord is God; there is no other besides him' (Dt. 4:35,39); 'I am the Lord, and there is no other' (Is. 45:5). Clearly the one name is not a matter of linguistics but of theology. When all nations give their allegiance to the Lord they will be admitting that any glimpses of the truth they had before came from this one God.

10. The mountains which are round about Jerusalem hide and protect it (Ps. 125:2), but because they will no longer be needed as a defence they are to be levelled, so that the city dominates the land, as befits the capital city of the King of the whole earth. *Geba* was six miles north-north-east of Jerusalem and marked the northern boundary of Judah (1 Ki. 15:22; 2 Ki. 23:8). *Rimmon* or En-Rimmon (Ne. 11:29; *cf.* Jos. 15:32, where the names Ain and Rimmon should probably be combined into En-Rimmon), 'spring of the pomegranate tree', is identified with Khirbet Umm et-Ramâmîm, about thirty-five miles south-west of Jerusalem, where the hill country of Judah slopes away into the *Negeb* or south.

The Gate of Benjamin, leading to Benjamin's territory, is likely to have been in or near the north-east corner of the wall (Je. 37:12,13). *The place of the former gate* is unknown, but as the *Corner Gate* marked the western limit, the former gate was possibly a site in the north wall. *The Tower of Hananel* (Ne. 3:1; 12:39) was the most northerly point of the wall, and *the king's winepresses* were to the south, near the King's Pool (Ne. 2:14) and the king's garden (Ne. 3:15). Thus the naming of landmarks on the east, west, north and south walls emphasizes that the whole city is included.

11. *And it shall be inhabited.* There are indications that after the exile the population of the city was small (Zc. 2:4; 8:5,6). Even as late as Nehemiah's time pressure had to be brought to bear on the Jews to inhabit the city (Ne. 7:4ff.; 11:1,2). Here the thought is that the city will never again be depopulated by being put under the *curse* or 'ban' (Heb. *ḥērem*). It was according to this ban that Canaanite cities were totally destroyed at the time of Joshua's conquest (Jos. 6:17,18). The loss of life and deportation at the time of the destruction of the city were interpreted as a similar curse (Is. 43:28). The prophet has indicated that distressing experiences are in store (Zc. 13:8,9; 14:1,2), but once the Lord comes as King there will never again be such a threat. *Jerusalem shall dwell in security,* whether there are walls or not, when the Lord is the glory within the city (Zc. 2:5).

12. Having related in restrained prose the awesome coming of God as King, and the mysterious changes that are to take place in the landscape in and around Jerusalem, the prophet now returns to those who oppose His rule. In pictorial language, suggested perhaps by the epidemic that swept through Sennacherib's army outside Jerusalem in Hezekiah's time (2 Ki. 19:35), he sees all the opposing armies of the nations reduced to helplessness by a sudden wasting disease.

13. Both the plague and the ensuing panic are *from the Lord.* Secondary causes are not ruled out, but they are too insignificant to mention, for God's day of judgment has come. So terrible is the experience that, in the intense desire to escape, one kills another (Hg. 2:22; Zc. 11:9).

14. *Even Judah will fight against Jerusalem.* See the note on 14:3. It makes much better sense to translate the preposition *be* 'in', as does NEB, *Judah too shall join in the fray in Jerusalem.*[1] A quick glimpse at Jerusalem shows her inheriting all the spoil from the battlefield, including her own possessions taken by the enemy (14:1,2). The Hebrew verb *'āsap* means both 'to collect' and 'to remove', hence the NEB, *and the wealth of the surrounding nations will be swept away;* but the more usual translation gives the more likely sense.

15. As he envisages the collection of booty the prophet thinks of the animals left in the enemy camp. They too suffer in the epidemic, and so cannot provide transport for escape. The language is symbolic, but a literal fulfilment is not thereby ruled out. There is no way now for any man to avoid judgment, except the way of conversion implied in the last few verses.

a¹. The Lord worshipped as King over all (14:16–21)

There is a similarity between the last paragraph of Part I of the book (8:20–23) and this final section. There are to be

[1] So also S. R. Driver, *CB*, p. 279; T. T. Perowne, *CBSC* (1888 edition), p. 146; C. H. H. Wright, p. 502.

survivors from among the nations who live to worship the Lord of hosts. 'The somewhat objective way in which this conversion is described should not blind one to the sublimity of the idea.'[1] This conversion is expressed in Old Testament terms, of course, but it is significant that the nations are not depicted as submitting to circumcision, nor even to keeping the law of Moses. The point is that they worship the one King and God. Finally, when God reigns all aspects of life are sacred.

16. *Every one that survives of all the nations.* The previous verse had not suggested that there would be any survivors from the plague, but this is figurative writing. Some of all nations are converted and so spared. The one festival uniting all nations in worship is to be the *feast of booths*, which was probably the oldest pilgrimage festival (Jdg. 21:19; 1 Sa. 1:3), and celebrated the sovereignty of the Lord, the giver of the crops (Dt. 16:13–17). It was open to all, including 'the stranger', and continued in importance during the post-exilic period (Ezr. 3:4; Ne. 8:14–18). The reference in Nehemiah shows that the festival was not only a thanksgiving for the harvest, but also an occasion for hearing the law read. This means that the covenant was renewed. In God's kingdom the gentiles would be brought within that covenant when they came to worship in the Temple *the King, the Lord of hosts*, who is now given His full majestic title (*cf.* Is. 6:5; Ps. 24:10).

17. The symbolism of drought and rain occurs in section *c* (9:11 – 10:1), where an adequate rainfall is connected with the prosperity of the Messianic era. In 13:1 a fountain cleanses from sin, while the rivers of 14:8 are part of the eschatological transformation of Jerusalem. It would be strange if *rain* were meant to be taken literally. Water-pouring ceremonies were part of the ritual at the Feast of Booths in post-exilic times, and are thought to have occasioned Jesus' promise of living water (Jn. 7:38). Water from the pool of Siloam was brought to the Temple in solemn procession by the priests, and poured out as an offering at the altar. The ritual may have been accompanied by prayers for rain after the long dry summer. How early this ritual was observed is not known. Evidence for it comes from the Mishna.[2] The prophet is anxious to indicate

---

[1] R. C. Dentan, *IB*, VI, p. 1113.
[2] Sukkah 4:9. For more detail see *IDB*, I, pp. 455f.

that the worship of the nations will continue, and rain sym-bolizes the essentials of life, for which the nations have learnt to depend on the Lord. Once worship stops they will be aware of their need and so apostasy will be avoided.

18. Egypt was an exception among the nations because it depended for water not on rainfall but on the Nile. As Egypt had experienced plagues at the time of the Exodus, and through them had been brought to acknowledge God's sovereignty, so *plague* was a fitting symbol of disaster in the new era. Difficulties in the Hebrew are reflected in the rather obscure translations of AV, RV. The Greek and Syriac give the reading adopted by RSV, JB, NEB, and this is likely to be the meaning intended.

19. Egypt is not singled out as the only people to suffer punishment. Any nation which fails to worship God meets disaster. The repetition, *that do not go up to keep the feast*, may be the result of scribal error, but it could equally well be intentional insistence on the supreme importance of worship.

20. *Holy to the Lord* was engraved on the plate of gold worn on the turban of the high priest (Ex. 28:36) as an expression and reminder of his consecration, but it was meant to be true of all Israel (Ex. 19:6; Je. 2:3). Once God's reign is established holiness will characterize not only the people but their animals. *Horses*, no longer needed for war, will bear the inscription on their jingling harness as they provide transport for pilgrims. *The pots in the house of the Lord* are the cooking utensils used by worshippers to cook for their own meal the sacrificial meat intended for them from the peace offerings (Lv. 7:15f.). Facilities were provided within the Temple courts for families to take part in such communion feasts (*cf.* Ezk. 46:21-24). The cauldrons in which the cooking was done are going to be as sacred as the *bowls* used to sprinkle the sacrificial blood on the altar.

21. Indeed all cooking utensils will be *sacred to the Lord of hosts*. There will be no distinction between sacred and secular, and therefore no shortage of utensils for use in the Temple. It may be inferred that there were shortages in the prophet's day; particularly would it be likely at festivals, with prices rising accordingly. Deep resentment may have prompted the final sentence, *And there shall no longer be a trader in the house of*

the Lord of hosts. Trader is literally 'Canaanite' (see note on
11:7). In this context the word applies, not to a particular
nationality, but to those who make extortionate profits out of
the worshippers. Once the King comes, money-making will no
longer mar the Temple courts, nor merchants' greed take the
joy out of sacrificial giving (*cf.* Mt. 21:12,13 and parallels).

Using symbolic language still the prophet is depicting
'Utopia'. For him the essential is that God should be King, not
only in the life of the individual, but of the whole human race.
When that condition is fulfilled everyday life will be 'holy to
the Lord', and all human problems solved.

MALACHI

INTRODUCTION

WHEREAS most of the prophets lived and prophesied in days of change and political upheaval, Malachi and his contemporaries were living in an uneventful waiting period, when God seemed to have forgotten His people enduring poverty and foreign domination in the little province of Judah. Zerubbabel and Joshua, whom Haggai and Zechariah had indicated as God's chosen men for the new age, had died. True the Temple had been completed, but nothing momentous had occurred to indicate that God's presence had returned to fill it with glory, as Ezekiel had indicated would happen (Ezk. 43:4). The day of miracles had passed with Elijah and Elisha. The round of religious duties continued to be carried on, but without enthusiasm. Where was the God of their fathers? Did it really matter whether one served Him or not? Generations were dying without receiving the promises (*cf.* Heb. 11:13) and many were losing their faith.

Malachi's prophecy is particularly relevant to the many waiting periods in human history and in the lives of individuals. He enables us to see the strains and temptations of such times, the imperceptible abrasion of faith that ends in cynicism because it has lost touch with the living God. Even more important he shows the way back to a genuine, enduring faith in the God who does not change (Mal. 3:6), who invites men to return to Him (3:7), and never forgets those who respond (3:16).

I. THE PROPHET

Who Malachi was we do not know. His name could equally well be translated 'my messenger' or 'my angel', as it is in Zechariah 1:9, 11, *etc.*, though the latter meaning can be disregarded in this context. Malachi then would be a *nom de plume* or maybe an editor's title for an anonymous book, borrowed for convenience from 3:1. Not that the prophet identified himself with that coming messenger, and for this reason the theory is not altogether convincing. Moreover, since the rest of the sentence is in the third person the sense would

demand 'the word of the Lord . . . by his messenger', an
an alteration which was made by the LXX translators, who took
the word to be a common noun. This fact, however, only
serves to reinforce the originality of the MT.

Though the name Malachi occurs nowhere else in the Old
Testament, similar names do occur with an 'i' ending, such as
Ethni 'my gift' (1 Ch. 6:41), Beeri 'my well' (Gn. 26:34; Ho.
1:1). Whereas sometimes two forms of a name suggest that the
'i' ending expects the addition of 'jah' (*e.g.* Abi 'my father' in
2 Ki. 18:2 appears as Abijah 'the Lord is my father' in 2 Ch.
29:1), there is no such longer form used to correspond to
Ethni and Beeri. It is therefore by no means certain that
Malachi would necessarily be short for 'Jah is my messenger',
a meaning which commentators have pointed out to be
inappropriate.[1]

The arguments which convince most modern scholars that
Malachi is not a name are: (*a*) the fact that it is not found
elsewhere in the Old Testament (but neither are Jonah and
Habakkuk); (*b*) the absence of any precise description of him,
such as 'son of . . . ', or 'the prophet' (but the same is true of
Obadiah); (*c*) the fact that in Zechariah 9:1, 12:1 'oracle of
the word of the Lord' has been commonly interpreted as a
mark of anonymity. If, however, as has been argued in this
commentary, the last six chapters of Zechariah are an integral
part of his book and not anonymous, this argument falls to the
ground.

Evidence from the Targum shows that the Aramaic translators understood Malachi as a name or title of Ezra the Scribe,
a viewpoint adopted by Jerome and by Rabbi Rashi (1040–
1105). Calvin was inclined to think that Malachi was Ezra's
surname.[2] While there is no evidence that Malachi is to be
identified with Ezra the tradition is strong that Malachi is a
personal name, and in the absence of compelling arguments
to the contrary it is logical to accept that the prophet was
called Malachi.[3]

Though the editor does not indicate Malachi's date, it is
possible to deduce from internal evidence the approximate

---

[1] *E.g.* W. Neil, *IDB*, III, p. 229, who calls this form of the name 'an
impossible concept'.
[2] J. Calvin, *Twelve Minor Prophets*, V (Edinburgh, 1849), p. 459.
[3] This is the conclusion reached by Chary (pp. 223, 233), and he cites
A. van Hoonacker, H. Junker and A. Deissler as being of the same opinion.

date of the prophecy. The post-exilic era is indicated by the mention in 1:8 of a governor (Heb. *peḥâ*), the word used in Haggai 1:1 to describe Zerubbabel, and in Nehemiah 5:14 to indicate Nehemiah's rank; the term is almost entirely confined to post-exilic writings. The absence of any reference to the rebuilding of the Temple, and the fact that worship has degenerated into mere routine suggest that some considerable time has passed since its rebuilding took place. Socially conditions are reminiscent of the time of Ezra-Nehemiah. There is the same unwillingness to part with money for the Temple funds (Mal. 3:8; *cf.* Ne. 10:32–39; 13:10); advantage was being taken of the poor and oppressed (Mal. 3:5; *cf.* Ne. 5:1–5); and, most characteristic of all, intermarriage with non-Jewish families was threatening the survival of the covenant faith (Mal. 2:10,11; *cf.* Ezr. 9:1,2; Ne. 13:1–3,23f.). This parallel evidence has proved convincing, and there is a general consensus of opinion that Malachi belongs to the same approximate period as Ezra and Nehemiah.

Only when attempts are made to date Malachi more precisely do differing viewpoints arise, to which uncertainty about the date of Ezra's arrival in Jerusalem and his relationship to Nehemiah contribute. The absence in Malachi of reference to recent legislation such as Ezra and Nehemiah introduced (Ezr. 10:3; Ne. 13:13,23–27) suggests that Malachi preceded them in time. If Ezra came to Jerusalem in 458 BC, Malachi might belong to the previous decade. This would explain the otherwise surprising reaction to Ezra's day of repentance and fasting, before he himself had had opportunity to preach (Ezr. 9:1 – 10:5). The words of Malachi had already quickened the public conscience. Those who think that Ezra followed Nehemiah would date Malachi a little later, some time before 445, or between Nehemiah's two visits, that is, after 433 BC. It is not possible to be more specific.

II. HIS BOOK

There can be little doubt about the essential unity of this book, for it is marked by distinctive traits which are present throughout, most notable of which is the disputation method, reflected at the beginning of each main section. The method was not new. Some find disputation in Amos 5:18–20; it lies behind Micah 2:6–11, where the prophet quotes his opponents; and

Jeremiah frequently refers to exchanges with his contemporaries (Je. 2:23-25,29ff.,35f.; 8:8,9). The same is true of Isaiah 40:27,28 and of Ezekiel 12:21-28.[1] Malachi reveals the same sensitivity to the thoughts and feelings of his contemporaries as did his predecessors. It is extremely unlikely that the words he puts into the mouth of his opponents were in fact voiced. Such remarks as 'How hast thou loved us?' (1:2), 'How shall we return (to God)?' (3:7), 'It is vain to serve God' (3:14) are rarely heard in public debate. Malachi reads the attitudes of his people and intuitively puts their thoughts into words, so gaining their attention before driving home his word from the Lord.

This method of presenting his message was used by Malachi, not merely on occasion, but regularly and systematically. He records a positive statement; the response of his hearers is countered and sometimes they question a second time (*e.g.* 1:7) before he makes his accusations or promises. The short sentences and direct style characteristic of Malachi are marks of the spoken word, so that, even allowing for a certain amount of editorial arrangement, the impression remains that the very words of the prophet are here recorded.

Unlike Zechariah Malachi does not employ any particular literary structure in order to convey his meaning. The subjects with which he deals follow one another apparently haphazardly, and yet there is a logical progression from election and privilege (1:2-5) to the inevitability of judgment (3:13 – 4:3). The last three verses, which form a fitting conclusion to our Old Testament and anticipate the New, are commonly thought to have been added to the book after Malachi's time. Before the prophetic collection was finally edited no-one would have known that Malachi would bring it to a conclusion, and, moreover, LXX has a different arrangement of these verses: 5,6,4. But if these verses were added as a later appendix, they are in keeping with the concise, hortatory style of the rest of the book, and could have come from Malachi's hand. The alteration of the order in LXX most likely reflects an attempt to end the book on a less threatening note rather than a different original order.

Emphasis on the law of Moses (4:4) and on the figure of Elijah (4:5,6) summed up all that God's servants had stood for

---

[1] C. Westermann, *Basic Forms of Prophetic Speech* (Lutterworth, 1967), p. 201, includes a section on 'The Disputation'.

throughout the centuries. When the law and the prophets were put together in one collection of sacred texts, these twin references looked forward to the consummation of the purpose for which both were given.

Other verses sometimes queried as later additions to the text are 2:11–13a; 3:1b, and indeed James Moffatt in his translation puts double square brackets round these small sections to indicate that he regards them as editorial additions or later interpolations. To these may be added all or part of 1:11–14, said to teach a universalism which contradicts the particularism elsewhere in the book (*e.g.* 2:11).[1] These verses, however, neither teach universalism nor do they conflict with the rest of Malachi's message (see the commentary on these verses). Evidence for regarding the other verses mentioned as later additions is so slight and so dependent on subjective factors that it is best to accept the text as it stands in our EVV.

Two verses (2:15,16) show signs of an attempt at an early period, before the versions were made, to make their meaning more palatable (*cf.* the commentary). Otherwise the Hebrew appears to be well preserved. German scholars have attempted to translate Malachi as poetry in the belief that the original oracles were in poetic form, and that it is possible to arrive at the poetic original.[2] EVV, including Moffatt and NEB, have translated the whole book as prose, in keeping with the Hebrew.

No direct light on the Hebrew text is provided by the Qumran MSS. The LXX in general keeps so close to the Hebrew, even translating literally when the Greek had a more appropriate word, that it lends support to the Hebrew text, and where the Old Latin deviates from LXX it keeps even more closely to the Hebrew.

III. HIS MESSAGE

It has become usual to disparage Malachi and belittle his message by saying that the creative period of prophecy had passed, and that he was more like a scribe or a casuist than a prophet, interested merely in the details of the ritual and in

---

[1] K. Elliger (*ATD*, p. 189) and F. Horst (*HAT*, p. 261) think verses 11–14 to be from another hand; Chary questions only verse 14 (p. 226).
[2] *E.g.* K. Elliger, *ATD*, p. 189; F. Horst, *HAT*, pp. 264-274; H. Frey, *BAT*, pp. 140–180.

applying the letter of the law. Men like Amos, Isaiah and Jeremiah, by contrast, belonged to the first rank of prophets.[1] The yardstick by which such judgments are made is not specified, and it is questionable whether comparisons between one prophet and another are meaningful. True, Malachi belonged at the end of the prophetic era, but each prophet had his specific role to play in his own historical setting, and it is more important to see how he fulfilled his task and to appreciate, ponder and apply his message than to allot him a grade in the prophetic pass list. As R. W. Funk says, 'The word of God, like a great work of art, is not on trial.'[2]

Fundamental to Malachi's teaching is the concept of covenant. It is implicit in the opening theme, the Lord's love for Israel (1:2–5), and the book ends with a call to fulfil the obligations of the covenant as expressed in the law (4:4). The Lord, who initiated the covenant, and on whose dependability it was established, is the central figure and chief spokesman. Out of a total of fifty-five verses, forty-seven record in the first person the address of the Lord to Israel (the exceptions being 1:1; 2:11–15,17; 3:16). This use of the first person presents a vivid encounter between God and the people, unsurpassed in the prophetic books.

By virtue of the covenant relationship the Lord refers to Himself as a father and implies that Israel is His son (1:6; 3:17; *cf.* 2:10). His desire is to bless His sons with all good things (3:10–12). He wants them to find true satisfaction and be like the ideal priest portrayed in 2:5–7, accepting daily His gifts of life and peace, responding with awe to the privilege of belonging to Him, and in his turn passing on to others the good things he enjoys. A living relationship with the Lord is utterly essential if Israel's covenant destiny is to be fulfilled.

Jacob's basic sin lay in jeopardizing this relationship. Twice Malachi specifies sin as covenant-breaking: the priests corrupted the covenant of Levi (2:8) and the people as a whole profaned the covenant of their fathers (2:10). Far from responding with warmth and spontaneity to the personal love shown to them, both priests and people were apathetic, bored with worship (1:13) and mean in their giving (3:8). In short, they despised the Lord (1:6), cheated Him of vows and robbed

---

[1] So, *e.g.*, W. Neil, *IDB*, III, p. 231; R. C. Dentan, *IB*, VI, p. 1120.
[2] R. W. Funk, *Language, Hermeneutic and Word of God* (Harper and Row, 1966), p. 11.

Him of dues (1:14; 3:8). Having failed to love God, they failed also to love their neighbour. A broken relationship with God led on to broken relationships in human society, inter-marriage and divorce being the examples of unfaithfulness quoted by Malachi. The objection to intermarriage was not on racial but religious grounds. Surrounding nations worshipped 'a foreign god' (2:11), and therefore to enter into marriage alliances with them was *ipso facto* to be unfaithful to one's own covenant God (2:10). Similarly, divorce was hateful to God because it involved breach of covenant. Malachi's description of marriage to the wife of one's youth as companionship (2:14) bears incidental witness to a high view of family life, based on the lifelong partnership of one man with one woman. The wife is valued for the worth of her own personality and not merely for her physical attraction. The upbringing of children is a shared responsibility (2:15) and children are to honour both parents (Ex. 20:12). Thus family relationships illustrate love and loyalty, and make the divine covenant comprehensible to man, while divorce, by contrast, typifies broken faith and severed relationships.

Lest the concept of God as Father should be misused, Malachi sets over against it God's rights as Master and King (1:6,14). The composite picture guards against over-familiarity on the one hand and a too distant subjection on the other. The note of judgment is intended to warn each individual so that none based hopes of salvation on a false confidence, but was prepared for the testing fires which even the faithful had to expect (3:3). The God of justice (2:17) is about to do a new thing. His intervention will in some way bring the nations to worship Him (1:11), He will come to His Temple (3:1), appropriately heralded by a forerunner, and there will perform His twofold task, to refine and to judge (3:2-5). Ultimately all that resists the refining process will be burnt up (4:1). This eschatological expectation was not presented as some distant goal but as an imminent event, and so acted as a powerful spur to repentance and reformation of life in preparation for the 'great and terrible day of the Lord' (4:5).

Malachi has nothing to say about the judgment of the nations. His concern is to keep faith alive in Israel, and the nations are not part of his brief (1:1). This does not mean that he was indifferent to the wider world. He knew that the Lord's dominion extended beyond Israel (1:5) and that all nations were to witness the intervention of the Lord, acknowledge Him and fear Him (1:14; 3:12). They would even bring Him a pure offering, surpassing the levitical sacrifices, which were never so described (see commentary on 1:11), but meanwhile his burden was to urge Israel to be true to the covenant lest history should culminate in destruction instead of blessing.

That Malachi was not teaching any doctrine of merit-making is obvious from his handling of the objection that it is vain to serve God (3:14). Those who are spared are not said to have deserved special favour. They find favour because they have 'feared the Lord and thought on his name' (3:16). Similarly it is misleading to say that in this book we find 'great stress laid upon the legalistic and cultic.... Thus fundamentally Malachi is simply a precursor of later Judaism',[1] if by that is meant that Malachi was preoccupied with the letter of the law rather than the spirit in which it was meant to be kept. Far from being legalistic Malachi has penetrated to the core of both the law and the prophets. His one great plea is for a personal relationship with the living God, who seeks men to 'walk with Him' (*cf.* 2:6).

Malachi's remarkable ethical thrust has lost none of its cutting edge through the passing of time. His teaching, both negative and positive, strikes at the heart of nominal, easy-going Christianity as it did at that of Judaism. Can it be that the book is disparaged because 'With man as the filter through which the word must pass, or, if you like, arbiter of the meaning of the word, it is inevitable that he will censor out what he does not wish to hear and audit only what he is predisposed to hear'?[2]

---

[1] C. Kuhl, *The Prophets of Israel*. Trans. R. J. Ehrlich and J. P. Smith (Oliver & Boyd, 1960), p. 169.
[2] R. W. Funk, *op. cit.*, p. 11.

ANALYSIS

COMMENTARY

I. THE HEADING (1:1)

Every word of this succinct opening sentence needs comment. *The oracle of the word of the Lord.* The first Hebrew word *maśśā'*, treated by RSV in Zechariah 9:1; 12:1 as a title, is somewhat inconsistently taken here as an integral part of the sentence (Hebrew construct state), so changing 'an oracle' into 'the oracle of' (contrast JB, NEB, which keep 'an oracle' in all three places). (For the meaning of *maśśā'* see Additional Note on The burden of the word of the Lord, p. 162.) The same word introduces oracles against the nations in Isaiah 13–23, characterized by eschatological judgment. The last six chapters of Zechariah are deeply eschatological, and though Malachi is in a different literary category from them, they share the same conviction that God's coming to judge the world is imminent. The 'burden' which weighs on the prophet is meant to weigh on men's consciences till they prepare for 'that day'.

Israel, the name used for a while of the Northern Kingdom, never ceased to be applicable also to the whole nation, which was represented by the few who had returned to Judah. *Malachi* has been treated as a proper noun in EVV generally, except that Moffatt translates 'by his messenger'. The arguments for and against anonymity are given in the Introduction (pp. 211f.), but there is no adequate reason for rejecting Malachi as the name of the prophet. It is difficult to escape the impression that these chapters have been taken less seriously than they deserve partly because of the widely accepted belief that their author is unknown.

II. A PRIVILEGED PEOPLE (1:2–5)

Since Malachi's ministry is to Israel (verse 1), it is fitting that his book should begin with an affirmation of God's continuing love for the covenant nation. The scepticism with which it is greeted indicates that the sermon is relevant. The atrophy of human love in the community (2:13–16) has undermined confidence in the divine love, and there is no appreciation of the providential overruling of God which has made possible the return to Jerusalem and the rebuilding of the Temple.

2. God's love is popularly thought to be a revelation first made in the New Testament, but this is far from the truth. It is implicit from the beginning, and especially from the time of the covenant with Abraham (Gn. 12:1–3; 17:1–8). It becomes explicit in Deuteronomy, a book that records theological reflections on the covenant implications of the Exodus events, brings out the elective sense of the verb *love* (Heb. *'āhēḇ*) (Dt. 4:37; 7:7,8; 10:15) and teaches that Israel should love God in return (Dt. 5:10; 6:5; 11:1,13). That God loves men and women is undoubtedly one of the hardest truths to grasp, for all that it is preached so often. Israel's reply, *How hast thou loved us?* expresses incredulity if not cynicism, and compares with the modern assertion that statements such as 'God loves men' die the death of a thousand qualifications. The less philosophically minded dismiss them as wishful thinking, mere sentiment.

The prophet appreciated that historical evidence was necessary to faith. His question *Is not Esau Jacob's brother?*, expecting the answer that he was not only his brother but his twin, emphasized their equality of opportunity as Isaac's sons of entering into the blessing covenanted to Abraham. By natural right Esau had the advantage of being the elder. *Yet I have loved Jacob.* The Old Testament nowhere teaches that Jacob was more lovable than Esau, or more pleasing to God than Esau, though it was a fact that Esau had so lightly valued his birthright as to sell it to his scheming brother (Gn. 25:29–34). No fuller explanation of God's choice of Jacob can be found than that God delighted to love him (Dt. 10:15), insignificant though he was (Dt. 7:7,8). The price Jacob (Israel, Gn. 32:28) paid for such favour was high. God was never satisfied with Jacob's response to Him, hence the shattering experience of the exile, which Esau, father of the Edomites (Gn. 36:1), had not had to undergo. While Jerusalem was capitulating to the Babylonians the Edomites were on the side of the invader, acting as informants, looting and cutting off the escape routes (Ob. 10–14). Edomites moved into Judah's vacated territory and apparently had the better of their enemies.

3. *But I have hated Esau.* The verb 'hate' is to be understood in the light of God's electing love. The very fact that Jacob was chosen, 'loved', meant that Esau was rejected, 'hated', rejection being implicit in the exercise of choice. Personal animosity towards Esau is not implied. Esau and his descendants, however, by nursing resentment and showing hostility towards Jacob, did bring God's judgment on themselves.

By the time Malachi was writing Jerusalem had been restored and the Temple rebuilt for some sixty or seventy years (see Introduction). Meanwhile invaders from the desert, Nabateans (1 Macc. 5:25), had ransacked Edomite territory, forcing its population to take refuge in the Negev, to the south of Judah. Their country, later known as Idumea (1 Macc. 4:29; 5:65; Mk. 3:8), had Hebron as its capital.[1] When the Nabatean invasion took place is not known, but it may have been as early as the sixth century,[2] and this means that it is likely to have happened before the time of Malachi. It was the Nabateans who built Petra, the city in the cliffs, which seems to have been begun during the fourth century BC.

Time has shown that Edom did not go unpunished for taking advantage of Judah. God's providential ordering of events proved His justice.

4. If Edomites are confident of their ability to return and rebuild their cities in their own traditional territory, as Judah has done, the prophet is to shatter their illusions. Such a privilege God can give or withhold, and it is not to be given to Edom. Let Judah take note and rejoice in her privileges, instead of bemoaning her lot. The name by which Edom is to be known, *the wicked country*, contrasts with the name given by Zechariah to Judah, 'the holy land' (Zc. 2:12). Whereas Judah would be cleansed (Zc. 5:5–11), Edom would be *the people with whom the Lord is angry for ever*, a terrible judgment, which should cause Judah in all humility to be thankful for God's love to her. Malachi is undoubtedly aware of Ezekiel's prophecy concerning Edom (Ezk. 35), with 'desolation' (Heb. *šᵉmāmâ*) as its *leit-motiv*. Malachi uses the same word in verse 3 '*laid waste* his hill country', and 'perpetual desolation' (Ezk. 35:9) suggests the continuing rebuke 'for ever' at the end of this verse. On *the Lord of hosts* see Additional Note, page 44.

5. Malachi chooses as proof of God's love evidence which

---

[1] So most authorities, but M. Noth implies that Lachish was the capital. *The History of Israel*. Trans. S. Godman (A. & C. Black, 1958), p. 343.

[2] S. Cohen, *IDB*, III, 'Nabateans', p. 491.

can be tested out in Israel's own experience, under their very eyes. They might have seen it earlier, but preoccupation with their own internal difficulties had prevented the necessary wider look at God's dealings with another nation. The Lord's domain is not restricted to Israel, says Malachi with irony. If Israel were more outward-looking she would come closer to a knowledge of God's love, and see, by contrast with the experiences of other nations, how wonderfully God had dealt with her. When the recipient of God's love failed to see that God loved her, there was little hope of her having any testimony to the nations (Gn. 28:14). Malachi therefore expects to see a 'conversion' away from apathy to new conviction, and it may well be that he expected an eschatological event which would demonstrate once and for all the universal dominion of the Lord.

III. A PRIVILEGED PRIESTHOOD (1:6 – 2:9)

Malachi was a bold man to attempt to bring home to the influential priestly class the deficiencies of their service. Who was he to take upon himself the authority of speaking in the name of the Lord of hosts when the priests were already His messengers (2:7)? Only with the deep conviction of his God-given authority would he have dared to speak as he did, especially if he was a 'layman', and the way he addresses the priests (1:6; 2:1) suggests that he did not class himself among them. By subjecting all in authority in Israel, royal family, prophets, priests, to criticism from 'outsiders' God exercised His final authority, and saved Israel from the corrupting influences of absolute power vested in any particular group.

Having first addressed the nation as a whole the prophet turned to those set apart for God's service, whose greater responsibilities involve them in greater accountability (Lk. 12:48). Like Ezekiel's executioners he was to begin at the Lord's sanctuary (Ezk. 9:6).

a. Indictment (1:6–14)

6. Malachi is skilful to win the assent of his hearers before he brings accusations against them. Since the majority of the priests would have sons of their own, and since the law of Moses was axiomatic, he would have whole-hearted support for his first proposition, *a son honours his father*. This appeal to the fifth commandment kept God's covenant requirements to the fore. The *servant* honoured *his master* because he belonged to him by right of purchase, and had no option but to obey. The question is whether the priests regard the Lord of hosts as their father or their master. Either way there are inescapable obligations.

A father–son relationship between God and Israel is implied at the beginning of the Exodus deliverance, 'Thus says the Lord, Israel is my first-born son' (Ex. 4:22). Hosea saw Israel as an ungrateful son (Ho. 11:1), and Isaiah's prophecy opens with a complaint of the heavenly Father against His rebellious sons (Is. 1:2). Like his prophetic predecessors Malachi realized that the heart of the trouble he was probing was a broken relationship with God. Instead of affection and trust there was antipathy to God's nature and will. That is why the priests failed to honour Him with worthy sacrifices. Malachi was not concerned about the minutiae of the cultus but about the refusal of reverence for a Father and obedience for a Master who was great 'beyond the border of Israel'.

How have we despised thy name? Sinful attitudes are most often 'secret faults', secret, that is, from the consciousness of the sinner, but they are not excused on that ground.

7. *By offering polluted food* (RV *bread*). Animal sacrifices were meant, as verse 8 proves, and the verb *offer* (Heb. *niggaš*) is Malachi's characteristic word for offering sacrifices (1:8,11; 2:12; 3:3). *Polluted* (Heb. *mᵉgo'āl*) has primarily a ritual meaning (Ezr. 2:62, 'excluded as unclean'), but these sacrifices are polluted in the first place by the attitude of mind of the offerers, and only secondarily by ritual imperfections. *How have we polluted it* (RV *thee*)? When the Israelite spoke of God's name he was speaking of His person. If God's name was despised or polluted He was polluted. The Hebrew 'polluted thee' (supported by the Syriac and Vulgate) is likely to be original, but the harsh expression offended Greek ears, and so LXX, followed by the Old Latin, read 'polluted it'.

The Lord's table (*cf.* verse 12) is an expression used only by Malachi in the Old Testament, though the idea is present in Psalm 23:5 and Ezekiel 44:16. The prophet was not referring to the table for the bread of the Presence (Ex. 25:23) because he had blood sacrifices in mind, but to tables mentioned by

Ezekiel (Ezk. 40:39-43; *cf.* 44:16). These were provided at the gates of the inner court for the purpose of slaughtering the sacrifices, but the Zadokite priest entered the sanctuary and approached 'my table' (Ezk. 44:16). No doubt all these tables were regarded by the prophet as 'the Lord's'. *May be despised.* Clearly the priests would never have said that it was permissible to despise the Lord's table, but Malachi is trying to bring to the surface subconscious attitudes by drawing out the implications of unworthy actions.

8. Though our attitudes of mind are largely hidden from us the actions to which they lead are out in the open for all to see. Every sacrificial animal was to be without blemish (Ex. 12:5; Lv. 1:3,10, *etc.*), and the law expressly forbad the offering of *blind, lame* or *sick* animals (Lv. 22:18-25; Dt. 15:21). A little thought should have established that blemished goods could not be presented to a human *governor* (Hg. 1:1,14; 2:2, 21; Ne. 10:1), much less to God. Malachi prefers this argument from human life to giving a rationale of sacrifice.

9. There is irony in the prophet's invitation to *entreat the favour of God*, the expression used by Zechariah (see commentary on Zc. 7:2), *that he may be gracious to us*. The Easterner offers gifts not only to acknowledge kindness received but also to secure favour in the future (Pr. 18:16), but to offer unworthy presents is to invite trouble. *With such a gift from your hand* is an interpretation of the cryptic Hebrew expression (lit. 'from your hand was this') in the light of the main subject, offerings. NEB is less specific *if you do this*, while JB takes these words as a parenthesis (*this is your own fault*) and in a footnote attributes them to a gloss, excluding the prophet from blame (*cf.* RV, *this hath been by your means*). Some commentators interpret verse 9 as a genuine plea for repentance,[1] but the ironical interpretation best agrees with the context. The offering of gifts was not in any case a means of securing God's favour (Ps. 40:6-8).

10. Malachi is serious when he says that it would be better to *shut the doors* rather than to perpetuate worthless worship. He is indignant that such ritual should be thought to have any value, and so give false confidence. It is better that all should know that the Lord has *no pleasure* (Heb. *ḥēp̄eṣ*) in them.

[1] Including the Jewish commentators Abraham Ibn Ezra (1092-1167) and David Kimchi (1160-1235).

Occasionally the Lord is said to take a delight (*ḥēp̄eṣ*) in a man (Pss. 22:8; 41:11; *cf*. Is. 53:10) or in the land (Is. 62:4; *cf*. Mal. 3:12), but it is surprising to read that Cyrus, a pagan ruler, is to fulfil all God's purpose (*ḥēp̄eṣ*) (Is. 44:28). The contrast between Israel's lack of obedience and the achievement of those outside the covenant may have been already in the prophet's mind (*cf*. verse 12).

The *doors* were probably at the entrances to the court of the priests, where the tables for sacrifice were situated (Ezk. 40:39-41). If these doors were shut no offerings could be made. In practice no-one was bold enough to take such a step. *Kindle fire upon my altar* refers to the part of the priests in worship, not to the slaying of the animals, which was done by the offerer (Lv. 1:5; 3:2; 4:24,29). The prophet has in mind throughout this passage the responsibility of the priests. This verse is referred to by the Qumran Community, who took it as a basis for rejecting the validity of the sacrificial system at Jerusalem.[1]

11. These much-quoted words are far from easy to interpret, and a few scholars have denied that they belong to the original book,[2] on the ground that, by denying the necessity of Temple worship, the verse contradicts what the prophet has already said. Horst thinks that 1:11-14 addressed to the laity reproaches already levelled at the priests. Against these arguments must be set the fact that the introductory word 'for' connects the verse with what has gone before, and the contrast between 'the nations' and 'you' (verse 12) links it with what follows.[3] There is no reason to reject the validity of this verse, or to argue that the priests are no longer being addressed.

The passage is important for the sanction it appears to give to the popular twentieth-century notion that all worship, to whatever god it may be addressed, is in reality offered to the one God of the whole earth. The late Chief Rabbi commented, 'even the heathen nations that worship the heavenly hosts pay tribute to a Supreme Being, and in this way honour My Name;

---

[1] G. Vermes, *The Dead Sea Scrolls in English* (Penguin, 1962), 'The Damascus Rule', VI, p. 103. 'None of those brought into the Covenant shall enter the Temple to light his altar in vain. They shall bar the door, forasmuch as God said, "*Who among you will bar its door?*" And, "*You shall not light my altar in vain.*"'

[2] F. Horst, *HAT*, pp. 265-267; K. Elliger, *ATD*, pp. 194, 195; C. Kuhl, *The Prophets of Israel*. Trans. R. J. Ehrlich and J. P. Smith (Oliver & Boyd, 1960), pp. 167, 168.

[3] Chary, p. 241.

and the offerings which they thus present (indirectly) unto Me are animated by a pure spirit, God looking to the heart of the worshipper. This wonderful thought was further developed by the Rabbis, and is characteristic of the universalism of Judaism.'[1] Christian comment in a similar strain is represented by W. Neil, 'We may be grateful to this unknown author . . . for his daring and, for these times, astounding recognition that worship offered in sincerity and truth under the auspices of any religion whatever is in effect offered to the one true God (*cf.* Acts 10:35).'[2] Now if this is the correct interpretation of Malachi's words he is the only biblical writer to express the idea that pagan sacrifices may be regarded as offered to God.

From the rising of the sun to its setting could not be more comprehensive in scope. Similar phraseology is used twice in the Psalms (50:1; 113:3) and twice in Isaiah (45:6; 59:19), in each case to convey the universality of God's reign, and the imminence of His disclosure of Himself to the nations as Maker, King, Redeemer. As Th. Chary notes, this orientates the text of Malachi towards the future.[3] It is unlikely that the prophet would have used this expression if he had had in mind the worship of Jews of the Dispersion or proselytes,[4] for they could hardly be said to have been scattered over the whole earth, even taking into account the limited geography of the period.

My name is great among the nations. Four times in this chapter the prophet describes God as *great* (verses 5,14 and twice here) because he wants to be sure that the truth will register. The Hebrew needs no verb, and whether present or future tense is to be understood depends on the verb in the next clause. *In every place.* 'Place' (Heb. *māqôm*) can possibly mean 'sanctuary' (*cf.* Gn. 12:6; Dt. 12:5,14, *etc.*). *Incense is offered* represents a difficult Hebrew expression made up of two participles, but EVV solve the problem by taking the former as a noun 'incense'[5] (*i.e.* 'that which is made to smoke'). The second, also passive and causative, means 'is caused to be offered', though the

---

[1] J. H. Hertz, *The Pentateuch and Haftorahs*, I (Oxford University Press, 1929), p. 474.
[2] W. Neil, *IDB*, III, 'Malachi', p. 232.
[3] Chary, p. 242.
[4] J. M. P. Smith, *ICC*, concludes that the prophet was most likely to be alluding to the scattered Jewish community (p. 31). So also D. R. Jones, *TBC*. W. E. Barnes, *CB*, thinks proselytes are meant.
[5] See BDB, *muqṭār*, p. 883.

tense is flexible and not necessarily present (*cf.* AV, RV mg. *shall be* offered).[1] The context has to be the decisive factor. But even if the future is used it has the sense 'is about to be offered', indicating that the event is near at hand and sure to happen. There is, therefore, an eschatological element in this verse.

The fact that the prophet says the Lord's *name* is great among the nations is significant in view of the special importance attached by biblical writers to names, and particularly the divine name. The name in the Old Testament denotes the essential being. 'Those who know thy name put their trust in thee' (Ps. 9:10). A change of name indicates a change of character (*e.g.* Gn. 32:28). The name Baali, which simply meant 'my master or husband', could not be allowed by Hosea (Ho. 2:16) because it was connected with debased cults. It is, therefore, inconceivable that a prophet should suggest that the nations of his own day were worshipping the Lord under another name (Is. 42:8). Rather is he proclaiming that the nations will come to know the God revealed in the Scriptures.

The sacrificial vocabulary used in this verse must also be examined. It has already been pointed out that the prophet chose an unusual way of saying 'incense is offered'. Strictly 'that which is made to smoke' could as well be the burnt-offering as incense, but the participial form of the verb, used only here, is very close to the form *miqṭār*, used in Exodus 30:1 for the altar of incense. The indication is that the prophet had in mind the sacred rite of incense offering which was the special prerogative of the high priest (Nu. 16), and that he was not thinking in terms of animal sacrifices. *A pure offering.* The word *offering* (Heb. *minḥâ*) is the most general term for a gift of any kind, and used alongside other offerings stands for the grain offering (*e.g.* Ex. 30:9; 40:29; Lv. 7:37). The adjective *pure* is *ṭāhôr*, a word which is not used elsewhere to describe offerings. The usual adjective is *tāmîm* 'without blemish', that is, ceremonially pure, whereas *ṭāhôr* means morally and physically as well as ceremonially pure. At their best the levitical sacrifices were never described in these terms (much less the defec-

---

[1] A clear example of the Hoph'al participle having future sense is in 2 Sa. 20:21, 'shall be thrown'. *Cf.* GK, §116 p. See also William F. Steinspring, 'The Participle of the Immediate Future and Other Matters Pertaining to Correct Translation of the Old Testament' in H. T. Frank and W. L. Reid (Ed.), *Translating and Understanding the Old Testament* (Abingdon, 1970), pp. 64–70.

tive offerings of Malachi's priestly contemporaries), but to maintain that pagans could offer pure offerings to God when the God-given sacrifices were not so described is indefensible. It is not possible, therefore, to accept the view that Malachi is using rhetorical language and maintaining that heathen offerings, though contemptible, are *relatively* pure. The prophet had no sentimental illusions about the moral standards of Israel's neighbours (Mal. 1:1–5; 2:11).

To sum up this rather detailed study we note (*a*) that the prophet expects to see God's name honoured among the nations; they will come to know God. This was not a new idea, for Isaiah had foreseen such a conversion (Is. 2:2–4; 11:10; *cf.* 42:6; 49:6; 55:3–5; 66:18–21), and Ezekiel's frequent refrain in his restoration prophecy was 'the nations will know that I am the Lord' (Ezk. 36:23; 37:28; 38:23; 39:7). (*b*) Where Malachi went further than his predecessors was in foreseeing that this world-wide worship would not be dependent on the levitical sacrifices offered in Jerusalem (contrast Is. 66:18–21; Zc. 14:21). (*c*) The context requires the participle 'is offered' (the only verb expressed in the sentence) to be understood as an imminent future. Just as Malachi expects the sudden coming of the Lord to His Temple, so he has in mind the culmination of imperfect sacrifices in a pure offering which will transcend all previous offerings both in worthiness and efficacy. He does not say who will offer it, but uses the passive 'it is about to be offered'. Thus the inadequacies of the sacrificial system, which had so troubled the prophets, were seen by Malachi as about to be transcended, as indeed they were in the sacrifice of Jesus Christ. Through this sacrifice those who were strangers to the covenants of promise would be reconciled to God (Eph. 2:11–22).

12. By contrast with what is about to happen Malachi turns to the sacrifices offered by the priests of his own time; *you* is emphatic. Malachi strips away all self-deception by putting into blunt language the motives he discerns: *you say that the Lord's table is polluted*, better *may be defiled* (NEB); the clause is parallel to *the food for it may be despised*. This was the Lord's assessment of their intentions.

13. He noted their boredom with the ritual (and the Christian has much less cause to be bored with worship), and its implication *you sniff at me*, that is, 'look in contempt at me'.

As in 1:7 'me' is likely to be original rather than the less striking 'it' (RSV mg.).[1] We should say 'you turn up your nose at me'. When a man presumes on God's favour this is the attitude which results. It is the notion of 'cheap grace', summed up before that phrase was coined in Heine's words, 'God will forgive me; it's His job'.[2]

First among the unworthy sacrifices Malachi lists *what has been taken by violence* (Heb. *gāzûl*), that is, caught and mutilated by a wild animal (*cf.* 1:8, where the blind are first mentioned). Mauled animals were considered unfit for human consumption, and were to be thrown to the dogs (Ex. 22:31). To offer them to God was an open insult. Moreover, as substitutionary offerings blemished animals were useless, for they would not be accepted (Lv. 22:20,25). Only when sacrifices represented penitence and faith had they any value to God or efficacy for man. It is sometimes argued that the fault lay with the people who brought such offerings, but it was still the responsibility of the priests to reject them.

14. The particular example given in this verse is the voluntary offering, vowed under stress as a thanksgiving if God will grant deliverance (Gn. 28:20–22; Nu. 30:2; Jon. 2:9). A *male* animal is specified for such a sacrifice in Leviticus 22:19. Priests, people and resident aliens were permitted to pay vows (Lv. 22:18), and all were open to the temptation to offer a cheap substitute when the time came to fulfil them (*cf.* Ps. 76:11, 'Make your vows to the Lord your God and perform them'). The provision of pasture land for flocks round the levitical cities (Nu. 35:3; Jos. 21:2) indicates that the priests and Levites had animals of their own.[3] The *cheat* who attempted to deceive God when paying his vows was *cursed*. The recitation of the blessing and the curse was an integral part of the ceremony of covenant renewal in Joshua 8:34 (*cf.* Dt. 27; 28; 2 Ki. 22:13). The word *cursed* (Heb. *'ārûr*) is used in the ritual curses of Deuteronomy 27:15–26, and ways in which they would

---

[1] 'This passage is one of the eighteen *Tikkunê Sopherim* enumerated by the Rabbis, *i.e.* emendations of the Jewish Scribes to avoid an expression which seemed to border on blasphemy.' E. Cashdan, *Soncino Commentary*, p. 341.

[2] Princess della Rocca, *Souvenirs de la vie intime de Henri Heine* (Paris, 1881), p. 125. 'Dieu me pardonnera: c'est son métier.'

[3] Confidence in the historicity of the levitical cities has largely been restored. See W. F. Albright, *Archaeology and the Religion of Israel* (Johns Hopkins Press, 1942), pp. 121–124; G. Henton Davies, *IDB*, III, 'Levitical Cities', p. 116.

work themselves out are enumerated in Deuteronomy 28:15–68. To be cursed was no empty threat, therefore, but led to death, whereas the blessing bestowed life (Dt. 30:19). The man who trifled with God would not go unpunished, but would find out that He was *a great King* as well as father and master (verse 6), and that He did not spare those who flouted His majesty.

Among the nations where the Lord's name was known there is evidence of individuals who *feared* it. Rahab bore witness to fear of God (Jos. 2:9–11); Ruth the Moabitess recognized His claims on her (Ru. 1:16); the Ninevites responded to Jonah's preaching (Jon. 3:5–9) as did the awestruck sailors (Jon. 1:16), and Babylonian and Persian rulers learned, as Pharaoh did before them, that the Lord was God of gods (Dn. 2:47; 3:28; 4:37; 6:26,27; *cf.* Ezr. 1:2).[1] By contrast Malachi was referring here, as in verse 11, to the imminent conversion of the nations, who would come, perhaps in a procession of homage, to the great King.

b. Judgment (2:1–9)

1. Even if the indictment included others beside the priests, the judgment is addressed expressly to them. The mode of address, *O priests*, is ominously reminiscent of pre-exilic judgment speeches (*e.g.* Ho. 5:1; Am. 3:1; Mi. 1:2). *This command* (Heb. *miṣwâ*) implies that there can be no mitigation of the punishment about to be pronounced.

2. *If you will not listen.* Though the sentence opens with conditional clauses, the end of the verse reveals that the possibility of avoiding punishment is passing, the probation period is coming to an end. The construction may have been suggested by the familiar wording of Deuteronomy 28:15, a passage of which the prophet would be reminded by mention of *the curse*, which the Lord *will send*. This verb is in the intensive form and could justifiably be translated 'hurl' or 'let loose'; the curse will descend irrevocably because once pronounced it takes effect and, like the blessing, is irreversible (Gn. 4:11–14; 27:37). *I will curse your blessings* has been understood in two ways. On the one hand 'blessings' are interpreted to mean the

---

[1] Whatever view is taken of the way in which this acknowledgment is expressed, the fact remains that these pagan rulers fulfilled God's purpose, and so 'obeyed' Him, albeit unwittingly.

material resources, perquisites, which came the way of the priests as recipients of the people's tithes (Nu. 18:21), and on the other hand as the words of blessing which it was the prerogative of the priests to pronounce (Nu. 6:24–26). In either case the blessings would recoil as a curse upon them; indeed Malachi says the Lord has already carried out the threat because they *do not lay it to heart*. The expression is similar to Haggai's 'consider' (Hg. 1:5,7; 2:18).

3. Malachi now expands further what the curse will involve. *I will rebuke your offspring* (lit. *seed*). AV, RV take this to mean that the harvests will be poor and so the tithes and other offerings will decrease, whereas RSV takes 'seed' to mean descendants (*cf.* Je. 31:27). Other exegetes have changed the vowel points to arrive at the sense adopted by JB, 'Now watch how I am going to paralyse your arm', and NEB 'I will cut off your arm', that is, render you powerless to officiate as priests (1 Sa. 2:31; Ps. 10:15; *cf.* 1 Ki. 13:4). The Hebrew, however, with its double meaning has much to commend it. A steady decline in numbers and income was less dramatic but no less effective a means of inflicting God's judgment.

And spread dung upon your faces, the dung of your offerings. The offal from sacrificial animals was to be removed from the sanctuary and burnt (Ex. 29:14; Lv. 4:11, *etc.*), but so revolting to God were those who offered to Him sacrifices of no value that they and their offerings were to end up on the dung-heap, excluded from God's presence. It is hardly surprising that the Targum dispensed with the metaphor and translated 'I will make visible on your faces the shame of your crimes'. The imagery was boldly uncomplimentary to those whose birth and training had set them apart for sacred duties, and was no doubt resented. The invective of the eighth-century prophets against the cultus (Is. 1:11–15; Ho. 4:6–10; Am. 4:4,5; 5:21–23; Mi. 6:6–8) was polite by comparison.

4. The Hebrew text and all the Versions agree that this command was given *that my covenant with Levi may hold*, that is, it was meant to lead to repentance and so make possible the continuation of the covenant with Levi. All the warnings of the Bible are similarly positive in their aim (Ezk. 18:32). JB and NEB, however, introduce the negative: 'It is I who have given you this warning of my intention to abolish my covenant with Levi' (JB); 'my covenant with Levi falls to the ground'

(NEB). This 'correction' involves the alteration of one letter (Heb. *miḥᵉyôṯ* instead of *liḥᵉyôṯ*; *cf.* 1 Sa. 15:26),[1] but it is by no means certain that this is the sense here, though those who argue for it cite in support 1 Samuel 2:31, a judgment pronounced on the house of Eli, and the supposed attempt to exalt the priesthood in Zechariah 3 and 6:9–14. If there was an alteration in the original Hebrew it took place before any of the Versions was made, with the purpose of removing the threat to the authority of the priests.

The making of the *covenant with Levi* is not formally recorded in the Old Testament. Indeed there is nothing complimentary to Levi either in the Genesis narratives (Gn. 29:34; 34:25,26) or in the poem of Jacob (Gn. 49:5–7). The fact that Moses and Aaron were of the tribe of Levi (Ex. 2:1f.; 4:14) brought the tribe into prominence, and it was Levites who carried out Moses' orders after the incident of the golden calf (Ex. 32:26–29; *cf.* Dt. 33:8–11). The 'covenant of peace' mentioned in Numbers 25:11–13 is in connection with Phineas, the Aaronite, and not with the Levites as a whole, so the earliest mention of such a covenant is Jeremiah 33:21 (*cf.* Ne. 13:29), which presupposes a covenant with them from early times. The blessing of Moses on the tribe of Levi (Dt. 33:8–11) commissions them for the task of giving guidance through the Urim and Thummim, teaching and officiating in worship, but it is not called a covenant. As time passes, experience of the constancy of God's saving purpose and appreciation of the work of the Levites 'raises the divine promise to Levi out of its private and limited context and makes it yet another instance of the concern of the covenant God for His whole people'.[2]

In assessing the meaning of this verse the vital question is whether Malachi is likely to have pronounced that God would break His covenant, whether with Abraham, David or Levi. Of the many references to broken covenants in the prophets, in every case it is men who fail to keep covenant (*e.g.* Is. 24:5; 33:8; Je. 11:10; 31:32; Ezk. 44:7); God had sworn never to break His covenant (Lv. 26:44; Jdg. 2:1). It is against this

---

[1] This emendation, put forward by Budde and adopted by Bulmerincq, is quoted by F. Horst, *HAT*, p. 266. Very occasionally in the niphʿal *hāyā* can have the meaning 'come to an end' (Dn. 2:1; 8:27), but the verb is not in the niphʿal here, and therefore MT would not suggest this translation.

[2] W. Eichrodt, *Theology of the Old Testament*, I. Trans. J. A. Baker (SCM Press, 1960), p. 65.

background that the words of Jeremiah 33:20,21 are to be understood. Though the Davidic covenant appeared to have been broken (Je. 22:30), the prophet knew that this could not be so, for God's covenants were as certain to be fulfilled as were the laws of nature (Gn. 8:22). In view of this positive assertion throughout the Old Testament that God would never break His word it is advisable to keep the MT here, as in AV, RV, RSV. All evil priests had to repent or be swept away from the sanctuary in order that the covenant with Levi might stand.

5. God's intention in choosing Levi was to establish *a covenant of life and peace*, an expression used only here. It is the special emphasis of Deuteronomy that total commitment to God's way leads to fullness of life (Dt. 4:40, 'that you may prolong your days'; 6:2; 30:15–20; *cf.* Je. 21:8), but it is axiomatic in the Psalms (Pss. 1:3; 5:11,12; 16:11; 21:4, *etc.*) and in Proverbs (Pr. 3:2, where life and peace follow the man of obedient heart; 4:10,22; 6:23, *etc.*). These blessings were granted to Levi *that he might fear* (*cf.* 1:6). Malachi knew in his own experience the awesome awareness of God's blessing that expresses itself in deep reverence for God. This reaction of *awe* at God's *name* was far removed from the insolence of those who offered that which cost them nothing (1:8,13), were bored with worship (1:13) and yet had utmost confidence in themselves (1:6c).

6. The man whose reverence for God is evidenced by meticulous care in outward worship has one basic qualification for giving *true instruction* (Heb. *tôrâ*). Clearly the teaching involved more than intellectual knowledge, though even this demands integrity in the teacher. The priest of God's choice not only knew God's law but lived by it himself (*cf.* Ezr. 7:10). *No wrong was found on his lips*. That words are an index of character is a theme of the Scriptures (Ps. 15:2,3; Pr. 12:17ff.; 18:4), but especially of the New Testament (Mt. 12:33–37; Lk. 6:45; Jas. 1:26; 3:2–12). *He walked with me*, an expression denoting close communion with God, but used sparingly (Gn. 5:22; 6:9), *in peace and uprightness*, that is, both keeping and enjoying the covenant. Such a man was an influence for good, turning *many from iniquity* (Mal. 4:6) as much by his example as by his words.

7. *Knowledge* of God's law was traditionally part of the priest's equipment (Dt. 17:9; 33:10) and Hosea complained that the priests of his day had forgotten it (Ho. 4:6); on the other hand, in the time of Jehoshaphat princes, priests and Levites fulfilled an itinerant preaching programme (2 Ch. 17:7–9), and in the time of Ezra Levites assisted him in his explanation of the law (Ne. 8:7,8,11). Malachi assigns to the priest the role of personal counsellor, sought after by individuals who needed guidance in particular situations, and for this personal experience of God together with knowledge of His law was essential. *He is the messenger of the Lord of hosts*, one who has been in His presence and can therefore bring a message from Him. The designation 'messenger' is first given to the priest here, though Haggai the prophet is so described (Hg. 1:13; *cf.* Is. 42:19). Malachi's own name could have suggested the description. Zechariah's fourth vision depicted the high priest with access to God's presence, and so equipped to be a messenger (Zc. 3:7).

8. Returning now to the realities of his own time Malachi traces the decline from such a high calling. Failure began in the personal lives of the priests when they *turned aside from the way*, an expression that shows godliness to be commitment to a total way of life (*cf.* Acts 9:2; 19:9, *etc.*). Once that way had been abandoned their public ministry suffered, and instead of turning many away from wrong they *caused many to stumble* by misinterpreting the word of God (Heb. *tôrâ*). God was misrepresented first by their unworthy lives and then by their erroneous teaching. This terrible possibility of causing others to miss the way called forth from Jesus one of His sternest warnings (Mt. 18:5,6), and it is those with positions of leadership who are in greatest danger of misleading others. That is why James humorously advised, 'Let not many of you become teachers' (Jas. 3:1).

Finally, Malachi saw that *the covenant of Levi* had been *corrupted*; the verb means 'to corrupt morally' (Gn. 6:12), 'to destroy' (Mal. 3:11), and is applied only here to a covenant. It has already been argued that God never violated a covenant, and therefore Malachi cannot be implying that the covenant with Levi is annulled, even though the priests have violated it. As was the case when the covenant with the nation was violated by Israel, judgments are to fall on the covenant-breakers, but God's covenant will still stand.

9. Retribution falls on those who despised God's name (1:6) for they are *despised*. Having courted popularity by modifying God's requirements for some, they found themselves *abased*, humiliated. The common people recognized godliness when they saw it, and were not slow to scorn the hypocrisy of compromising priests. This discernment and its consequences were ultimately from God, who said *I make you despised* (*cf.* Mt. 7:2; Lk. 6:37,38). The prophet ends the section by reiterating the twofold error of God's representatives: failure to walk with God and the desire to curry favour with men.

IV. THE IMPORTANCE OF FAMILY LIFE (2:10–16)

Themes from three different sermons may have been put together in this section, for the prophet begins (verse 10) with a question that bears on the nation as one family. He continues (verses 11,12) to see the nation as a spiritual family, and in the last four verses turns to individual family life within the nation. Alternatively the theme may have been covenant loyalty, the sermon being prompted by the specific examples of unfaithfulness to which the prophet refers.

10. *Have we not all one father?* The context must be allowed to determine the meaning of this question. Mention of *the covenant of our fathers* indicates that the *one father* could well be one of the patriarchs, either Abraham or Jacob (Israel). There is scriptural precedent for 'Abraham your father' (Is. 51:2), an interpretation favoured by Jerome and Calvin, and Malachi makes frequent mention of Jacob (1:2; 2:12; 3:6), from whom the twelve tribes (fathers) descended. There can be little doubt but that Malachi intended *we* to mean fellow Jews, so, even if he had in mind God as the one father, he was not thinking in terms of 'the universal brotherhood of man'. His concern was rather for evidence of brotherly loyalty within the nation of Israel. *Has not one God created us?* The twin ideas of fatherhood and creation are found in Deuteronomy 32:6 and Isaiah 63:16; 64:8 (*cf.* Mal. 1:6), but always with Israel in mind because the nation was meant to reflect the character of the Father, who had taught it to walk in His way (Ho. 11:1).

Why then are we faithless . . . ? implies a general tendency to disregard promises and agreements of all kinds, in business, marriage or social affairs generally (Is. 24:16). Contrast the upright man who never lets his neighbour down (Ps. 15:4c). Irresponsible behaviour profaned the national covenant. The verb is different from that used in verse 8, but the meaning is similar; another covenant had been violated.

11. Narrowing now from the general to the particular, the prophet turns to a practice which through the centuries had undermined spiritual life in Israel, namely marriage into a family of a different religious and cultural background. There was no objection on racial grounds to intermarriage. A mixed multitude went out of Egypt with the Israelites (Ex. 12:38), but by submitting to circumcision and keeping the passover they committed themselves to the God of Israel (Ex. 12:48; Nu. 9:14). Boaz married Ruth the Moabitess, but she had forsaken Chemosh for Israel's God (Ru. 1:16). Malachi puts his finger on the crucial objection when he says *and has married the daughter of a foreign god*. 'Daughter of' implied 'bearing the character of' a deity whose whole ethos was diametrically opposed to the righteousness of Israel's God, and since a married couple must come to a common understanding in order to live happily together, one or other partner had to compromise on the matter of religion. It had been proved in Israel's experience that in practice the less demanding standards prevailed (1 Ki. 11:1–8; 16:31; Ne. 13:23–27), and apostasy quickly became the fashion. Since apostasy had been responsible for the exile it was unthinkable that the whole community should be put at risk again.

The use of the names *Judah* and *Israel* indicates that the prophet sees the repatriates in Judah as the contemporary inheritors of the ancient promises. Yet they have committed an *abomination*, a strong term used for idols and for the practices connected with their worship (Dt. 32:16; Is. 44:19). Even nations like Egypt separated themselves from a culture different from their own (Gn. 43:32; 46:34), and peoples who worshipped manufactured gods did not abandon them (Je. 2:11), but Judah *profaned the sanctuary of the Lord* by indulging in idolatrous worship and then approaching His presence. In the time of Ezra priests and Levites were involved in intermarriage with pagan nations (Ezr. 9:1,2), and Malachi, by mentioning the sanctuary, seems to have been including them. Some, however, have understood *sanctuary* (Heb. *qōḏeš*, 'holiness') to refer to the people, the 'holy seed' (Is. 6:13; Ezr. 9:2), the

Lord's portion (Dt. 32:9). Certainly it is they whom He *loves*, and on balance this interpretation is to be preferred to that implied by RSV.

12. Malachi prays that the Lord will remove the evil from the land by allowing no posterity to the offenders. *Any to witness or answer* is an idiom, the exact meaning of which is uncertain, though various suggestions have been made. One is that the metaphor arose from the rote learning of pupil from teacher (*cf.* Vulg.; AV *the master and the scholar*); another, reflected in RV *him that waketh and him that answereth*, envisages a nomadic custom of keeping watch round the tents at night; this agrees with the mention of *the tents of Jacob*; *nomads or settlers* (NEB) is based on Arabic. Though the Targum interprets rather than translates with the paraphrase 'son and grandson', this is the meaning the prophet wanted to convey. The idolater, left with no-one belonging to him in his old age, would so obviously not be blessed that other people would be discouraged from following his example, and no children of his would survive to perpetuate his sin.

13. The prophet now draws attention to another blatant example of unfaithfulness, *this again you do*; but first he comments on excessive displays of emotion, intended, apparently, to move God into granting long-awaited answers to prayer. Since lay people had no access to the altar it is argued that the words are meant figuratively, but if there were priests who were guilty there is no problem. The inference of the Targum, followed by Jerome, that it was the deserted wives who were weeping, is untenable because they had not yet been mentioned.

14. Weeping and wailing would achieve nothing because moral wrong was hindering access to God: marriage vows had been broken. The Law of Hammurabi decreed that marriage was a legal contract to be drawn up with the appropriate documents,[1] but the Israelite saw it as a *covenant* to which *the Lord was witness* (Gn. 31:50; Pr. 2:17) and for that reason the more binding. This spiritual dimension should have contributed to the stability of home life. The loyalty of each partner to the covenant God was a uniting bond which created a lasting companionship between the partners. The word *com-*

---

[1] *ANET*, p. 171, No. 128. *Cf.* the marriage contracts found among the Elephantiné Papyri, *ANET*, pp 222, 223.

panion, which is often used in the masculine of a close friend, with whom interests, good or bad are shared (Ps. 119:63; Pr. 28:24; Ct. 1:7; 8:13; Is. 1:23; Ezk. 37:16, AV, RV; Dn. 2:17), is used only here of a wife. Malachi is a quiet witness to a mutually satisfying marriage relationship which, though begun in youth, does not become jaded with the passing of time. Though it is true that to insist on the binding nature of the legal ceremony and to deny the opportunity for divorce cannot create such a companionship, yet there is a close connection between loyalty and faithfulness as a character trait and the building up of the mutual trust essential to a stable marriage. It was this trust which Malachi was accusing his contemporaries of betraying.

15. Here the text becomes difficult, having suffered perhaps at the hand of scribes who took exception to its teaching. One guide to interpretation is that it must agree with the clear intention of Malachi, expressed at the end of the verse, to encourage husbands to remain true to their first wife. It is impossible to make sense of the Hebrew as it stands, and therefore each translation, including the early versions, contains an element of interpretation. The problem is partly that the word 'one' can be taken in different ways. It may be the subject of 'made' and stand for *one God* (so RSV, NEB), or it may be the object of the verb, the subject (God) being understood: *did he not make one?* (RV; *cf.* AV, RSV mg.), that is, one flesh (Gn. 2:24).[1] The interpretation of the next clause 'having a remainder of life (or spirit)' depends on the way the first clause has been taken, but none is very satisfactory. A suggested emendation which involves the change of one vowel point (*šeʾēr* for *šeʾār*) turns the word 'remainder' into 'flesh', though not the word used in Genesis 2:24 (*bāśār*). This emendation has been adopted by JB, *Did he not create a single being that has flesh and the breath of life?* and NEB, *both flesh and spirit?* It certainly makes good sense. God made two human beings one with the specific purpose of giving them *godly offspring*. Only when both

---

[1] A further possibility, favoured by Jewish interpreters, is that 'the One' refers to Abraham (*cf.* 2:10), who, some protested, married Hagar and so set a precedent for taking a second wife. The prophet would then have replied that Abraham's motive was different. He wanted a godly seed. R. Cashdan, *Soncino Commentary*, develops this and similar viewpoints. The disadvantage of these interpretations is that they do not provide the prophet with a very strong case for his main argument.

parents remain faithful to their marriage vows can the children
be given the security which provides the basis for godly living.
The family was intended to be the school in which God's way
of life was practised and learned (Ex. 20:12; Dt. 11:19).
Because a divine institution was being threatened Malachi
urged that *none be faithless to the wife of his youth*.

16. But there is one further compelling factor: *For I hate
divorce, says the Lord*. English Versions agree that this is the
prophet's meaning, even though the Hebrew in fact reads 'if
he hates send (her) away', a sense found also in the ancient
Versions. Evidently the text suffered early at the hands of
some who wanted to bring Malachi's teaching into line with
that of Deuteronomy 24:1, which permitted divorce. Such a
reading undermines all that the prophet is seeking to convey.
The God of Israel, a name used only here by Malachi, is appropriate because the subject concerns the future of the chosen
race. He sees divorce to be like *covering one's garment with
violence*, a figurative expression for all kinds of gross injustice
which, like the blood of a murdered victim, leave their mark
for all to see.

JB makes the last sentence very meaningful: *Respect your own
life, therefore, and do not break faith like this*. It is in the best
interests of the individual as well as of the community that
families should not be broken by divorce. Malachi's plea
prepares the way for the teaching of Jesus (Mt. 5:31,32;
19:4–9).

V. THE LORD IS COMING WITH JUSTICE
(2:17 – 3:5)

The age-old problem raised by the apparent prosperity of the
evil man was a live issue in Malachi's day. It appeared that
God favoured the wicked, and both Jeremiah (Je. 12:1) and
Habakkuk (Hab. 1:2–4) had questioned God's just ordering
of providence, while at the same time maintaining their faith
in God's ultimate righteousness. Malachi's contemporaries, by
contrast, had become cynical and unbelieving, and because
they had given up all intention of taking right and wrong
seriously the prophet faces them with coming judgment. It is
noteworthy that he does not attempt a theodicy in order to
justify God's ways. That would merely appeal to the mind,

whereas the prophet knew that he needed to quicken the conscience.

17. Disillusionment had followed the rebuilding of the Temple because, though decade followed decade, no supernatural event marked the return of the Lord to Zion. So far as could be judged the Jews had done their part, but God failed to fulfil His promises (*cf.* Zc. 8:3). His delays were being taken as an excuse for atheism. The question *Where is the God of justice?* was tantamount to doubting His existence. It was on account of this failure of faith that they *wearied the Lord with their words*; He is never said to be wearied with human prayers and questions but only with human sin (Is. 43:24).

3:1. In response to the implied challenge of the question the Lord Himself speaks. *Behold* is literally 'Behold me', 'Here I am, about to send my messenger'. In the end no man will avoid confrontation with God, and it is of His goodness that warning of that event is given. Just as preparations are made in advance for a royal procession, so the Lord's coming would be heralded by a forerunner to indicate the route (Is. 40:3) and summon the population to fill up the ruts and remove the boulders (Is. 57:14; 62:10), that is, *prepare the way.* Malachi leaves the hearer to apply the metaphor. The identity of *my messenger* is not revealed. In that he was seeking to bring men to repentance, Malachi would be aware of fulfilling that role, but so had all the prophets. It is unlikely that he was thinking of himself, but rather of someone with a unique mission as forerunner (*cf.* 4:5), who himself must be distinguished from *the messenger of the covenant.*

When the preparations are completed *the Lord* (Heb. *'ādôn*) *will suddenly come to his temple.*[1] The promise suggests that there was continuing disappointment with the second Temple, despite the encouragement of Haggai and Zechariah (Hg. 2:7; Zc. 2:10, *etc.*), and it was a healthy reaction to be looking to God to do something greater than they had yet seen. When the Lord comes Ezekiel's vision of the glory returning to fill the house (Ezk. 43:1–5) will be completed, and the purpose of the rebuilding of the Temple fulfilled. But who is intended by *the messenger of the covenant*? The title occurs only here, so there is no aid to interpretation apart from this context. He comes

[1] That *'ādôn* is interchangeable with Yahweh is proved by such verses as Zechariah 4:14; 6:5, ' *'ādôn* of the whole earth'.

simultaneously with the Lord, if indeed he is not to be identified with Him (so AV, RV), a view encouraged by a Messianic interpretation in the light of the New Testament. The prophet, however, may have been thinking that, as the angel of the Lord was instrumental in establishing the Mosaic covenant (Ex. 3:2; *cf.* Is. 63:9), so he would be needed to institute the new covenant (Je. 31:31; Ezk. 37:26). Jewish commentators explain him as the angel appointed to avenge the breaking of any covenant, or as Elijah.[1]

In whom you delight is probably ironical. Just as Amos had had to point out that the day of the Lord was to be dark and not light (Am. 5:18), so the coming of the messenger of the covenant would be less than welcome when the implications of his coming were experienced. The fact that he will come *suddenly* is ominous, for suddenness was usually associated with a calamitous event (*e.g.* Is. 47:11; 48:3; Je. 4:20, *etc.*).

2. *Who can endure the day . . . ?* The question implies a searching ordeal, and the second question *who can stand?* is borrowed from battle imagery (2 Ki. 10:4; Am. 2:15) and means 'who will stand his ground?'. The prophet suggests that no-one will pass the penetrating tests which the Lord will impose. Yet the purpose of the *refiner* was not to destroy but to purify, and the *fuller's soap*, or rather alkali (soap in our sense was not yet in use), was applied in order to whiten cloth. According to these metaphors suffering fulfils a divine plan to remove impurities of character. The picture of the refiner is a persistent one in the prophets (Is. 1:25; 48:10; Je. 6:29,30; Ezk. 22:17–22). 'The beauty of this picture is that the refiner looks into the open furnace, or pot, and knows that the process of purifying is complete, and the dross all burnt away, when he can see his image plainly reflected in the molten metal.'[2]

3. The refiner who sits and concentrates all his attention on the metal in the crucible depicts something of the concern of the Lord for the holiness of His people. He begins at His sanctuary (*cf.* Ezk. 9:6) with *the sons of Levi* to purify them *till they present right offerings*, or, more literally, *offerings in righteousness* (AV, RV). Both senses are needed. Once character has been

---

[1] R. Cashdan, *Soncino Commentary*, p. 349.
[2] J. Neil, *Everyday Life in the Holy Land* (Church's Ministry among the Jews, 1913), p. 163.

transformed and purified the offerings (Heb. *minḥā*) will both be worthy and be offered in the right spirit.

4. Only then will the rest of the population, who no doubt also undergo the purifying process, be able to offer what is *pleasing to the Lord as in days of old*. The last phrase is indefinite, being used to refer both to the time of Moses (Is. 63:9,11; Mt. 7:14) and of David (Am. 9:11). Malachi is almost certainly thinking of the Mosaic period as the ideal era (Je. 2:2,3), when the Israelites depended directly on God.

5. What is a refining process for some will for others bring *judgment*. It is the community that is being refined, and, as in the case of metal, the base elements must be removed. The Lord is both *witness* and judge in the law suit against those who refuse to take correction and so are condemned 'in that day'. No other witness is needed because no other could be competent (2:14; *cf*. Je. 29:23). The word *swift* would be better translated 'expert'. The speed results from training. *Cf*. Ezra 7:6, where 'skilled' is from the same root. Malachi is the faithful pastor who faces his people with the possibility of ultimate rejection but hopes all the time to win them.

With the possible exception of the *sorcerers*, who perpetuated ancient superstitions, all the groups listed were responsible for social evils. Malachi dealt in detail with *those who swear falsely* in his sermon on unfaithfulness (2:10–16), and would probably have considered among the *adulterers* those who divorced their wives. The wage-earner in Malachi's day was 'oppressed' by being underpaid or by being kept waiting for his wages (*cf*. Lv. 19:13; Dt. 24:14,15), and *the widow and the orphan*, who had no-one to shield them, were at the mercy of the unscrupulous (*cf*. Zc. 7:10). All these were always the Lord's special concern (Ex. 22:22–24; Lv. 19:10). The *sojourner* would be known these days as the settler or the immigrant. He also had his rights, and God would judge the man who robbed him of them. All who ride roughshod over other people reveal that they *do not fear* the Lord of hosts, but when He 'draws near for judgment' the question 'Where is the God of justice?' (2:17) will be answered.

VI. THE LORD LONGS TO BLESS (3:6-12)

There is a close connection between these verses and what has gone before. They form a parenthesis between two sermons concerning God's justice, the sequence of thought being that Israel has the opportunity to question His justice only because He is unchanging in His patient provision of opportunity for repentance. The prophet suggests a way by which the whole people can prove for themselves that this is so. The action he has in mind will so touch their pockets that their repentance will be costly and therefore genuine. The response of the Lord to this repentance will be measurable in material terms also when the next few harvests are reaped, and the man who puts his possessions at God's disposal will find tangible evidence to prove that He accepts and blesses the giver.

6. The two halves of this sentence balance one another. The Hebrew reads 'For I the Lord do not change, and you, sons of Jacob, have not ceased'. It is easy to see why the EVV have usually translated the last verb *are not consumed*, which is one meaning of the verb, but also why NEB can read *I am the Lord, unchanging; and you, too, have not ceased to be sons of Jacob*, that is, wayward. The fact is that neither God nor Israel had changed. There is utter consistency in God's dealings with men. He who once loved Jacob (1:2) did not cease to love his sons, though they continued to take after their father and were cheats and supplanters (Gn. 27:36; *cf.* Mal. 3:5). The antithetic parallelism accentuates God's goodness.

7. Malachi is far from idealizing past generations (*cf.* Ezr. 9:7; Zc. 1:2). All had shown the same rebellious attitude to God's *statutes* through which He revealed His will (Dt. 4:4-7). The call to repent is worded in Zechariah's phraseology (Zc. 1:3), but it meets no response because there is no awareness of any shortcomings.

8. Malachi's method of quickening conscience into conviction of sin is to lay stress on one more indisputable manifestation of unworthy attitudes. *Will man rob God?* The verb translated 'rob' (Heb. *qāḇaʻ*) is rare in the Old Testament, though it is well established in the Talmudic literature to mean 'to take forcibly'.[1] Modern scholars are inclined to transpose the consonants to give the verb *ʻāqaḇ*, 'to circumvent,

[1] R. Cashdan, *Soncino Commentary*, p. 351.

assail insidiously', the root from which 'Jacob' is formed. JB *Can a man cheat God?* and NEB *May a man defraud God?* accept this emendation, which is supported by LXX. Attractive as is the play on words with the name Jacob, the Hebrew, supported by Vulg., has the advantage of a bluntness that rings true, and should be retained.

The English word *tithes* means 'tenths'. The practice of giving a tenth of one's possessions to a superior is evidently an ancient one, for there is testimony to it in Genesis, when Abram gave a tenth of the spoil to Melchizedek (Gn. 14:20), and Jacob made his vow at Bethel (Gn. 28:22). The law decreed that a tenth of all produce was 'holy to the Lord' (Lv. 27:30) and was intended for the Levites (Nu. 18:24), who themselves gave a tithe to the priests (Nu. 18:28). From the legislation in Deuteronomy it is clear that others benefited also, and that every three years a community feast was held at the time of offering the tithes, to which the needy were invited as well as the Levites (Dt. 14:28,29). When tithes went unpaid the widow, the fatherless and the sojourner were amongst those who suffered (*cf.* verse 5).

Offerings were the portions of sacrifices set apart for the priests (Ex. 29:27,28; Lv. 7:32; Nu. 5:9) and the voluntary gifts for a special purpose (Ex. 25:2–7). One of Nehemiah's tasks was to ensure that the supplies intended for support of the Temple ministry did not fail as they had done during his absence (Ne. 13:10–13). When no gifts were brought the Levites had no option but to give up their ministry and earn their own living by farming.

9. A proverb taught that the man who gives grows all the richer, while the one who withholds what he should give only suffers want (Pr. 11:24). This was the outworking of the curse on the stingy giver, for God cannot bless the individual, church or nation that can spare Him nothing. Moreover, God so identifies Himself with His servants that to withhold from them is to rob Him.

10. Let those who have been doubting God's existence begin to take seriously His demands, and honour Him with substantial gifts, for the tithes were at least as costly as a tenth of a modern wage packet, *that there may be food in my house.* If God's larders are empty His people are to blame; at the same time they are depriving themselves of one of the joyful rights of His servants, a share in His work. They also miss the personal discovery that God pours out *an overflowing blessing*, out of all proportion to the human gift. *The windows of heaven*, which opened to rain down the flood (Gn. 7:11), will at God's command shower an overwhelming supply of God's gifts.

11. The prophets traditionally promised God's blessing in terms of *the fruits of the soil* (*cf.* Hg. 2:19; Zc. 8:12). Malachi added that these would be protected from *the devourer*, probably a member of the locust family, though the word is as general in Hebrew as in English. Three kinds of locust do damage[1] and it was because of these destructive qualities that the locust was so much feared (Joel 1:4). The *vine in the field*, the most important representative of the fruit trees, would also bear grapes without fail (*cf.* Hg. 2:16).

12. Good harvests alone, however, would not make a country *a land of delight*. Although the prophets spoke in material terms there were spiritual counterparts to the fruits of the soil. Not that the material blessings are to be spiritualized away. God promises literally to prosper the man who gives liberally (Lk. 6:38; 2 Cor. 9:6–11), but the benefit to the personality of the giver is beyond price (Pr. 11:25). What is true for the individual is true also in the community. Contrast the grabbing attitude, which wants to take all and give nothing. That is what tends to poverty (Pr. 11:24).

VII. GOD'S JUDGMENT WILL BE FINAL
(3:13 – 4:3) (Hebrew 3:13–21)

The prophet now returns to the subject of judgment, but at a more profound level than in 2:17 – 3:5. He shows that there is a fundamental difference between the man who serves God and the one who does not, not only here and now but, even more significantly, in the day of God's great assize. Injustices and inequalities are to be seen in the light of that final judgment, when innocence and guilt will be exposed and opportunity for repentance will have passed. Malachi is virtually saying, live in the light of that day.

13. Malachi begins in his usual way with God's accusation against a section of the community which has grown dis-

[1] G. S. Cansdale, *Animals of Bible Lands* (Paternoster Press, 1970), pp. 240f

illusioned in God's service, and has, apparently unwittingly, spoken *stout* (NEB *hard*) *words*, against Him. Unguarded conversation has undermined morale.

14. Opinions differ among commentators as to whether the prophet is dealing here with the 'righteous' or the 'wicked', assuming that there is always a hard and fast line between them. The attitude described here is one to which God's servants are particularly prone when times are hard, and they are no longer in the first flush of youthful enthusiasm. The people Malachi had in mind were *keeping his charge*, that is, living by God's commandments. The expression is used to refer to the covenant requirements generally (Jos. 22:2,3), though sometimes to more specifically priestly duties (Lv. 8:35; Zc. 3:7). It would be understandable if these were Levites who had suffered as a direct result of the failure of tithe income (3:8). They had walked *as in mourning before the Lord*, in repentance lest they were at fault, but had continued to experience shortages.

There is a degree of uncertainty about the exact meaning of the phrase 'as in mourning' (Heb. *qᵉdōrannîṯ*) because the word occurs only here in the Old Testament. Translators have usually connected it with the verb 'to be dark' (Heb. *qādar*), hence the idea of mourning, but there is another verb (Heb. *qādaḏ*) meaning 'to bow down', which would indicate an attitude of deference, but this involves an emendation in the text, slight though it is. D. Winton Thomas[1] arrives at a similar meaning, however, by deriving the word from Arabic *qadara*, 'measured', which, like Latin *modeste* from *modus*, 'measure' means 'moderately, temperately, discreetly'. NEB *behaving with deference* has adopted this meaning, though JB *walking mournfully* has kept the more usual interpretation. In this 'affirmation of virtue' the more forcible expression is to be preferred.

15. There is genuine dismay that those who defied God, *the arrogant*, seemed to enjoy every security. The psalmist faced the same difficulty (Ps. 73:2–14), 'envying the arrogant . . . and watching the wicked get rich' (verse 3, JB), who asked ' "How will God find out?" ' (verse 11). The scandal was that the advocates of evil had their own way and God appeared to

[1] 'The Root ṣn' in Hebrew, and the meaning of *qᵉdōrannîṯ* in Malachi III:14', *JJS*, I (1948–49), pp. 182–188.

condone their crimes. They *put God to the test* by seeing how far they could go in evil. Contrast God's invitation in verse 10 to see how far He would go in blessing.

Pre-exilic prophets were given the certainty of the exile to preach as an incentive to repentance. The psalmist took comfort in the righteous outworking of God's providence, and in the joy of conscious communion with Him (Ps. 73:17–28). Malachi has his own characteristic way of expressing the answer God gave to Him.

16. In brief, his assurance is that God knows and cares. *Those who feared the Lord* are not necessarily a different group from those who had been complaining, but they are those who have taken the rebuke, and they begin to encourage each other to renewed faith. It is this groping after faith that *the Lord heeded and heard.* The *book of remembrance* recorded not righteous deeds, as in a Persian king's chronicles (Est. 6:1,2), but the names *of those who feared the Lord and thought on his name.* Like Abram they believed God (Gn. 15:6) and in so doing found themselves accounted righteous (verse 18).

The idea that the Lord keeps a record of the names of His people occurs as early as the Exodus (Ex. 32:32,33; *cf.* Ps. 69:28; 87:6; Dn. 12:1), but only Malachi calls it a 'book of remembrance'. His thought is that not one believer will be forgotten by God.

17. The high privilege God will bestow is to make these believers His own possession; *mine* is emphatic in the Hebrew, and *my special possession* further endorses the point. These words, quoted from the covenant inauguration (Ex. 19:5) and later referred to in that connection (Dt. 7:6; 14:2; 26:18; Ps. 135:4), draw attention to the original election of Israel. The purpose which God had in first choosing a people is shown in the last of the prophets to be about to be fulfilled. The father–son simile emphasizes God's compassion for His less than worthy servants (*cf.* 1:6).

18. Parallelism here identifies the *righteous* with *one who serves* God and *the wicked* with *one who does not serve him.* The righteous has nothing to his credit but has been 'spared' (verse 17). Ultimate judgment turns on a man's relationship to God, and that is determined by his response to God's invitation to 'return' (3:7).

4:1. Malachi had used the imagery of a refining fire (3:2) but now speaks of a destructive fire. *The day* will be one of tropical heat, when parched vegetation suddenly catches fire and dry fields become one vast oven in which even the roots of the plants are reduced to ash. *The arrogant and all evildoers* who refuse to repent will find no escape.

2. The metaphor now changes. The Lord addresses personally *you who fear my name* (*cf.* 3:16), that is, those who have repented and long to see His cause triumph and right prevail. For them the sun which caused the heath fire (verse 1) will be *the sun of righteousness*, bringing health and healing to those who love righteousness (Is. 57:18,19). Like calves released from their stall into the sunlight they will leap about with sheer relief and exuberance that right has triumphed.

Only here in the Bible does the term 'sun of righteousness' occur, and the imagery of *wings* representing the sun's rays recalls the winged sun disc which appears on many Near Eastern monuments.[1] It is a particularly apt figure to claim for the Lord of hosts as He reveals Himself as judge in all His power.

3. The amazing reversal in which the wicked are no more is best appreciated by those who, because they are righteous, have suffered at their hand. Forbidden to avenge themselves (Dt. 32:35; Pr. 20:22), they endure with no hope of relief. In every age persecuted believers long for the dramatic *dénouement* when God's eternal order will be vindicated. The prophet longs that this should be prefaced by world-wide repentance, but if not, the alternative, destruction of the unrepentant, is inescapable.

VIII. CONCLUDING EXHORTATION
(4:4–6) (Hebrew 3:22–24)

The last three verses of Malachi form a fitting conclusion to this book, which itself completes the 'Book of the Twelve'. Though the Hebrew Bible concluded with the Writings and

---

[1] At least sixteen plates in *ANEP* from Egypt, Syria and Assyria depict the winged sun disc presiding over the event recorded. Sometimes it is stylized, as in the Stele of Merneptah (342) and Shalmanezer's Black Obelisk (351), but sometimes it is realistic, as in 477 from Byblos.

not with the Prophets, there is an appropriateness about this ending to our Old Testament, which follows the order of books in the Greek and Latin Versions. In the references to the law of Moses and to Elijah the prophet, with both of whom Jesus conversed on the mount of transfiguration (Mt. 17:4 and parallels), there is a backward glimpse to the covenant requirements and a forward look to one who will work for their fulfilment. The promise of the coming of 'Elijah' ensured one more prophetic voice before the end came.

Remarkable as these complementary verses are, it is frequently argued that they represent two later additions to the book (see Introduction, p. 214). The continued ethical emphasis, however, and the style of writing are in keeping with the rest of the book, and point to Malachi as the likely author.

From early times attempts have been made to avoid the harsh ending of the book. Greek MSS placed verse 4 after verse 6, while Hebrew liturgical use led to the repetition of verse 5 after verse 6. Hebrew Bibles continue to print verse 5 a second time at the end of the chapter.

4. The whole of the Pentateuch is summed up in this verse, phrased in Deuteronomic terms. The exhortation *Remember*, used thirteen times in Deuteronomy to direct attention to experiences of God's saving acts, now calls *all Israel* to observe *the law of Moses*. This term primarily refers to the obligations undertaken at the time of entering into the covenant (Jos. 8:32; 23:6; 1 Ki. 2:3), but later it is used of the Pentateuch, more or less complete (2 Ch. 23:18; 30:16; Ezr. 6:18; 7:6; Ne. 8:1). *Statutes and ordinances*, strictly the categorical law and case law, is a very common way of referring to the law of God in general (Lv. 26:46; Dt. 4:1,5, *etc.*; Ezr. 7:10,11; Ne. 1:7; Ps. 147:19). The name *Horeb* as an alternative name for Sinai is often said to be Deuteronomic, but it occurs in Exodus 3:1; 17:6; 33:6, and Sinai occurs in Deuteronomy 33:2. If Israel will not listen to Malachi's prophecy, let them remember that the law of God is *commanded*, and a great King's commands are not neglected with impunity.

5. Having looked back to what was commanded, Malachi now looks forward to *the great and terrible day of the Lord*, an expression used in Joel 2:31. There will, however, be a warning first. The choice of *Elijah* to typify the coming prophet may have been suggested by the mention of Horeb, for, like Moses, he had a revelation of God there (1 Ki. 19:8–18). Then again Elijah served as a moral catalyst to the nation. No other prophet so dramatically changed the attitude of his contemporaries, nor so influenced the destiny of the nation. If the messenger of 3:1–3 was in mind, Elijah had called down fire from heaven (1 Ki. 18:38), had witnessed the Lord's wind, earthquake and fire at Horeb (1 Ki. 19:11,12) and had been taken from Elisha in a chariot of fire. The fact that he did not experience death suggested that he still lived to carry on his work (*cf.* 2 Ch. 21:12).

6. The future ministry of the coming prophet is described in terms of bridging the generation gap. The fifth commandment implied that the home was essentially the school of the community. There, in a 'world in miniature', authority and submission, love and loyalty, obedience and trust could be learned as nowhere else and, with the word of God as guide in the home, society could be changed. The dread alternative constituted Malachi's last word, God's *curse* (Heb. *ḥērem*). Connected with the idea of holiness the word 'curse' represents the taboo which set apart for destruction any person interfering with whatever had been vowed to the deity and was therefore 'holy', excluded from secular use (Jos. 7:11–15). The cities and population of Canaan which had belonged to other gods were also put under the curse and were to be utterly exterminated (Dt. 13:12–18; 20:16f.). This harsh fate later became associated with the terror of final judgment, to be set free from which was the height of blessing (Zc. 14:11; Rev. 22:3).

Words from this verse are quoted by Ben Sirach (Ecclus. 48:10) in his description of Elijah, and by Luke in the record of the angel's message to Zechariah, father of John the Baptist (Lk. 1:17). Jesus identified the messenger of Malachi 3:1 as John (Mt. 11:10) and Elijah as John (Mt. 11:14), yet it is true that John repudiated the suggestion that he was Elijah (Jn. 1:21), and J. A. T. Robinson believes that John thought of Jesus as the man of fire (Mt. 3:12; Lk. 3:17).[1]

Whatever may have been the truth about John's understanding of his role, he believed that the Messianic age was

[1] J.A.T. Robinson, *Twelve New Testament Studies* (SCM Press, 1962), pp. 28–52.

being ushered in, and that only through a process of testing by fire could anyone escape final judgment (Mt. 3:11,12). He undoubtedly knew the message of Malachi and was profoundly influenced by it. In the life of Jesus the expectation of John was not fulfilled. An interval separated the first and second comings and the day of grace was extended to delay final judgment. This does not mean, however, that judgment has been averted. The warning that ends the Old Testament is not absent at the end of the New (Rev. 22:10–15), but the difference is that there grace has the last word (verse 21).